Understanding Language Classroom Contexts

ALSO AVAILABLE FROM BLOOMSBURY

Reflective Language Teaching: From Research to Practice, Thomas S. C. Farrell
Foreign Language Learning with Digital Technology, edited by Michael Evans
Teaching Teachers: Processes ad Practices, Angi Malderez and Martin Wedell
Planning for Educational Change, Martin Wedell

Understanding Language Classroom Contexts

The starting point for change

MARTIN WEDELL

AND

ANGI MALDEREZ

B L O O M S B U R Y

LONDON • NEW DELHI • NEW YORK • SYDNEY

Bloomsbury Academic
An imprint of Bloomsbury Publishing Plc

50 Bedford Square
London
WC1B 3DP
UK

175 Fifth Avenue
New York
NY 10010
USA

www.bloomsbury.com

First published 2013

British Library Cataloguing-in-Publication Data
A catalogue record for this book is available from the British Library.

ISBN: PB: 9781441133076
HB: 9781441198372
ePub: 9781441102454
ePDF: 9781441160591

Library of Congress Cataloging-in-Publication Data
Wedell, Martin.
Understanding language classroom contexts : the starting point for change / Martin Wedell and Angi Malderez.
pages cm
Includes bibliographical references and index.
ISBN 978-1-4411-3307-6 (pbk.) – ISBN 978-1-4411-9837-2 (hardback) – ISBN 978-1-4411-0245-4 (ebook) – ISBN 978-1-4411-6059-1 (ebook)
1. English language – Study and teaching – Foreign speakers. 2. School improvement programs. I. Malderez, Angi, 1950– II. Title.
PE1065.W346 2013
428.0071–dc23
2012042325

Typeset by Newgen Imaging Systems Pvt Ltd, Chennai, India
Printed and bound in India

Contents

List of figures

List of tables

Acknowledgements

Our interactions and discussions over the years with teachers and with our students (especially those studying on the MA TESOL (China)), have provided the impetus for us to grapple with trying to clarify the complexity that is context. We thank them all for the questions, suggestions and comments which have contributed to this work.

More practically, our thanks to Gerry te Meij and Jeff Malderez for help with the diagrams, and to Sue Haines for last minute layout salvation!

Finally our love and thanks to our families (Gary, Jeff and Jan) for their contributions to our writing context.

Introduction

English is unique among the many foreign languages that are taught in state education systems around the world because it is a subject in almost every state education curriculum, and is therefore a feature of education in the widest range of contexts. Whilst much of what we write here will be of relevance to language teaching, or even any teaching more generally, our examples and main focus are on English Language classrooms.

As any reader who works in language teaching will know, policy-led changes to how teachers are supposed to teach, what they are supposed to teach, what resources are available to use in their teaching and what their learners are supposed to achieve, rain down from on-high with bewildering speed. Meanwhile some of the changes teachers *want* to make at classroom level happen more or less as planned, while others seem much more difficult or even impossible to achieve.

Understanding as much as possible about the existing context of a particular classroom (for teacher initiated change) or of the region or nation's classrooms (for larger scale, externally initiated change) is, we believe, *the* prerequisite for any effective change. Such an understanding is needed both to develop an appropriate, clear rationale for the change and its hoped-for outcomes, and to develop appropriate processes to enable the aims of the change to be achieved. We believe that this understanding of the change context, and so of the challenges that any proposed change is likely to pose for that context, needs to inform both the initial planning and the implementation of any change in a language classroom, at whatever level it is initiated.

This book explores and illustrates how what happens in a language classroom is both influenced by and an influence on the contexts in which it is situated. These interconnections in turn help explain why changes constantly occur in (and to) language classrooms worldwide. They also provide a framework for understanding why effective implementation of planned changes (whether planned by a teacher or educational professionals at other levels) does or does not occur in a particular context.

Have you ever . . .

- Become frustrated because changes you have tried to make in your teaching haven't worked?
- Wondered why the training you have provided seems to have had no lasting impact on teachers' actual practice?
- Worried about the difficulties of getting schools and teachers to implement the new curriculum?

If you recognise any of these (and many other similar issues) this book may help. We don't claim it will solve your problems for you, but it should help you to better understand more about why they exist. This understanding is the first vital step in working out possible contextually appropriate solutions.

In remainder of this short introductory chapter, we say a little about who we are and why we have written this book, some more about who we hope will find it useful, provide a summary of the contents and finally suggest some ways you might use the book.

1. Who we are and why we have written this book

Together we have more than 70 years of experience of working broadly in English Language Teaching. We have had a range of roles and worked in every continent apart from North America and Australasia. As a result, we have participated in many national attempts to effect change. On the whole, these have had little success in terms of seeing widespread implementation of the desired changes in most classrooms. In addition, we have met thousands (by now, we think this is not an exaggeration!) of teachers who although wanting to make changes to what happens in their classrooms have found themselves unable to do so. So, we have been puzzling over why planned change – whether planned by ministries or teachers – seems to be so difficult to effect. Through our work with many groups of teachers, we now believe the reasons are many, but that all relate more or less directly to visible or invisible aspects of the contexts in which teachers work. This book is therefore the product of many minds, and is an attempt to share our understanding more widely. It is an understanding we have found of very practical use in our work.

2. Who might find this book useful?

As teachers motivated us to write this book, our primary intended readership is English language teachers. We hope that a better understanding of 'the whole picture' of their work situation, and so of what it is worth trying to change (or not), will ultimately contribute to helping them to remain positive members of the profession and avoid burnout, frustration or cynicism.

- Teachers of teachers, too, will find this book of interest. First, it can help them to more fully understand some of the contextual realities which influence the teachers they teach (and so enable them to provide more appropriate and relevant programmes and teaching). It can also help them to understand the limits of what it is possible to achieve in a particular teacher education context, and so help to preserve *their* professional sanity.
- Those studying on undergraduate or postgraduate TESOL, Applied Linguistics, Language Teacher Education or Educational Leadership and Management programmes will also find this book relevant. The picture that the book develops of the 'whole' educational context will help to highlight and reinforce the links between many of the other modules that they are likely to study on their programme.
- Finally, we believe the book has messages for educational change 'managers' either when initially planning the scale, scope and speed of a change or when considering how a planned change might be effected in practice. In other words, we believe that a 'whole picture' understanding of their context will help them plan more realistically and so avoid some otherwise likely disappointments.

3. What is in the book?

Other authors have written in depth about certain *aspects* of the relationship between change and context, for example in relation to the use or roles of language, the language teaching-learning process or the planning and implementation of new curricula.

What practitioners seem to find helpful when thinking about change (at whatever level) is to consider context as a whole. Everything, and importantly the connections between the parts, impinges on a teacher's work. This book is therefore 'long and thin' – 'long' because we cover and try to link many different areas (not because it goes on for ever!), and 'thin' because none of them are treated in the same depth as in existing books which specialise in fewer areas (otherwise it *would* go on for ever!).

Throughout the book we often suggest that you put your own ideas about various concepts, issues or topics into words before reading what we have to say. We don't do this for rhetorical style. Rather, it is because we believe that the reading will be both more interesting and easier if you have your own consciously formulated ideas at the forefront of your mind as you read. This will allow the dialogue between us and you to occur more easily as inevitably you will be contrasting and comparing all the while. (And the wonderful thing about having a dialogue with a book is that you are not going to hurt anyone's feelings when you shout at it, or expose yourself as silly if you later come to agree with a point of view you first thought was nonsense!) We will also be inviting you, the reader, to explore your own context, through undertaking tasks using the lenses/ideas introduced in each particular chapter.

What follows is a more detailed description of the focus of each chapter.

4. Chapter outlines

We start the book with a description of a context. Most aspects of this description have the potential to make a difference to what happens in a classroom and to what it is and is not (or not easily) possible to change. We come back to most these aspects in later chapters. In the first chapter, Components of Context, we introduce a framework for beginning to describe the visible and invisible features of a context, and show how the framework relates to the description we began with.

In Chapter 2, we explore the 'invisible' (culture(s)) that are part of, and strong influences on, any context. As cultures cannot avoid being part of any context, there are many possible levels at which the term may be used. We suggest that most of us in education are simultaneously members of more than one culture. We then consider how some of what happens in classrooms can be explained from the point of view of culture(s).

Chapter 3 looks at language as an aspect of context from a number of different points of view. We look at one theoretical framework for the role of language (any language) in the teaching and learning process, and at possible relationships between language and thought. We consider languages in different contexts, in terms of what languages exist and are used for in different parts of the world, and why countries vary so much in the languages that they use and teach. Finally, we look at the roles that English may play in different countries and education systems and at how this may affect the local language learning and teaching context.

Chapters 4 and 5 discuss the main changes that have taken place in language teaching methods and approaches (in theory, anyway) over the past half-century or so. This is not to provide a 'history of methods' for its own sake, as this has been done elsewhere and will anyway be a different 'history' in each context. We do so rather to provide readers with tools to identify the prevailing approach in their context, in order to, for example, better understand the challenges that any planned changes might entail. In Chapter 4, we look at how changes of emphasis in the aims of language teaching and the roles of teachers and learners in the language classroom resulted in different methods of language teaching being proposed. We discuss how these affected methodologies, and how the belief in a 'best language teaching method' reflected research in all disciplines based upon belief in universal and decontextualised truths. In Chapter 5, we look in some detail at the implications for methods of our growing understanding of the nature of language. We see that if we believe that language use varies with the context of its users, then language teaching and learning methodologies (including in English language teaching (ELT)) also need to be tailored to the context in which the language is being taught. One outcome is that the earlier, apparently more uniform, teaching methods have been replaced by a far greater variety of teaching approaches.

Chapters 6 and 7 consider the micro context of the classroom. We explore the idea that the relationship between teachers, learners and context is complex and that the people in any classroom can be thought of as being both *part* of or even *creating* their context as well as *influenced by* it. We discuss in some detail who teachers are, and how they come to be that way, and then consider characteristics of and influences on learners. Finally we look at the how the grouping of different people, as individuals and 'types' can produce very different affective and cognitive contexts for learning – for both learners and teachers – and at how all the aspects discussed in these chapters do, in combination, contribute to creating a unique classroom culture, which will affect the ease with which particular changes can be introduced.

Chapter 8 again focuses on the micro-context of classrooms and institutions, this time considering how observable physical conditions within these, as well as the often less visible influences of a institutions' different organisational cultures, may affect what happens in the language classroom.

Chapter 9 revisits earlier themes to highlight some of the factors that may help or hinder the implementation of change at the classroom, institutional or national levels. We end the chapter with a proposal for how externally initiated changes which usually require large numbers of people (not only teachers) to be learning over time, might be managed.

In the Conclusion, we try, very briefly, to review ideas in the book from some different perspectives to illustrate that the way in which we have presented and ordered the material is itself a product of the writers as individuals in their own particular context. The reader, too, is asked to consider (again) how their own contexts and cultures may have influenced the sense they have made of 'the whole picture' presented. Readers are also invited to recall any ideas for changes in their own practices that their reading of the book may have provoked, and to imagine their first steps towards taking the necessary action.

5. Ways to use the book

Of course, as authors, we would recommend starting at the beginning and reading carefully through to the end, undertaking all the proposed tasks as you do so! Having said that, your context (and immediate perceived needs) might suggest a number of different approaches to making use of what is in this book.

For example:

If you want to discover the prevailing approach to English language teaching in your context.

You could start by reading Chapters 4 and 5

If you are a manager (at any level) of classroom change decided by anyone other than teachers.

You could start by reading Chapter 9, and then whatever other chapters you discover you need

If you are a teacher of teachers (whether formally supporting teachers to learn and adapt to externally-initiated changes, or not).

You could start by reading Chapters 6 and 7, and then whatever other chapters you discover you need

If you are in a (peer support) group which has agreed to work with this book.

You could all agree to complete a particular context exploration task by a certain time and share the outcomes.

So what do we mean by 'context'? The first chapter attempts to give an overview.

1

Components of contexts

Introduction

This chapter provides an overview of the many aspects of context that can affect teaching. We introduce them all briefly here to illustrate the 'whole picture', before, in later chapters, looking at many aspects in more detail.

The thing about context is that it is easy to take it for granted. Teachers do notice and comment on aspects of their immediate context – for example the numbers of pupils in each class, or the availability of facilities. Every teacher experiences the differences between the classes they teach, but have you ever worked in different schools? What about moving to different parts of your country or indeed to another country? Have you had to work with a new curriculum? Have you changed the age or level of learners with whom you have worked? The more often you have answered yes to any of the questions posed, the more likely it is that you are already aware of some of the ways in which the broader context can affect language classrooms.

As an understanding of context is so often taken for granted it is often given too little attention. For us, an explicit understanding of context needs to underpin the work of any English Teaching (ET) professional (teacher, textbook writer, curriculum developer, ministry planner, teacher of teachers, tester and inspector), since how each plays their role influences what happens in classrooms.

1. Description of a context

What follows is the type of description of a context that all the above ET professionals (at whatever level) might find particularly useful prior to making plans for the implementation of changes in language classrooms. Although it is not a full description, nor one of a single 'real' context, and although in many respects it may look 'old-fashioned', in our experience it continues to represent a typical sketch of many English language teaching environments in the world today.

It is the kind of sketch that could be written by visitors to a context who have walked around a school and the town in which it is situated, observed classes, spent some time talking to a range of school staff and done some basic background reading about the region and the country.

Readers might like to consider, as they read, which aspects of the description are or are not 'true' for their own situation.

(i) This classroom contains fixed tables and benches, and 51 learners, aged between 14 and 15, although one or two look rather older. There is a blackboard in the room and most learners have a copy of the national textbook (new or second-hand) which is the basis for all teaching. The English 'blurb' on the back cover of the textbook says that its goal is to develop learners' ability to understand and use English. The teacher and learners are formally dressed (learners in a more or less complete uniform). The teacher stands behind her 'teacher's desk' or at the blackboard. The teacher uses a mixture of her mother tongue and English in class. She uses English when she is reading directly from the book, but she doesn't use it for classroom management. (She does not talk fluently when answering visitors' questions.) Oral drills, textbook grammar exercises and pupils reading texts aloud can be seen in most English lessons. Learners copy grammatical explanations and vocabulary items which the teacher has written on the board into their notebooks. Learners remain sitting in the same seats throughout the lesson, except when nominated by the teacher to answer a question, when they stand up. During the lesson, learners only speak when asked or instructed to do so by the teacher, and from what they say, they seem to have different levels of English proficiency. The teacher says that this class obtains lower results on tests and exams than other classes in the same year.

(ii) The teacher, in her mid-twenties, graduated five years ago from a provincial teacher's college, and has had no further formal support for development. Learners have had between 3 and 5 years of formal English lessons (some learners began learning English at primary school).

(iii) The junior secondary school, of which this classroom is part, looks like all the other schools in the area. It is built in three main blocks, around a central playground. Two of the blocks have three floors with classrooms. Staircases and corridors are covered, but open, and as most classroom windows are also open for most of the year, noise carries easily between classrooms. There is a small gender-segregated toilet block between the two classroom buildings. The third smaller blockhouses staff rooms and administrative offices. The twenty-five full-time teachers have tables in one of two staff rooms (shared with their part-time colleagues). The head teacher has a private office and a secretary in an adjacent room, which houses the only copier in the school reserved for the head's use only. The deputy head also has an office. There is also a larger formal room for staff meetings and for meetings with visitors. The caretaker and his assistants also have storerooms in this building. There are slightly more than one thousand students, and three full time English teachers in the school, with a geography teacher also giving some English lessons. All learners have at least three periods of English a week, with final year students (approximately a third of the student population) who are aiming for a high stakes English exam that will determine their entry to senior secondary, having five, mostly taught by the most senior teacher. The full-time English teachers teach a minimum of twenty lessons a week. During their non-teaching periods they do not necessarily remain in school. Classes start at 7 a.m. and end at 1.30. The school leaders communicate with teachers through a staff meeting at the start of each of the three terms, and any necessary bulletins are posted on the staff notice board. Each subject has a lead teacher who acts, amongst other things, as a channel through which teachers can communicate with school management. We are informed that such communication happens rarely.

(iv) The school is situated on the outskirts of a medium sized town in a largely rural region, 80 kilometres from the regional capital. There are important historical sites nearby. There are two main languages used in the town, a national lingua franca and the local language. English can be seen on some shop fronts, and is used in the growing tourist industry. In addition, English is needed by some personnel in the exotic vegetable export business. The climate is fairly hot and humid most of the year, with most rainfall concentrated in the summer months. Agriculture of one kind or another was the principal occupation of almost all inhabitants of this region until very recently, and remains important.

(v) The country itself is industrialising rapidly. There are many consequent infrastructure problems, including that of power supply. The gap between the rich and the poor is widening. The President of the country is keen to promote the country's global competitiveness and universal English proficiency is deemed an essential component of the development strategy. There are few higher education institutions and a shortage of graduate (and postgraduate) level personnel within the country.

(vi) There is a national curriculum for English and government-approved and supplied textbooks to support its teaching. However, according to the teachers the content of the high stakes English exams does not reflect the goal of learning English as expressed in the curriculum documentation.

(vii) Teacher training colleges report increasing difficulty in recruiting good quality applicants. Although teaching is traditionally highly respected, industrialisation and the growth of alternative opportunities for employment mean that teachers' low incomes deter many. We were told that the school recently lost a very promising and enthusiastic English teacher (a graduate from one of the best colleges) to the local tourist industry. There is no national curriculum for initial English teacher preparation, so there is some difference between graduates from the different institutions. However, most initial preparation for teachers consists of language proficiency development and lectures in literature and linguistics, together with some general courses in education, and, perhaps, one or more, often largely theoretical ('A History of Methods'), courses on English Language teaching methodology. The preparation programmes in general refer little, or not at all, to local textbooks or the national English curriculum. Student teachers are expected to make their own arrangements for the usual period of 'teaching practice' which in most cases is undertaken, largely unsupervised, at the end of the programme. Graduating English teachers are generally not very confident in either their own language proficiency or their own teaching skills.

(viii) There is an inspectorate drawn from the teaching workforce. They receive no specific training for their role which, as well as 'providing support to English teachers', involves reporting to the Ministry on teacher supply and the quality of teaching (largely judged on students' exam results, and one observed lesson). These reports affect teacher promotion.

(ix) There is no systematic provision of in-service development opportunities for teachers, although there are occasionally ministry and/or donor-funded workshops led by staff from teacher training colleges or non-governmental organisations (NGOs). These are attended by only some teachers, often the lead teacher and are usually connected to a major change (such as when the new English curriculum and textbooks were launched seven years ago).

(x) The country is situated in a part of the world that has historically not had a large influence on world affairs or been visibly influenced by them. Now however, its aspirations for modernisation mean that it is increasingly turning to the wider world for financial and technical assistance as well as strategic support for development. This is a part of the world in which the old are traditionally respected for their wisdom, and the good of the group is considered to be far more important than the self-realisation of the individual.

(xi) Official documentary rhetoric states that education should encourage all learners to flourish in their own way. However, our conversations and observations suggest that many people working in the education system see their role to be to maintain the status quo (conserve things as they are) and equip young people to fit harmoniously into the existing social structures and norms.

(xii) The school in which our classroom is situated seems to be run on hierarchical lines. For example, staff tell us that everyone follows the Head teacher's instructions. It is noticeable that the Lead English teacher, who is considerably more experienced than the others (and for whom initial teacher preparation was unavailable at the start of his career) is deferred to by his colleagues.

At first sight, anyone (e.g. inspectors, planners, head teacher, etc.) might assume that what the teacher in the description above did and did not do in the classroom, was a result purely of her own professional understandings (or lack of them) and her own linguistic confidence. However as the description continues, it seems very likely that there are much more complex reasons for the observed classroom behaviour. It could be that her practice is largely a function of the atmosphere in the school, the Head teacher's instructions, the nature of the exams, the nature of her initial teacher preparation or some combination of these or other factors. It is likely that the teacher in our description above is not consciously aware of many of the factors in her context that affect her existing practice or her ability to make classroom changes, whether motivated by her own experience or required by others.

The rest of the book will be trying to illustrate ways that you might make sense of your context for your own purposes. In the next parts of this chapter, we try to provide a systematic overall framework for understanding the 'whole picture' of any context, and in subsequent chapters, go into more detail on different parts of that 'whole'.

2. Developing a framework for understanding context

Before we go any further, did you recognise any aspects of your own context in the description that we gave? Were there any parts of the description which made you realise that you didn't have enough information about your own context to say whether or not it was similar? Why might this be?

2.1 The impossibility of describing context completely

Describing context is complicated. It is made more so by the fact that contexts are not static, but changing over time. This means that even some of the visible components may not remain constant for long enough to make the effort of describing them in detail worthwhile. Just how difficult any attempt to describe the complete context of an educational setting can be, is suggested by Fullan when he states that any such context has:

> . . . a huge number of variables and their interactive change nature is so large that it is logically unfeasible to get all the necessary information, and cognitively impossible for individuals to understand the total picture, even if the information is available. (Fullan 1993:208)

Therefore, we have to accept that we cannot look at every component of context from every perspective, and that whatever is described on one day or week or year will have changed, at least to some extent, by the next. If this is so, why even try? A former colleague of ours (Alan Maley) once said, referring to attempts to describe what was meant by the then new concept of 'communicative competence': 'you can't get at the essence of a rose by pulling off its petals'.

There is a sense in which pulling a concept such as 'communicative competence' or 'context' apart only gives the illusion of a complete understanding, since there will always be parts left out. For example, important factors may be missing due to the complex relationships between the person doing the pulling apart and what is being examined. These relationships can considerably alter the form of, or the emphasis within, the descriptions ultimately reached. Taking the quest to understand the 'essence of the rose' as an example, one person's 'essence' may be strongly influenced by, for example, the memory of the pain of a thorn, while another's may be influenced by memories of having been given a red rose on a romantic occasion, or catching the beautiful perfume on a summer evening.

What use then is the 'pulling apart' that we are now embarked on? Well, to begin with we could not have talked about the part of the 'rose' that caused us pain if someone had not noticed and named a thorn. If nobody had studied the part of the rose we call roots, or the effects of cutting back rose stems during winter, we would not know how to care for roses in ways that produce the types of flowers we want. And the analogy could go on. The point is that making an attempt to undertake the process of noticing the various parts and the ways that they affect each other is worth it, as Alan Maley went on to note. In the process of examination, the language to label the parts is developed (coined by the first 'examiners', and learnt by those who follow) which in turn enables later thinking and talking about parts, their connections and the whole, as part of an ongoing process of understanding.

This ongoing re-examination is particularly necessary when it comes to 'context' because, as noted earlier, context is never static. The effort involved in the ongoing attempts to understand a context, will, of course, need to be supported by a personal purpose that provides the motivation for the detailed work of examining parts, their connections and the whole.

So, what is your 'personal purpose'? How would a better understanding of your context benefit you?

In this book, we have had to make choices about which parts of the (English Language) Classroom Context to explore, using and building on parts which have already been labelled. We have included those which we have found most useful when wanting or being expected to make or plan changes in English classrooms, and that we believe will be most useful to most readers with regard to understanding the main features of the context in which their English teaching and learning takes place.

2.2 *Identifying components of context*

To begin with, we base our discussion on two ways of describing English Teaching (ET) contexts BANA and TESEP proposed by Holliday (1994). Although these terms were coined some time go, they remain useful since they not only highlight differences that are frequently commented on in the still relatively limited 'ET context literature', but also offer an initial way of differentiating between two still current (in 2012) broad ET realities.

A way of viewing the ET profession is as a continuum with the extreme ends represented by, at the one end:

- The minority of English Teachers in the world who work in university departments, higher education language units or private language schools, in Britain, Australasia and North America (BANA) who:
- share many features of their educational cultures.
- have developed many of the current ET approaches and methodologies.
- control most of the internationally recognised journals.
- write most of the widely influential 'methods' books, including (still) textbooks.
- teach small classes and have access to a wide range of materials and equipment.
- have a wide range of professional experience as a result of being expected to make decisions about what and how to teach, based on their understanding of their learners' needs.
- teach mainly teenage / adult groups of paying learners with clear (usually instrumental) aims for learning English.

and at the other end

- The majority of English teachers worldwide who work in tertiary, secondary or primary level (TESEP) institutions within the state sector in non-English speaking countries who:

- represent a variety of different educational cultures.
- teach learners who are learning because it is part of the curriculum, and who, even where there are 'school fees' to be paid, are not paying specifically to learn English.
- often teach larger classes.
- often have much less access to a variety of materials and/or equipment.
- usually have less freedom to make decisions about what to teach or how to do so, and so have a more limited range of professional experiences.
- are often expected to use materials and/or methods emerging from BANA contexts.

Of course, between these two scenarios, are a range of others. For example, there are increasingly large numbers of teachers in private language schools or NGO personnel working outside BANA countries who, to varying extents, share features of both scenarios.

So where are you? Are you working in a BANA or TESEP context, or are you somewhere in between?

Holliday uses this BANA/TESEP contextual distinction in a discussion of appropriate teaching methodologies. For example, he suggests that the teaching methodologies devised by BANA professionals may not be appropriate for TESEP contexts without considerable modification. However, he points out that nonetheless, due to the continuing prestige of BANA ideas and practices in many parts of the world (as those working in BANA contexts are both mostly native speakers of English, and representatives of 'the North' or 'developed' countries), there has been a tendency to assume that BANA methodologies *can,* and even *should* be transferred wholesale to TESEP contexts. In many cases, attempts to do so have been very disappointing. Our experience suggests that what Holliday said, almost 20 years ago as we write, still holds true.

Holliday also uses the terms "Macro" and "Micro" contexts to refer to different aspects of the whole context that we might want to investigate. The Macro context is the wider context of the educational and national culture and the socio-economic environment in which any individual educational institution is situated. The Micro context refers to the specific features of the individual school or classroom.

We find these ways of thinking about context (BANA, TESEP, Macro and Micro) useful for thinking about all the many factors that might influence what does or does not happen in classrooms, and so will refer to them in this book. However, we have found we need a more detailed framework than these provide for understanding 'whole' contexts, which we now begin to discuss.

2.3 Core components of context

English Teaching (ET) is concerned with the teaching and learning of language, and language is essentially human. *People* are therefore central to any discussion of the context of ET. People behave according to their own conscious or unconscious 'thinking'. This thinking is influenced by the meanings that they have made of experiences they have had, which in turn are coloured by the norms of the culture(s) to which they belong (see Chapter 2).

The physical environment, or *place*, in which they find themselves, can also influence how people behave, as you may have noted in the example description above. (For example, perhaps one of the reasons for the teaching methods in the description above was connected to climate in the *place*, causing the open windows and corridors in the school design and so the desire to avoid disturbing other classes with 'too much noise').

In addition, when we describe the way people think and behave, and the environments in which they work, what we are describing is inevitably situated at a point in *time* in terms of individual biographies or of the history of the place or of ideas. Also, since any teaching is about actively *encouraging* changes in what people know and the way people think and behave over time, teaching itself needs to take into account the stage in learning that has been reached at a given point in *time*. In other words, what people (can) think and do is influenced by the point in *time* at which the teaching occurs.

All this leads us to conclude that the three central, interdependent contextual elements that influence and may be influenced by, what happens in any classroom (whether described as BANA or TESEP or somewhere in between) are **People, Place and (point in) Time.**

Although we believe **People** to be the central component of any teaching and learning context, in the past, when we have asked teachers to talk about their working context, the ideas they have mentioned first have been those to do with the notion of **Place**. So, as we are now going to look in more detail at these three elements, we will centre the discussion in this chapter on the context of **Place**.

3. The context of place

Starting from the classroom (that many teachers first mention when asked about their teaching context) we can 'zoom out' geographically (Google-Earth fashion) theoretically as far as the boundaries of planet Earth!

From the classroom, (the micro), which forms the centre of any education system, we can move outwards to the school or institution in which the classroom is situated, to the city or town and region, and at the outer macro layers to the country and its physical, geopolitical position in a particular part of the world. All of these geographical, immediately visible aspects of *place*, will influence, for example, the prevailing types of economic activity, the prosperity of the *place* and so the funding available for education. Geographical location will often also affect the culture at all levels (see Chapter 2), and the languages that are used officially and unofficially, that are needed for different domains in life, and taught in schools, (see Chapter 3). In addition, features of *place* will affect the physical structures in which education occurs (see Chapter 8) and when, each day, children are at school. If you read the description at the start of the chapter again, you will notice that almost all of these aspects of Place are mentioned.

So, the idea that most people have of context as Place – because this is the most noticeable, the most *visible,* aspect of context, is not 'wrong' – place does matter – but so do other aspects.

3.1 People and place

There is also an *invisible* dimension to each of the above layers of the Place context. This invisible dimension is a result of the (often unspoken) meanings given to each of the Place layers by the people working in them. For example, what happens in a classroom is determined by beliefs (often unspoken) about what is, and what is not, appropriate behaviour for language teachers and learners. What is considered to be appropriate classroom behaviour is itself a result of deeper and more widespread societal beliefs at the level of nation or world region regarding, for example, the purpose of education.

To clarify, by 'visible' we mean aspects of context that it is physically possible for an outsider to notice relatively quickly, (through observation: seeing and listening; or reading or questioning), that is, using the eyes and/or one or more of their other senses. 'Invisible' aspects of context are, we consider, equally real, but are not directly accessible to the senses, and therefore take longer and more effort to understand.

TABLE 1.1 Context as place: visible and invisible layers

Visible aspects of the context of 'Place'		Invisible aspects of the context of 'Place'
Classroom	P	Group dynamics
School/institution	E	Institutional culture
Village/town/city	O	Local attitudes
Region	P	Regional educational culture
Country	L	National educational culture and socio-political belief system
Part of the world	E	Balances of power and philosophical tradition
World		Human-ness

(At points in) TIME

Table 1.1 presents a way of describing the various layers of 'visible' and 'invisible' Place, to illustrate some possible interactions at each layer. If read top down, the table moves from the micro-context out to the macro.

In both of the above lists, the extent to which the influence of each layer will be apparent to the individual teacher or learner is likely to decrease as they move away from the immediate classroom and classroom group towards the wider world outside. This means it is much easier for teachers (and we include ourselves here) to be aware of many visible (and some invisible) influences of particular classes and institutions on what happens in our classrooms, than it is to realise how these micro-contextual influences are themselves a result of beliefs and behaviours in the macro-context.

In the section that follows, we will look in a little more detail at some of the aspects of context that might be included at each of the layers listed in Table 1.1.

3.2 Some features of the visible layers

3.2.1 The classroom

It does not take a great deal of imagination to realise that if there are no tables or desks in a classroom (for example) it will make a difference to what happens. Features of the classroom that may have a bearing on the kind of teaching and learning that occurs include: number of people in it, its size, weather and sound-proofing, and availability of various facilities – IT equipment, boards, desks, paper, electricity and other teaching/learning support facilities and materials.

3.2.2 The institution

Since budgets are generally held at institutional level (or above) the money available will determine many of the visible features of the classroom. In addition, the type of institution (school, college, university, ministry), or at a local level its name, whether it is a state or private school or whether it is affiliated to a particular religion, may all provide clues about the types of activities that may be carried out in its rooms and how such activities are likely to be conducted.

3.2.3 Village, town or city

Whether an institution is located in a broadly speaking rural or urban area is likely to affect its size, the number and type of people within it, and often the budget allocated to it.

3.2.4 Region

In most countries there are richer and poorer regions and differences in architectural styles of buildings, which may be due as much to climate and physical geography as to social and/or economic history. In addition, regions may be homes to different ethnic groups within the wider society who may visibly differ from each other.

3.2.5 Country and part of the world

Similarly countries have their own climatic and geographical characteristics and different socio-economic profiles. They have more or less money available for education, different periods of compulsory education, and put different amounts of effort into ensuring that children attend school. The proportions of each age group and the age distribution of people engaged in formal learning will therefore, differ. For example, UNESCO statistics for worldwide educational enrolment in 2008 show that different regions of the world have between 40 per cent and 210 per cent of their children of primary age actually attending primary school. The strange phenomenon of having more than 100 per cent of an age group at school is, as the World Bank has suggested, perhaps due to the inclusion in the figures of those repeating a year and of overage children.

3.2.6 The world

Despite the variation in actual school attendance seen above, most parts of the world, on paper at least, give education a high priority and are endeavouring to widen provision. All countries have places they call schools, where teaching and learning takes place, and governmental bodies responsible for education. We cannot compare the educational context on earth with that of any other planet!

We have chosen to work from the micro to the macro because our experience, as noted above, is that when people think about context, they all first think about their own micro working environment. It would of course have been equally possible to begin from the outermost layer. It might even have been more logical, in the sense that the macro layers determine many of the possibilities available to those working closer to the classroom.

This notion of the smaller units being part of, and therefore influenced by, and potentially at least influencing, the larger units within which they exist, may be better illustrated by concentric circles (rather than the lists suggesting a hierarchy) in which the classroom lies at the centre and the world is represented by the outermost layer. Figure 1.1 illustrates this. The dotted lines indicate the fuzzy, permeable nature of the boundaries between layers and (the potential for) a constant flow of influence between layers.

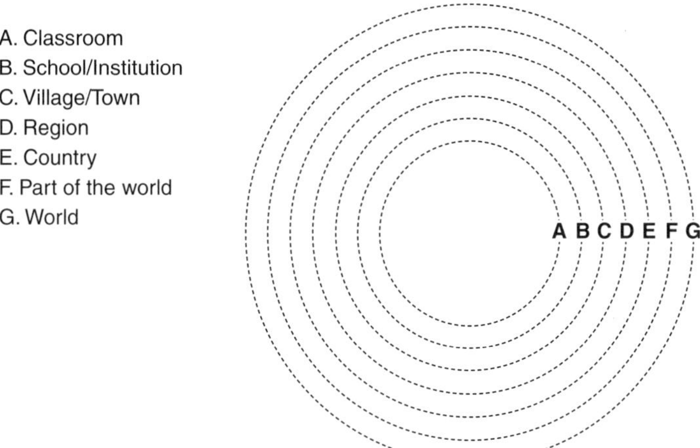

FIGURE 1.1 *The layers of the visible Place context.*

3.3 Some features of the invisible layers

We will now look at the right hand side of Table 1.1 and consider invisible influences on what happens in classrooms, this time beginning from the outer macro layers and working inwards towards the micro context of the individual classroom.

3.3.1 Humaness

Here again we run into the problem of only being able to compare ourselves with other life forms on this planet. The main feature of being a human that is relevant to this discussion, seems to be the use of language which enables each generation to learn as quickly as possible what previous generations have come to know and consider important to the society. Nowadays at least a part of this learning usually takes place in formalised systems that we call 'education'. (We will see in Chapters 2 and 3 that much informal learning through language occurs, for example, and perhaps especially, in the years before children enter their first classroom).

3.3.2 Balance of power and philosophical position

Now, as throughout history, not all parts of the world are equally powerful. Nowadays power, defined as the ability to make things happen as one wants them to, is most usually closely connected to economy, technology and access to information. The development of these, in turn, is increasingly perceived to be highly dependent upon an educated population. We see a connection here between our definition of power and Sen's (1999) view of Human Development as involving education that helps people become able to *do* what they want, rather than just *have* what they want.

In addition, different parts of the world have always held more or less different philosophical positions in terms of matters such as what is thought to be important in life, where truth can be found and what the ideal patterns of social organisation are considered to be.

3.3.3 National educational culture and socio-political belief system

The philosophical positions that predominate in different parts of the world have been interpreted in a variety of ways in different countries. For example, whether individual fulfilment or group harmony is thought to be of prime importance within a society varies considerably from one part of the world to another. Even where the individual is considered to be the most important, for example, there will be variations in the extent to which this principle is formally enshrined in written or unwritten national constitutions or evident in everyday life. Therefore national educational cultures will differ, at least in part, according to the different belief systems from which they derive. (The term 'culture' will be discussed in far greater detail in Chapter 2; for the present we are taking it to mean *the invisible belief system underlying the external social behaviour of a particular national group.*) For example, those countries that view the purpose of education primarily as producing new generations of socialised group members will have an educational culture which is distinct from those that see education principally as a means to enable each individual to reach his or her highest potential.

Broadly speaking each educational culture may be placed somewhere on a number of interconnected continua whose notional extremes represent different and complex ideas of the purposes of education and how they may be achieved. Kennedy 2011 (borrowing terms from Kalantzia and Cope 2008) proposes one such continuum which suggests that three main types of education systems currently exist in different parts of the world: the Didactic, the Authentic and the Transformative (p. 30). They differ from each other in, for example, their view of appropriate teaching approaches (structural-communicative or task based – see Chapters 4 and 5), where they believe that education can take place (only in schools; partly in schools, partly off site; or anywhere at all using technology) and in their view of the extent to which learners should be regarded as a uniform group or as individuals.

At a more fundamental level, educational cultures may differ in how they understand, for example, the concept of 'knowledge'. At extreme ends of another continuum one view of knowledge might be as a finite, unchanging body of 'true facts', while the other views knowledge as constantly being (re) constructed and so changing and expanding. The view of knowledge in turn affects attitudes to the learning approaches that are most common within the different levels of the education system. In some educational cultures the way in which knowledge is defined and the learning approaches that result may remain largely unchanged throughout the education system. In others there may be significant differences between, for example, primary school and university.

Coleman (1996:151, adapted from Ballard and Clanchy 1991) gives an overview of how cultural attitudes to knowledge may affect conceptions of learning and so what is expected of teachers. Table 1.2 highlights some of the options.

The top row of Table 1.2 shows a continuum of possible ways of thinking about knowledge. At the left, a 'conserving' view sees knowledge as a more or less finite and unchanging body of information to be passed on. At the right end, 'speculating', implies a view of knowledge as dynamic and changing

TABLE 1.2 Examples of how belief systems may affect what happens in the classroom

Attitudes to knowledge	Conserving ______		Extending
Learning approaches	Reproductive ______	Analytical ______	Speculative
Role of teacher	Exclusive source of knowledge, directs and assesses. ______	Coordinator of learning resources, questioner, critical guide, principal assessor. ______	Colleague, collaborator, preliminary critic, advisor.
Type of learning strategy promoted	Memorisation Imitation ______	Analytical and critical thinking ______	Speculating Hypothesising

and open to question. The rows that follow show some likely implications of these different views of knowledge for what is expected of teachers and what learning strategies are recommended, for example. We hope that you will see that differences in ideas about the nature of knowledge can therefore lead to very different visible behaviours in classrooms.

How do you see knowledge? Is this the same as or different from others in your context? How do you know?

3.3.4 Regional educational culture: Local attitudes to education

The factors mentioned under 'region' in the 'visible' layers may lead to variations on the national theme. For example, remote rural regions of any country are traditionally thought to be more conservative, in the sense of wanting to 'conserve' the present and keep things as they are. In the past, this has probably usually been largely due to lack of opportunities for contact with the wider world. Developments in technology now have the potential to change that, and in many places are doing so.

The economy or principal employment base of a particular place may mean that attitudes to education locally may be more or less favourable for children's learning. For example, if a particular place depends largely on agriculture, there may be a tendency to take children out of school during harvest periods, or for time after school to be used up on essential tasks to support immediate family needs rather than on homework. On the other hand, in an affluent, competitive, urban environment, parents might choose to pay for extra private teaching after school on top of what the state provides to try and ensure their children's educational success.

3.3.5. Institutional culture

The variations already mentioned at the layers above become further differentiated at the institutional level. Many readers will doubtless have had experience of working in different institutions and will therefore know how these may stress different aspects of the wider educational culture, expect and encourage different kinds of behaviours and appear to have different priorities. These differences may be a reflection of the region or town in which the institution is situated, but may equally be the result of the biographies of the different decision-makers involved (see Chapter 8).

3.3.6 Aspects of group dynamics in classroom groups

As may be imagined, all the above affect what actually happens in the classroom, and the way that the people in the classroom group think and behave, (see Chapters 2 and 6). All layers of the invisible context will contribute to classroom norms (what is considered to be appropriate behaviour), classroom relationships (how people interact with each other) and classroom goals (what results group members expect from time spent in the classroom).

In Figure 1.2, we again try to represent the 'invisible' context from the table in a way that demonstrates the part-wholeness of each of the layers. 'A' now represents the understandings people bring to and create in classrooms, and 'G' what it means to be human in the world. Once again the dotted lines in the diagram signify the ability of each layer to both influence and be influenced by the others.

As you will note, Figures 1.1 and 1.2 look essentially the same. However, each figure should be understood as representing different 'sides' of the **Place** context. Figure 1.1 offers a way of considering the many layers of the **Place** context from the physical visible perspective. Figure 1.2 takes the perspective of the many layers of the invisible, and often unspoken, meanings that influence what people living and working within particular **Places** expect from and invest in them. In Figure 1.3, we try to bring the two, visible and invisible, perspectives back together to represent the single, whole, multi-layered context of any **Place.**

Just as we said that the boundaries between each of the layers in Figures 1.1 and 1.2 are fuzzy and permeable, the same is true for the two 'sides' of the

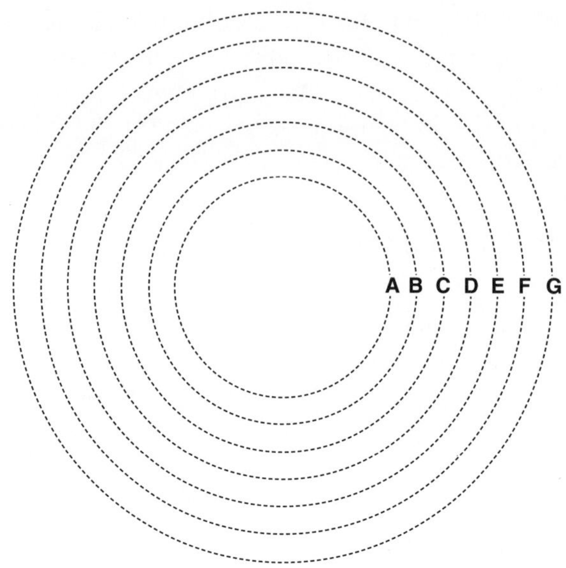

A. classroom groups B. institutional culture C. local attitudes (to education
D. regional educational culture E. national belief system
F. (balance of power) philosophical tradition G. human–ness

FIGURE 1.2 *The layers of the invisible Place context.*

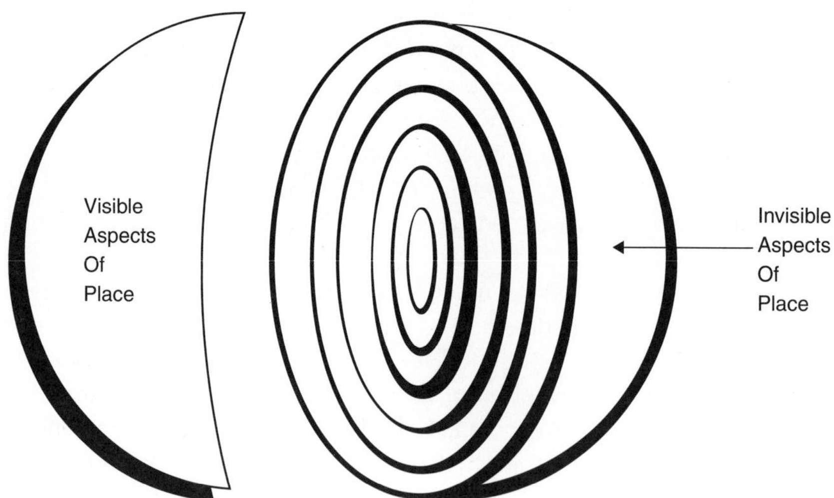

FIGURE 1.3 *The whole context of Place.*

whole. Here too, the 'invisible' and 'visible' are not neatly separated in the way the diagram above might suggest, but instead influence and are influenced by each other.

4. Time

As we have already mentioned, no layers of context are static. For example, at macro levels socio-political systems and the philosophical positions in which they are embedded are the result of historical processes and are continuing to change. As such changes occur, so their influence prompts changes in other layers.

Layers change at different speeds. Generally, the more powerful macro layers (where any 'top–down' or 'outside–in' change is initiated) themselves change more slowly. But changes to the macro-layers can also occur, apparently more quickly, as a result of 'bottom–up', or 'inside–out' influences stemming from changes within the micro layers. For example, if one individual (or small group) who has some power and/or influence in his/her layer of context begins to imagine and then talk about and/or demonstrate different ways of doing things and different ways of behaving, changes may start to happen (see Chapter 6). If, over time, a critical mass (Markee 1997) of individuals within the context begin to understand and support the new view, then changed attitudes and behaviours may begin to spread more widely, initially within that layer. In the longer term, provided they are not over-ruled by individuals or institutions in more powerful outer layers, these changes may eventually become a part of the educational culture (see Chapters 8 and 9).

Understanding a context therefore requires us to situate any event not only in terms of place but also in terms of when it takes place in the history of a class, an institution, an educational system or a country, as well as when it occurs with regard to the personal histories of the individuals (the teachers and learners) involved (see Chapters 4–6).

5. People

Most things about people relevant to understanding context have already been mentioned or alluded to in the previous sections. However, to summarise and review from this perspective:

- Societies are made up of groups of people, and cultures are a result of the meanings that unite people within these groups and within a society (see Chapter 2).
- Time affects peoples (national groups) and people as individuals. This is extremely relevant to education, as is clear if, for example, you think about how you would differentiate your teaching practices for a 6-year-old and a 26-year-old.
- Teaching is a human activity. We define teaching as purposeful activity designed to promote and support human learning processes, and human learning as something that happens within, between and mediated by people.
- Any context of teaching and learning entails **People** undertaking activities at a certain point in **Time** and in a certain **Place**. In other words, it is **People** who are central.

So, having illustrated how we developed our framework, we will now show you how it relates to the descriptive sketch of a TESEP context with which we began this chapter.

(i) *This classroom contains* . . . Everything in this paragraph relates to the MICRO, INNERMOST LAYER, mostly about PLACE (with some PEOPLE) and describes what is VISIBLE in the classroom.

(ii) *The teacher graduated five years ago* . . . This paragraph is again at the MICRO, innermost classroom layers, and describes what is VISIBLE in the same broad way as above. The focus here however is on PEOPLE and TIME.

(iii) *The junior secondary school of which this classroom* . . . This paragraph focuses on the next layer of the VISIBLE MICRO context, the institution, and describes aspects relating to PLACE, then PEOPLE.

(iv) *The school is situated on the outskirts of a medium sized town* . . . This paragraph begins to move towards more MACRO layers and describes VISIBLE aspects of PLACE, with some references to PEOPLE.

(v) *The country itself is industrialising rapidly* . . . We are now focussing on the National, MACRO layer describing VISIBLE aspects of PLACE and PEOPLE. There are some glimpses of the TIME element.

(vi) *There is a national curriculum* . . . Still describes VISIBLE features of the National MACRO level, with a focus on education.

(vii) *Teacher training colleges report* . . . Another paragraph describing mostly VISIBLE features of the Macro (national) context, relating to teachers and teacher education (PEOPLE) with references to PLACE (socio-economic conditions) and TIME (changing status of teachers)

(viii) *There is an inspectorate . . .* Again, describing VISIBLE aspects of the MACRO, National context, mainly relating to PEOPLE.

(ix) *There is no systematic provision . . .* as for the previous paragraph – but with the addition of some TIME information.

(x) *The country is situated in a part of the world . . .* MACRO, another layer out, VISIBLE, PLACE and TIME, then the beginnings of a discussion of PEOPLE in terms of their INVISIBLE 'thinking' in this PLACE.

(xi) *Official documentary rhetoric states that education should encourage all learners to flourish in their own way . . .* MACRO, but back to National PLACE layer, official 'visible', and some PEOPLE 'invisible' (though it would have needed some serious research to be able to assert that the main educational aim of most people was 'conserving').

(xii) *The school in which our classroom is situated is. . . .* MICRO, institution, PLACE layer, focus on the INVISIBLE and PEOPLE (with some VISIBLE examples of the likely influence of the INVISIBLE, and some reference to TIME and influences of next more MACRO layer of PLACE).

As you will have noticed in this analysis, the description we provided at the start of the chapter dealt in a lot more detail with visible aspects of place and people than with time, and dealt far less with the 'invisible' aspects of context. This is why much of what follows in this book will be focussed on developing lenses through which the 'invisible' behind the more easily accessible 'visible' can begin to be revealed.

6. Summary and task

- In this chapter we have introduced the idea that every (English language) classroom is at the centre of its own, partly visible, and partly invisible context, made up of many layers and three main interrelated components: **Place, People** and **Time**.
- Part of this complete context will be expressed in terms of the set of educational attitudes and behaviours that the **People** involved at the particular level of **Place** hold to be true and/or appropriate at that point in **Time.**
- Attitudes and behaviours are some of the fundamental markers of 'culture' which is the focus of our next chapter.

Task:

Look again at the description that started this chapter and at Figures 1.1 and 1.2 and the text that follows each. Make notes describing what you consider to be important features (because they influence what you do /do not do in the classroom and /or how you do it) of as many layers of your own visible and invisible context as you can. Where are there spaces? What do you need to do or find out about in order to fill them?

References

Coleman, P. H., ed. 1996. *Society and the Language Classroom.* Cambridge: Cambridge University Press.

Fullan, M. G. 1993. *Change Forces. Probing the Depths of Educational Reform.* London: Falmer Press.

Holliday, A. 1994. *Appropriate Methodology and Social Context.* Cambridge: Cambridge University Press.

Kennedy, C. 2011. 'Challenges for language policy, language and development'. In: H. Coleman, ed., *Dreams and Realities: Developing countries and the English language.* London: British Council, pp. 24–38.

Markee, N. 1997. *Managing Curricular Innovation.* Cambridge: Cambridge University Press.

Sen, A. 1999. *Development as Freedom.* Oxford: Oxford University Press.

UNESCO Institute of Statistics, 2008. [accessed 25 May 2012]. Available from: http://stats.uis.unesco.org/unesco/TableViewer/tableView.aspx?ReportId=183.

2

Exploring culture

Introduction

In Chapter 1, in explaining the invisible aspects of context, we made several references to the unspoken meanings that *people* in *places* over *time* create and share about how to 'be' (think and act). Here we will explore these ideas further, and relate them to definitions of culture.

You might like to think about (and note your responses to) the following before reading on:

> *How do you understand the word culture?*
> *Is it possible for one person to be a member of more than one culture at the same time? What makes you say so? Which cultures are you a member of?*
> *How do you see the relationship between 'culture(s)' and the 'invisible' aspects of context?*

In this chapter we explore these questions in quite a lot of detail. We think it is important because, as described in Chapter 1, the 'invisible' is a key part of context and has a huge influence on what happens in classrooms anywhere. We are now suggesting that what we have introduced as the 'invisible' aspects of context, equate to meanings associated with the term 'culture' which we explore in this chapter. By definition, the invisible cannot easily or simply be made visible, and there are no easy short cuts to explain what we want to mean here. As Williams noted (1976:87, in Kumaravadivelu 2008:9): 'Culture is one of the two or three most complicated words in the English language.'

We spend most of this whole chapter on discussing ways of understanding 'the invisible', 'culture' and 'cultures' – and, be warned, we do so in ways that may seem more academic and detailed than necessary. However, we believe that the complex understanding of 'culture' that will result if you stay with us throughout this chapter will be worth the effort. This is because 'culture' does powerfully influence all the visible layers of any context, although these influences are rarely taken sufficiently into account in descriptions of contexts. Also, because of its central importance not only to understanding context, but also to understanding what happens (or does not) when people try to make changes in classrooms, we use the term 'culture' frequently throughout the whole book. It is therefore important to come to a shared understanding of its meaning.

We begin by presenting two definitions of the term 'culture'. They are both ours, and the first we gave in the previous chapter. The second, the result of a process of study, is much more complex and detailed. We see the first of these as corresponding broadly to what Holliday (2011) calls an 'essentialist' closed view of culture, and the second to his 'non-essentialist' much more open view. We go on to describe how we got from the one to the other. The final section in this chapter demonstrates the use of a tool to support the investigation of the cultural influences on a classroom and shows how our revised, more flexible and detailed definition of culture can be used to help develop an understanding of some of the less visible but important aspects of a classroom context. A deeper awareness of the range of factors that may exert influence on what people do and think is necessary for anyone trying to make informed and realistic decisions about which teaching and learning approaches may be more less easily accepted by, integrated into, or effective in, their English teaching context.

1. Exploring CULTURE

Introduction

Here are two ways we have described 'culture'. The first 'just came' as we were writing Chapter 1, while the questions and answers that make up the second in the boxes below were the outcome of a period of 'desk research' and discussions.

1 'an invisible belief system underlying the external social behaviour of a particular national group'

2 What follows now is a description of how we got from the first definition to the other!

WHAT IS CULTURE?	Culture is a socially shared, underlying, often 'taken-for-granted' system of 'rules' which guide and control social behaviour, and which are very strongly held and affectively charged.
WHAT KINDS OF CULTURES ARE THERE?	Cultures can exist at all levels of context. In addition, occupations and educational disciplines can be said to have cultures which can exist across any particular contextual boundary of place.
HOW DO WE BECOME MEMBERS?	Culture is socially learnt (though never fully explicitly 'taught'), through interaction and the experience of living within the culture and behaving as a member.
HOW DO WE KNOW IT EXISTS?	Cultural 'rules' are invisible and rarely put into words. They can often be inferred from repeated observable behaviours (linguistic, interpersonal, physical etc.) in one group that are distinctive and different from those of another.
WHAT DOES IT DO?	Culture enables members to recognise each other, recognise 'outsiders', function with minimal social friction, intuitively and fundamentally understand each other and communicate 'in the same language'
WHAT IS IT FOR?	Culture ensures the smooth running of social groups, and contributes greatly to individuals' sense of belonging and identity.

For any reader on a course of study, **how** we went about expanding our understanding may be of as much interest as **what** we discovered and is outlined in the section, 'Process of exploring "culture"' at the very end of the chapter.

To understand anything, it is helpful to look at it from different perspectives. This is even more true with abstract 'things' because there are likely to be more perspectives to take into consideration in the first place. On this particular learning journey, we started to explore the concept of culture from three different angles (points of view).

We chose these initial three perspectives for very pragmatic reasons. The first was to look more closely at our original 'working definition' from Chapter 1. We then took a historical perspective, looking at different definitions over *time* (since when it comes to the development of ideas, *time* is one of the most influential aspects of context). Finally we considered 'culture' in terms of our purpose for investigating this concept – understanding the influence of 'invisible context' on the teaching and learning (of English).

1.1 Looking more closely at our previous definition

If we look again at our definition of culture and try to divide it up into the different component ideas, we find that it contains the following four parts:

> (1) an invisible (2) belief system (3) underlying the external social behaviour (4) of a particular national group.

Let's take each of these four parts of our definition in turn and consider the extent to which we might want to adapt them in the light of what other people have said.

You might like to try this same process with your own definition (if you made one when we asked you the question in the introduction.)

1.1.1 Culture as invisible

Taking the first idea, the notion of 'invisibility', let's see how central this is to other authors' understandings of the term. For example, Scollon and Scollon (1995:126–7) say the following:

> When we use the word 'culture' in its anthropological sense, we mean to say that culture is any of the customs, worldview, language, kinship system, social organisation, and other taken-for-granted day-to-day practices of a people which set that group apart as a distinctive group.

In this definition, it is clear there is some notion of invisibility, as a 'worldview' for example cannot be seen, it can only be inferred from what people say and do.

However, customs, language and social organisation are all more or less 'visible'. This gives us one perspective – but we need to consider at least one more. Goodenough (1957:167), for example, first defines culture as:

> whatever it is one has to know or believe in order to operate in a manner acceptable to its members, and to do so in any role that they accept for one of themselves.

It would seem that his understanding is that culture is 'invisible', because he goes on to say:

> Culture is not a material phenomenon; it does not consist of things, people, behaviour, or emotions. It is rather an organisation of these things. It is

the forms of things that people have in mind, their model for perceiving, relating, otherwise interpreting them.

These writers seem to see culture somewhat differently. The first one talks more about visible manifestations of a culture – mentioning some invisible parts. The second focuses almost entirely on the invisible role that culture plays in influencing particular behaviour and customs. Nonetheless it would seem that others broadly agree with our notion that a large part, at least, of the essence of culture is invisible.

1.1.2 Culture as a belief system

The second part of our working definition introduced the notion of a 'belief system' (2).

Many authors write about 'belief systems' in connection with 'culture'. They use expressions like 'patterns of thinking and frameworks of interpretation' (Cortazzi and Jin 1994:76), 'cognitive system' (Kay 1970:29), 'organised collection of rules' (Ciborowski 1979:102), 'models of perceiving' (Goodenough 1964:36), or 'common mental programming' (Hofstede 1991:112). More recently Spencer-Oatey and Franklin see 'the system' as less clearly defined, but still involving 'beliefs': 'a fuzzy set of basic assumptions and values, orientations to life, beliefs, policies, procedures and behavioural conventions' (2009:3).

Although authors use different words and metaphors, words like 'pattern', 'organised' 'model' or 'set' all seem to be close to the idea of some kind of more or less consistently connected system. In addition, words such as 'thinking', 'cognitive' and 'mental', suggest that this system relates to the idea of individual 'beliefs'.

1.1.3 Culture as underlying external social behaviour

That a culture's beliefs are perceived to be organised into a system is hardly surprising when we consider the next part of our definition 'underlying the external social behaviour' (3), since visible social behaviour could not be described as such if there were not observable patterns that could be noticed. In fact, according to Hofstede 'culture is always a collective phenomenon' (1991:112), although he continues by saying that individual behaviour within a culture is not always identical or totally predictable. At the individual level, he suggests that it constitutes *'a set of likely reactions of citizens with a common mental programming'*. (Hofstede cited above, our emphasis). Rather than being uniform, culturally determined reactions, he suggests, are simply likely to be found *'statistically more often in the same society'* (cited above). Similarly, Spencer-Oatey and Franklin (cited above) point out that culture 'influence[s] but do[es] not determine each member's behaviour and his/her interpretations of the 'meaning' of other people's behaviour' (2009:3).

Membership of a culture is therefore signified by external social behaviour. These commonly shared patterns of behaviour accomplish a number of things. They distinguish the members of one group or category of people from another. They make the actions of one group member 'intelligible to another' (Kay 1970:29) by providing 'the know-how that a person must possess to get through the task of daily living' (Wardhaugh 1986:211). Finally they give members 'a distinctive identity which is used to organise their internal sense of cohesion and membership' (Scollon and Scollon 1995:126–7). To summarise, culture can explain external social behaviour and be inferred from it, even though not all members of any culture follow all the cultural 'rules' all the time.

1.1.4 Culture as being a feature of a particular national group

Finally our definition concluded with 'of a particular national group (4)'. How far is culture always understood as being connected to national groups? Baker (1993:272) includes 'the umbrella idea of western culture' in his discussion of the concept, suggesting that it is possible to understand culture as being bigger than a mere national group. Furthermore, Cortazzi and Jin (1994:76) talk about culture in relation to 'thinking and behaviour of social or ethnic groups and also those of major occupational groups'. So, it seems that groups of people of any size, with shared and distinctive 'mental programming' (Hofstede 1991:112) can be thought of as members of a culture. If groups of differing sizes may be considered to be a 'culture', and if cultures exist at the level of occupational groups, this introduces the possibility that an individual may simultaneously be a member of more than one culture. We explore this further in Sections 2.3.2 and 2.3.3 below.

1.1.5 Conclusion

We have seen, then, that our original definition (although suiting its purpose at the time) was somewhat limited. First, we have seen that groups both larger and smaller than 'a nation' can share culture. Next, the invisible cultural belief system needs visible manifestations. This is mainly so that members can recognise others with whom they share cultural meanings. In addition, however, this not only allows outsiders to recognise someone as being from a different culture, but is also the reason why the concept of culture has any meaning. If there were no outward signs of cultural difference, the concept of culture would probably never have developed and perhaps instead we would talk about the meaning of 'being human'. Finally, as noted above, although cultures are socially shared, individual members of every culture also behave differently.

2. The historical perspective

Although we reached a 'conclusion' above which has already led to changes in our initial definition, we still have the other two perspectives to look at. So we now turn to how understandings of culture have evolved over time.

2.1 Early definitions

Writers early in the last century, such as Tylor (1924) defined culture as:

> that complex whole which includes knowledge, beliefs, art, morals, law, customs, and any other capabilities and habits acquired by man as a member of society.

This definition includes many of the visible and invisible factors already discussed, but is significant because it also includes 'Art', a symbol of another, very common understanding of the word 'culture'. In this understanding, the term is primarily used to mean the valued visible products created at some point in history by (members of) a particular national or ethnic group. These products may be literary, artistic, musical, architectural or artefacts such as textiles and pottery. Using the term in this sense, when people refer to Chinese culture, poetry, porcelain or the Terracotta Warriors may come to mind, Indian culture has magnificent architecture, or Moghul miniatures, French culture painting, German culture music, or British culture Shakespeare.

2.2 More recent definitions

Later definitions explicitly exclude this meaning of culture, as for example Wardhaugh (1986:211), who states:

> We do not intend to use the term culture in the sense of 'high culture', i.e., the appreciation of music, literature, the arts, and so on.

But Wardhaugh was not the first to exclude 'high culture' from definitions of the term. He deliberately acknowledges his debt to Goodenough, see above, who as early as 1957 not only omitted to mention 'high culture', but also explicitly excluded any 'visible' 'things, people, behaviour or emotions'.

2.3 The concept of culture extended

In more recent times, the notion of culture has been extended in various ways. Many of these seem relevant to our third perspective (understanding the influence of 'invisible context' on the teaching and learning of English) so we mention them here.

2.3.1 Culture contributes to identity and is not emotion-free

So far, when looking at what others say about culture human emotions and feelings have not been seen as part of 'culture'. The extracts below suggest that the invisible 'thinking' that members of a culture share (what we called 'belief system') is important for their psychological wellbeing and identity and is invested with emotion.

> It provides individuals and groups of individuals with psychological structure that guides various aspects of their life. It steers them in their intellectual, spiritual, and aesthetic development. It offers them a rationale for their behaviour, a prism through which to see it, and a measurement by which to evaluate it. It presents them with a basis for identity formation. (Kumaravadivelu 2008:10)
>
> Cultures are a collective phenomenon that embody people's responses to the uncertainties and chaos that are inevitable in human experience. These responses fall into two major categories. The first is the **substance** of culture-shared, emotionally charged belief systems that we call ideologies. The second is **cultural forms** – observable entities, including actions, through which members of a culture express, affirm, and communicate the substance of their culture to one another. (Trice and Beyer 1993:2)

As you can see, the authors propose the same visible and invisible dimensions of culture and emphasise the same notion of shared beliefs and meanings which guide behaviour. In addition, however, Kumaravadivelu highlights the importance of culture for identity formation and maintenance, and Trice and Beyer acknowledge the affective dimension of cultural beliefs when they call them 'emotionally charged'. As cultural beliefs are linked to identity, they are not emotion-free, but instead engage our feelings, to the extent that we may get upset if they are challenged, if our 'key meanings' (Blackler and Shinmin 1984) are questioned. (This is discussed further in Chapter 9)

2.3.2 Organisational cultures

Louis (1983) among others points out that the notion of culture can and should also be applied to understand the workings of organisations and institutions, for example, government departments, businesses, schools or universities.

> Organisations are culture-bearing milieux, that is they are distinctive social units possessed of a set of common understandings for organisational action (e.g., what we're doing together in this particular group, appropriate ways of doing in and among members of the group) and languages and other symbolic vehicles for expressing common understandings. (Louis 1983:39)

The members of organisations, therefore, like the members of other types of culture mentioned, to some extent at least share a particular worldview, certain beliefs and ways of behaving that 'outsiders' do not share. English teachers or other ELT professionals who work within a school or an education department for any length of time are also members of an organisation. They too are therefore, members of their organisational culture (which again we discuss in more detail in Chapter 8).

2.3.3 Occupational and disciplinary cultures

Cortazzi and Jin (1994), as we have seen above, suggest that occupational groups may also constitute cultures. Such occupational cultures may have members throughout the world, whose cultural identity is in part demonstrated through their use of a particular professional language

> Professional discourse is composed of various discourses which have been developed over time by different occupations, for example medicine, law, psychiatry, education, etc., as illustrated by the use of jargon, of certain communicative genres and of certain routines. (Grossen 2010:11)

For example, doctors the world over, wherever they come from, are members of an international culture of doctors. This is true to the extent that much of their professional language (professional languages are often known as registers) and many professional actions are based on the same set of underlying rules and beliefs, and are therefore mutually intelligible only to other doctors. Is this also true for teachers? Are they members of an occupational culture? Within teaching there do seem to be definite disciplinary or subject-specific cultures, with separate registers and ways of teaching based on sets of underlying beliefs about the teaching-learning process. If this is so, then English teachers can be said to constitute a disciplinary culture, since they too have their own register, and some shared teaching – learning beliefs about desirable classroom behaviours.

In Chapter 1, we referred to Holliday's (1994) distinction between BANA and TESEP. If we agree with this distinction, then we may not have a single disciplinary culture of English teachers. Indeed it is likely that individual teachers' membership of a disciplinary culture will vary according to the place and time aspects of context.

2.3.4 Individuals belonging to multiple cultures

Sections 2.3.2 and 2.3.3 above suggest that the beliefs and behaviours of organisational and/or occupational cultures are usually shared by a group of people in only part of their lives (that is the working environment). If the organisational and/or occupational culture governs only part of its members' lives, then this suggests that in the rest of their lives outside work they are also part of the larger culture in which they live. This has introduced the notion that a person may belong to more than one culture simultaneously. Thus now we are saying that as well as being a member of a *national* and/ or ethnic culture, many English teachers are members of an *institutional* culture, that of their school or their college, and may also, to differing extents (depending on the beliefs of their wider organisational and national cultures) be part of a shared national or even worldwide English Teaching *occupational* culture, with its own professional language and experiences.

2.3.5 Culture is dynamic, not static

Street (1993) wrote an article called *Culture is a verb* in which he suggests that our concept of culture should understand the term as something that people *do*, not just as a collection of unchanging objects. This parallels the difference between a view of culture as the belief system underlying what cultural groups at different levels actually do (and don't do) and the way they expect their members to behave, and the view of 'high-culture' as the collection of a national or ethnic group's visible, completed artistic endeavours. Although such high-culture tends to change more slowly and often looks backward into history, the individual's actual *do*ing of culture is continuous and constantly evolving in the light of changing circumstances.

Indeed, our quick trawl though the evolution of ideas about culture in the twentieth century shows that how it is understood has changed and is changing – and seems bound to continue to change. So, while we acknowledge that we cannot reach a final definitive understanding of the term, perhaps it is possible to find an acceptable definition for now, which suits our purpose in using it: that of understanding the influence of 'invisible context' on the teaching and learning of English.

3. Seeing the relevance of 'Culture' to our purpose

We have so far touched on several ways in which the concept of culture is relevant to (English) teaching and learning. In this section, our main aim is to understand how the invisible context may influence our work, so in our reading we have looked particularly for references, to, for example, schools, learning, teaching, classrooms or language.

3.1 Culture is learned, not innate

The first thing we discover is that culture itself is learned. Hofstede (1991:5) points out that 'culture is learned not inherited. It derives from one's social environment not from one's genes.' Previously Wardhaugh had already noted that:

> whatever a person needs to know in order to function in a particular society . . . is socially acquired; the necessary behaviours are learned and do not come from any kind of genetic endowment. (1986:211)

Scollon and Scollon (1995) explain this more fully and we draw on some of their main points here, as they are full of references to the key words that we said above that we would set out to look for.

First of all, the development of our worldview occurs as part of our learning to be members of the cultures into which we are born. There are two main ways in which we learn our culture(s): education and socialisation. Education represents the formal planned procedures for teaching and learning that have been more or less explicitly agreed by a particular culture and which are systematically used with all new members. Socialisation is the informal process whereby children in all cultures notice what others around them do, notice the comments that are made about their own and others' behaviour, and so 'learn' (in the sense of Krashen's 'acquire' 1981/2003) what is and what is not viewed as acceptable in their culture.

Scollon and Scollon further divide socialisation into:

1. Primary socialisation: the process of becoming a member of society that every child goes through when very young within the family setting.
2. Secondary socialisation: the continuing process of becoming a member of one or more cultures that takes place outside the home in the school and other environments, but that is not part of formal education. An example here might be learning how to interact with other children in the school playground.

Features of socialisation include that it begins at birth and it is never explicitly happening – nobody is 'teaching' it. Within education, too, the vast majority of cultural learning that happens is indirect – through the often-invisible influences of culture on for example, what it is thought valuable to learn, and how it is proper for teachers and learners to behave. One thing all teachers in all classrooms will be doing, probably unconsciously, is 'teaching' aspects of cultures. For example, Scollon and Scollon broadly contrast features of the Chinese and East-Asian, Confucian-influenced culture with the Christian influenced culture of Europe and North America in terms of their views of human nature and of the basic units of society and suggest that these result in very different educational cultures. We provide a crude summary of this below in Table 2.1 to illustrate how deep invisible 'worldviews' may influence the classroom (although we recognise, based on our experience in both contexts, that the polarised black and white distinctions made are in fact, as is always the case in the real world, labelled points on a continuum of shades of grey).

TABLE 2.1 How features of 'worldview' may influence 'educational culture'

	Confucian-influenced cultures	Christian-influenced cultures
View of the nature of humans	Human nature is basically good THEREFORE: Teachers tend to assume that learners are going to cooperate and try to do what is right. Learners have an intrinsic motivation to do the right thing	Humans are basically sinful THEREFORE: Teachers tend to assume learners are not going to cooperate, that they will try to undermine the teacher. Learners need to be motivated to do the right thing by reward or punishment and threats.
View of the basic unit of society	The individual is part of the wider family group which is in turn part of the larger units of society. THEREFORE: The success of the individual in the education system/ the classroom is seen in terms of its contribution to the needs of the wider social unit.	The individual is the basic unit of society. THEREFORE: Within education learners are encouraged to compete to be individually successful, even if this leads to a lessening of group harmony.

Chick (1989) expands on the conditions and process of this cultural learning. He notes that:

> 'People's world views are shaped by their contemporaneous life experiences, and in interacting they (people) confirm conventions by conforming to them, and establish new ones by finding ways of thinking and doing things together . . . (Cultural learning) is' 'both historically given and in the process of being created.' (1989:243)

Learning 'culture' thus involves both learning a set of previously agreed conventions and behaviours, and participating in the constantly evolving creation of new ones. Social interaction is a crucial component of cultural learning, which, like learning in general, is a lifelong process.

3.2 Language and culture

3.2.1 Language and cultural learning

If *interaction* is needed for culture to be learnt, then so too is language. In classrooms, teachers, of English or any other subject, try to reach shared meanings with learners through such interaction. Whether using first or second language the types of interactions that are thought to be appropriate in a particular classroom will be culturally influenced.

In all classrooms whatever the subject being taught, it is **language** (from the teacher, the textbook and fellow students) which is, as it were, the major tool for promoting both subject learning and every type of cultural learning (see Chapter 3).

3.2.2 Language as a marker of cultural membership

This brings us back to the idea of members of a culture sharing a common language. As we noted above it seems possible that everyone can be a member of more than one culture, each of which may have its own different 'language'. 'Language' here, may refer to 'world languages', for example, English, Chinese, Hindi, Bahasa Malaysia, or Xhosa or the languages/registers of, for example, particular professions (such as doctors' language or teachers' language).

3.2.3 Teachers' cultural memberships

The conscious or unconscious cultural affiliations of the individual people in any classroom will influence what happens within it. Indeed, in any classroom there will be a unique combination of teacher and learners, each bringing their personal understandings of their culture(s) to the classroom with them. This means that each classroom itself becomes a small culture. We discuss this further below.

While both teachers and their learners may be members of more than one culture, here we discuss the various cultures that an English teacher may be a member of, as in most contexts teachers are the more powerful members of classroom communities.

Any teacher will be a member of a national culture, and organisational culture and as suggested above a number of classroom cultures. They will also be members of other cultures. For example, in one occupational culture there may be different disciplinary cultures. You may have noticed that English teachers and Science teachers use what could be called a 'different language', at least when teaching or talking about their subject – and as we have seen, different 'languages' are a visible marker of different cultures. For example, Figure 2.1 illustrates different disciplinary cultures within the single occupational culture of teaching.

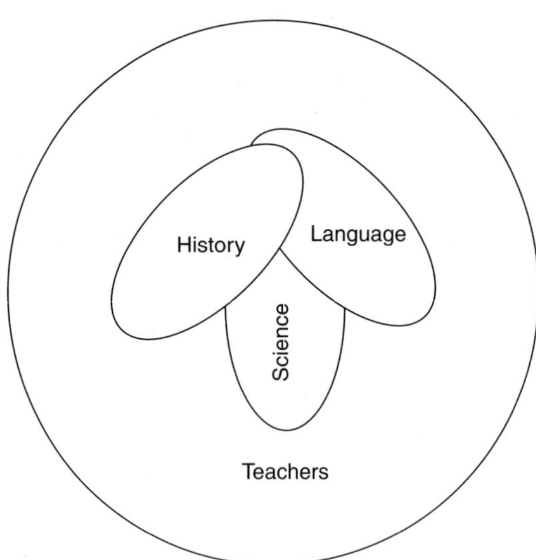

FIGURE 2.1 *Different disciplinary cultures within a single occupational culture.*

We can also, as in Figure 2.2, have different occupational cultures spanning a single discipline. For example, within 'Languages' we not only have teachers, but also, speech therapists, translators and experts in artificial intelligence etc.

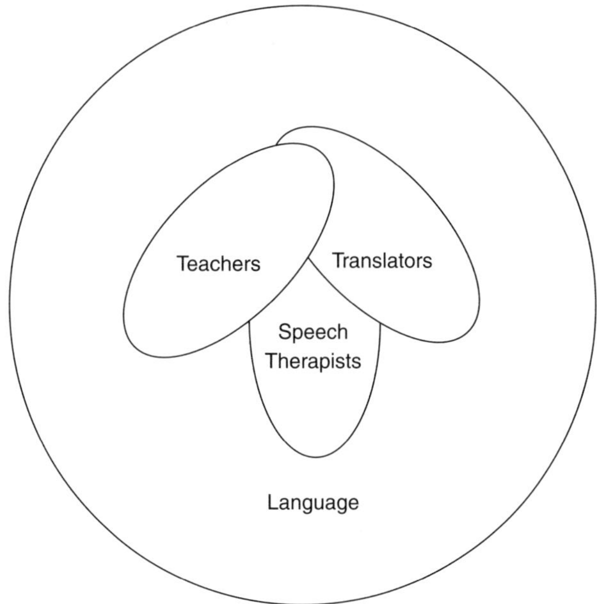

FIGURE 2.2 *Different occupational cultures within a single discipline.*

As well as being overlapping as illustrated in Figures 2.1 and 2.2, another noticeable feature of both disciplinary and occupational cultures is that they can extend beyond national boundaries to regions of, or even the whole, world. Potentially therefore, as shown in Figure 2.3, members of the same disciplinary culture, like English teachers, may in certain respects have more in common with each other (other English teachers anywhere in the world), than with other members of their respective national occupational cultures. English teacher B in Figure 2.3 below would be an example of this. English teacher A, however, would be an example of someone who has more in common with colleagues teaching other subjects in their own national culture, than with English teachers worldwide. English teacher C in Figure 2.3 offers a third possible option: that of an English teacher who has more in common with non-teaching aspects of the profession worldwide (materials writers or language testers, for example) than with fellow classroom teachers either globally or within their own context.

The concept of simultaneous membership of a number of 'embedded cultures' (organisational cultures within national cultures, occupational cultures within organisational cultures, classroom cultures within occupational cultures etc.) that we have developed throughout this chapter, is represented in Figure 2.4.

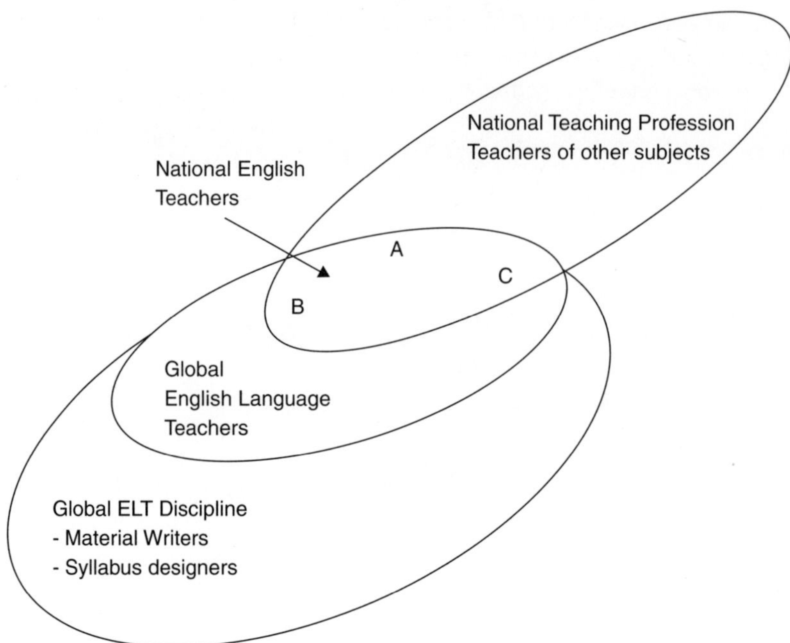

FIGURE 2.3 *Possible relationships between occupational/disciplinary cultures and the wider culture.*

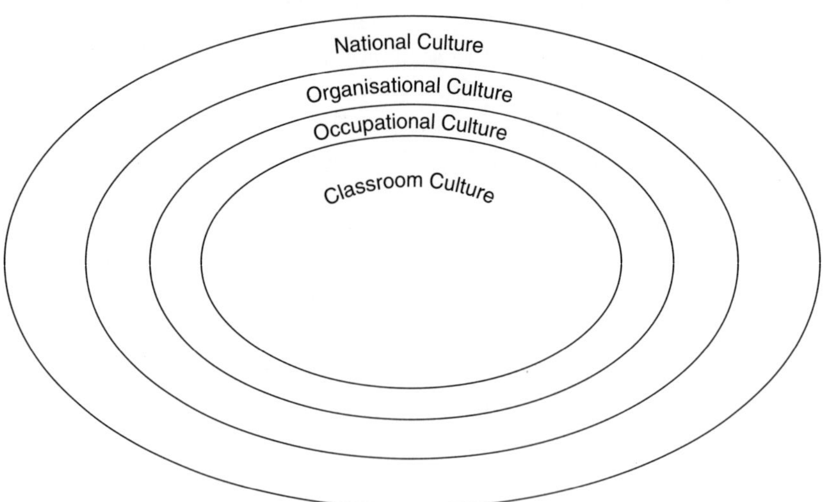

FIGURE 2.4 *Embedded cultures.*

You will no doubt have noticed that Figure 2.4 is very similar to Figures 2.2 and 2.3 in the previous chapter on aspects of contexts. In fact, and as we discovered, (when trying to avoid even using the word 'culture' in the previous chapter), it is almost impossible not to talk about culture when referring to context and vice versa. Every context contains and is affected by one or more cultures or levels of culture. Every culture can be manifest in many contexts. As with the layers of visible and invisible context in Chapter 1, we do not believe that the boundaries between the different levels / layers of culture that we each belong to are strictly fixed. Instead, they are 'fuzzy' (Spencer-Oatey 2000) and the behaviours and beliefs typical of one layer probably overlap with many of those at others (Signorini et al. 2009).

Finally, as a result of this process of exploration, and to get to our second more detailed definition (in 2.1 above) we developed the following questions.

- What *is* culture?
- What kinds of cultures are there?
- How do people become members?
- How do we know it exists?
- What does it do?
- What is it for?

How would you now answer these questions? Perhaps you might like to try to do this without first looking back at our table – which in any case does not provide 'the right answer', but rather how we answered the questions after the process we have described.

4. Classroom cultures

We said above that because every individual in a classroom brings with them their memberships of various cultures, the interactions in any one classroom will be influenced by these and so create a unique classroom culture, one which will nonetheless share some or many features with other classrooms in that school, city, region or country.

In this section, we look at how all the above theorising can be of use to teachers and other educational professionals in exploring and understanding what happens in classrooms.

4.1 Getting at cultural understandings through visible aspects of the classroom context

So what exactly can teachers look for? The invisible remains invisible, but there is a wealth of visible evidence to notice in schools and classrooms that can help them identify cultural influences on, and cultural learning in, the classroom. Scollon and Scollon (Section 1.1.1 above) talked about culture 'in the anthropological sense', and anthropologists when studying cultures spend time in the cultures just observing (using the visible as a starting point for understanding the 'invisible'). They look at, for example, what people do, what they use to do it, what they produce, their language and so on. Teachers can do the same. Examples of the kinds of visible things that can help teachers work out underlying cultural 'rules' and that you might notice in a classroom over time are given below.

- WHAT PEOPLE DO
  - writing, or drawing or talking?
  - sitting, standing or moving around?
  - all doing the same, people doing different things?
  - who is doing what?
- WHAT PEOPLE USE TO DO IT
  - textbooks and exercise books,
  - a blackboard, whiteboard or data projector?
  - desks, tables, chairs?
  - laptops, pens, pencils or chalk?
  - how many of each thing?
  - how distributed?
- THE PEOPLE
  - number?
  - clothing?
  - positioning in relation to each other?
  - movement during the class – all, some, when, how?

- PRODUCTS
  - what is produced?
  - e.g. spoken, written language, task outcomes etc.
  - who produces?
  - what is done with the products?
- LANGUAGE
  - who uses what language in what ways, to whom, when?
  - who uses language most?
  - what is language used for?
  - who initiates interactions?
  - what types of interactions are most frequent?
  - which language, in terms of first language and target language do different people use?
  - how often and what for?
  - how is language used in the sense of tone and volume of voice?
  - how is language used by the different people?
- OTHER FEATURES OF INTERACTIONS
  - gestures? who? when?
  - facial expressions? who? when?
- RITES AND RITUALS

Finally there is the area of classroom 'rites and rituals' that it may be possible to observe.

Does anything noticeable repeatedly happen – for example, at the starts or ends of classes or between phases in lessons?

Are there any further regular patterns observable in the manner in which different people behave to one another?

While we are suggesting that it is useful for teachers to take an anthropological stance from time to time to investigate (one of) their classroom cultures, it is also a useful perspective for outsider observers to take.

We, for example, used this framework when watching a DVD of an English class in West Africa. We are certain that we did not notice everything (even in that which *was* filmed) but some of what we did notice is:

What people do	The teacher remains standing throughout the lesson, sometimes moving between the board and her desk (on a dais) and once or twice moving off the dais to the front of the class. At one point she goes to the back of class when explaining the meaning of the word 'near' The pupils sit all the time (except when they stand up to answer questions); one or two are called to the front of the class to help illustrate the meaning of a word or phrase. The tasks given (implicitly) to the pupils throughout the lesson seem to be to listen to and try to answer the teacher. Pupils as a group are often told to repeat words or phrases modelled by the teacher. Almost all pupils put their hands up whenever the teacher asks a question. Pupils speak only to respond to the teacher's questions.
What people use	The teacher uses a blackboard and chalk. She uses the classroom, the things and people in it when explaining meanings. She looks at papers (lesson notes?) from time to time. We see exercise books in front of some students but they are not opened. The students sit, shoulder to shoulder, on benches which are attached to a desk top. There is one aisle between the rows of benches down the middle of the room which is used by the teacher and any pupils she calls to the front of the class
The people	There are at least 50 pupils. There seem to be equal numbers of boys and girls Some students are noticeably bigger and taller (older?) than others.

	Students wear different clothes, in a limited range of colours. Some students' clothes look newer/neater than others'. The teacher wears a brightly coloured, floor-length dress. She wears jewellery and a watch. Her hair is styled.
Products	The classroom walls are bare. There is writing on the board All pupils produce some repeated words or phrases orally, mostly chorally . . .
Language	The teacher initiates all language use in the classroom. She speaks the L2 (target language) at all times. She speaks almost entirely in single sentences, occasionally in linked sequences of two or three sentences. The interaction with the learners follows a sequence: • teacher asks a question • pupils give an answer • teacher tells or shows them whether the answer is right or wrong Pupils respond to the teacher's questions individually. There is also choral and some individual repetition of new words and phrases.
Rites and rituals	(Perhaps – because we only saw one class!) At the beginning of the class all pupils stand up together greet the teacher and ask how she is. The teacher replies. After each question from the teacher many students call out 'teacher teacher!' and raise their hands and sometimes their bodies. The nominated pupil stands up to answer.
Other message bearers	The teacher, when indicating who should answer, sometimes calls a student's name and sometimes says: 'You' and points.

We did not always find it easy to decide which category we should put what we noticed into. Some could probably be in more than one category. It is important to recognise that categorisations are ways of helping to organise a mass of information. They are rarely perfectly exact, separate and fully independent of each other.

4.2 Interpreting observations of classroom cultures

The next stage, after careful description, is to consider to what extent what we saw is specific to the classroom culture, or the institutional culture, or the culture of the particular system or more generally to the broader national or 'part-of-the world' cultures in which the classroom is situated. It may also be that elements of what we can describe might more accurately be attributed to the global 'disciplinary culture' of English Language professionals.

We next therefore, looked at the above information and considered what it suggested about 'cultures' at various levels. We did not find this easy to do, and again it was often difficult to decide which level or levels of culture were responsible for which of the things and behaviours that we noticed. So, again, we do not claim that our conclusions are 'right answers'.

English Language Teacher culture (occupational and disciplinary)	The teacher seemed to understand the need to contextualise the new language being introduced in order to support 'meaning'. Linked to this, she understood the role of 'realia', and how to exploit the classroom to provide contexts. She recognised the desirability of using the L2 in the classroom as much as possible. Patterns of interaction followed a sequence known as Initiation, Response, Feedback (IRF: Sinclair and Coulthard 1975). (This pattern is widely adopted in the broad occupational culture – that is, very common in classrooms all round the world. However, it has been criticised in parts of the disciplinary culture of ELT because it does not model or allow students to practise 'authentic' patterns of communication.)
	Choral Repetition is an aid to learning. Learning a language involves the learning (memorisation?) of words and phrases. It is not clear how important being able to use them is thought to be.
Classroom culture	The teacher was very much in charge. The pupils were not 'in awe' of the teacher, they seemed keen to participate

	The classroom was a hierarchy with clear roles accepted by both sides. The teacher used a few pupils' names, and her facial expression was serious throughout: suggesting to us a fairly distant teacher-pupil relationship (?).
Institutional/ school culture	Possible rules of the school culture include: • Teachers are supposed to dress smartly. • Pupils are not expected to wear uniform. • Pupils should show respect to teachers by, e.g. standing up and greeting them when they enter the room, and standing up to answer questions.
Educational culture	The teacher should stand at the front of the class (on the dais provided). The teacher is expected to initiate all learning activities and remain in full control of what everyone is doing all the time. Learners are not expected to initiate anything in the classroom. Their role is to follow whatever the teacher initiates. All learners need to learn the same things in the same way.
Wider regional or national culture	The number of children in the classroom and the lack of visible equipment and resources suggest a fairly poor country. From what we know, at the time of recording, English had no official role in the country (a Francophone country), so the fact that it is taught suggests a culture that believes English has, or will have, some importance for its citizens. The pupils' efforts to participate suggest fairly high motivation, possibly due to respect for education in the wider culture. The smartness of the teacher and students' deferential behaviour suggest that teachers have some status and are respected in the culture. Boys and girls sat side by side in the classroom. Numbers of each gender were more or less similar. This suggests a culture that sees the importance of educating all its citizens.

The above therefore suggests, in terms of influences of cultures on what happens in this classroom (following the 'invisible' layers of context):

- A wider culture that values education and those who work within it.
- An educational culture that assumes the teacher–pupil relationship to be a knower–learner one, in which the teacher will be in complete charge at all times.
- An institutional culture which reflects the hierarchical assumptions of the educational culture and expects learners to demonstrate their respect for the teacher through signs of politeness. Teachers are expected to dress formally.
- A classroom culture in which the teacher (and perhaps the pupils too?) does not wish to alter the fundamentally hierarchical relationships that exist. There is little sense of personal contact between teacher and pupils. The size of the class must make this difficult anyway.
- An English teacher disciplinary culture suggests itself in the teacher's use of L2 throughout (admittedly a very narrow range of language) and through her use of the few available resources to contextualise the language that she introduced and/or had students practise. Choral repetition is an aid to learning. Learning a language involves the learning (memorisation?) of words and phrases.

Given what the students are experiencing, there is also considerable cultural learning taking place (secondary socialisation) with regard, for example, to what (language) learning means, a child's role in that process and so on.

The above interpretation provides only a sketch of the possible cultural influences that exist or cultural learning that might occur in the classroom. It isn't 'right' or complete. If this is so, why then do we bother to do it? For us, it is the *process* of stopping to think about cultural influences that is valuable in itself. The product of any such process will be imperfect and incomplete. However, because 'cultures' underpin all thinking and behaviour, such a process, even though it can result in an only partial understanding, is crucial to any examination of context.

In this chapter, we have looked more closely at the 'invisible' side of our model for 'context'. We have already said, and will no doubt say again, that the separation of layers or perspectives is an artificial device to enable us to discuss aspects of context in linear words. In fact, of course everything is intertwined and influences and is influenced by everything else. Writing about pedagogical settings (by which we understand them to mean much the same as we mean by 'context of teaching and learning') Leach and Moon describe these connections as follows:

> It is the interdependence of all its parts over time that makes a pedagogic setting a single entity. Participants create, enact and experience- together and separately- purposes, values and expectations; knowledge and ways of knowing; rules of discourse; roles and relationships; resources, artefacts; and the physical arrangement and boundaries of the setting. All of these together and none of these alone. (1999:267)

THE PROCESS OF EXPLORING 'CULTURE'

For any reader on a course of study, ***how*** *we went about expanding our understanding may be of as much interest as* ***what*** *we discovered and this is outlined here.*

In this section we will provide a commentary on the process of exploring the concept of culture and arriving at our own understanding. Although we had tried not to mention culture in Chapter 1, we found ourselves unable to avoid it, and therefore had to provide a working definition. We say 'had' to, because we knew just how complex the concept was, and did not want to investigate it at that point, but we did need to give a working definition of the term to enable us to continue our argument. In this chapter, however, 'culture' is central and so we took what we had already written as the starting point for the first phase of our exploration of the term. This involved searching for similarities and differences between our initial working definition and those we found in the literature.

We next looked at the development of the concept in the literature over time. You may have noticed that certain writers, for example Goodenough, seem to have influenced other people's thinking. It is quite usual in the discussion of academic concepts to find that certain writers are referred to more frequently than others. This probably means that these are the people who are accepted as having added significantly to the general understanding of the concept under investigation. It is sensible therefore, in your own thinking and writing to also consult and refer to these authors.

The fact that people still refer back to Goodenough's definition suggests that he is one of these kinds of people. We noted that his definition was a considerable departure from previous definitions which included reference to 'high culture' and the 'appreciation of music, literature the arts and so on' (Wardhaugh 1986). We also wonder whether one reason that our intuitive definition was very close indeed to that of Goodenough may be because during the second half of the twentieth century, the Goodenough definition had filtered down into a general academic consciousness of which we are part.

A further point about this historical perspective is that it might be tempting to assume that the most recent definitions are necessarily 'the best'. However, it is too simplistic to say the later the better, after all the influence of Goodenough's definition lasted a long time. In addition, it is important when looking at recent definitions to ensure that they are building on what has gone before. Some may be exploring only a part of the whole, adding detail, as it were, while others, like us in Chapter 1, might be using an undeveloped 'working definition'.

Our purpose here was to define culture and then to relate what we found to the focus of this book: understanding contexts of teaching and learning English. We went through the following stages:

- We divided up our working definition (itself constructed as a result of the need to use the word 'culture' in Chapter 1) into separate ideas.
- We looked in the literature for references to these ideas.
- We adapted our ideas in the light of what we found.
- We added other ideas that we felt were relevant to our purpose.
- We looked for connections between cultures at different levels and teaching-learning in classrooms.
- We offered a revised definition of culture

We have described our process in some detail. Our purpose was to demonstrate the kind of (idealised) process that needs to be undertaken to arrive at a new, more complete understanding of a particular academic term – in other words to get at the shared academic meaning behind the term. We went through this process in order to demonstrate the relevance and practical use of a complex understanding of culture for anyone in Education (whatever their various cultural memberships) who seeks to investigate their context.

5. Summary and task

In this chapter we have:

- Explored the term 'culture' in more depth
- Considered the role(s)/influences culture(s) might have on/play in the teaching and learning (of English)
- Proposed a tool to help identify such roles/influences and, through demonstrating the use of this tool

- Shown how a deeper understanding of 'culture(s)' can in turn lead to a deeper understanding of the context of teaching and learning (English) in classrooms anywhere.

It is already clear is that culture cannot be disassociated from language. In the next chapter we shall look in more detail at ideas about:

- Possible relationships between language and culture.

We also consider

- Some of the huge variety of 'language contexts' that exist in different countries and regions of the world
- The extent to which English is perceived as a 'world language'
- How such perceptions may affect decisions made about English language teaching provision.

Task:

Looking at the section 'Getting at cultural understandings through visible aspects of the classroom context', observe a (language) classroom in your context. Describe what you noticed under the headings suggested. Then try to interpret what you have noticed in terms of what it can tell you about the culture in and of your context.

References and further reading

Ciborowski, T. J. 1979. 'Cross-cultural aspects of cognitive functioning'. In: Marsella et al., eds, *Perspectives on Cross-Cultural Psychology*. Waltham, Massachusetts:Academic Press, pp. 101–16.

Chick, J. K. 1989. 'Intercultural miscommunication as a source of friction in the workplace and in educational settings in South Africa'. In: O. Garcia and R. Otheguy, eds, *English across Cultures: Cultures across English: A Reader in Cross-Cultural Communication*. Berlin: Mouton de Gruyter, pp. 243–65.

Coleman, P. H., ed. 1996. *Society and the Language Classroom*. Cambridge: Cambridge University Press.

Cortazzi, M. and J. Lixian. 1994. 'Narrative analysis; applying linguistics to cultural models of learning'. In: D. Graddol and J. Swann, eds, *Evaluating Language*. Bristol: BAAL/Multilingual Matters, pp. 75–90.

Goodenough, W. H. 1957. 'Cultural anthropology and linguistics'. In: P. L. Garvin, ed., *Report of the Seventh Annual Round Table on Linguistics and Language Study*. Washington, DC: Georgetown University Press, pp. 167–77.

Grossen, M. 2010. 'Interaction analysis and psychology: a dialogical perspective'. *Integrative Psychological and Behavioural Science*, 44, pp. 1–22.

Hofstede, G. 1991. *Cultures and Organizations: Software of the Mind.* London: McGraw-Hill.

Holliday, A. 1994. *Appropriate Methodology and Social context.* Cambridge: Cambridge University Press.

— 2011. *Intercultural Communication and Ideology.* London: Sage Publications.

Krashen, S. 1981. *Second Language Acquisition and Second Language Learning.* Oxford: Pergamon Press.

— 2003. *Explorations in Language Acquisition and Use.* Portsmouth NH: Heinemann.

Kumaravadivelu, B. 2008. *Cultural Globalization and Language Education.* NY: Yale University Press.

Leach, J. and B. Moon, eds. 1999. *Learners and Pedagogy.* London: Paul Chapman.

Louis, M. R. 1983. 'Organisations as culture bearing milieux'. In: L. Pondy, P. Frost, G. Morgan and T. Dandridge, eds, *Organisational Culture.* Greenwich, CT: JIA Press, pp. 39–54.

Scollon, R. and S. W. Scollon. 1995. *Intercultural Communication.* Oxford: Blackwell.

Signorini, P., R. Wiesemes and R. Murphy. 2009. 'Developing alternative frameworks for exploring intercultural learning: a critique of Hofstede's cultural difference model'. *Teaching in Higher Education*, 14/3, pp. 253–64.

Sinclair, J. and M. Coulthard. 1975. *Towards an Analysis of Discourse.* Oxford: Oxford University Press.

Spencer-Oatey, H., ed. 2000. *Culturally Speaking.* London: Continuum.

Spencer-Oatey, H. and P. Franklin. 2009. *Intercultural Interaction: A Multidisciplinary Approach to Intercultural Communication.* London: Palgrave Macmillan.

Street, B. 1993. 'Culture is a verb: anthropological aspects of language and cultural process'. In: D. Graddol, L. Thompson and M. Byram, eds, *Language and Culture.* Clevedon: Multilingual Matters, pp. 22–44.

Trice, H. and J. Beyer. 1993. *The Cultures of Work Organisations.* Englewood Cliffs, NJ: Prentice Hall.

Wardhaugh, R. 1986. *An Introduction to Sociolinguistics.* Oxford: Basil Blackwell.

3

Language and languages in education

Introduction

In the previous chapter we suggested that the people in any classroom are members of one or more cultures. These affect their beliefs and behaviours, thus creating a unique classroom culture (even if its 'uniqueness' is not always very visible).

As we discuss below, the mother tongue or language of everyday communication (LEC) in any context, which generally becomes the language in which children think, is an essential tool for learning culture. In addition, in any language-learning classroom a language is also the subject being learned, and so how teachers and learners perceive the role of the language-as-subject (LAS) in the world outside the classroom will be an important part of the classroom and learning context.

In this chapter, we discuss two main issues relating to language(s) and the English classroom. In Section 1, we look at a view of (cultural) learning in which language (LEC) use is key, and consider how ideas emerging from this view can be used to guide and support what happens in LAS classrooms also. In Section 2, we consider the influence of the external language environment on the teaching and learning of languages in classrooms, especially with regard to the role(s) of (and attitudes towards) English in different parts of the world today.

1. Language and learning

In our experience, educational contexts continue to understand the notion of 'learning' differently. Very broadly speaking there are two main views of learning which are used by educational planners and policy-makers to guide their educational decision making. The first might be called a socio-cultural view of learning (often incorporating versions of constructivism) which we discuss below. The second might be called a behaviourist view (which very simply stated sees learning resulting from training learners to perform 'correct behaviours'). While particular educational contexts might in their published policy documents subscribe to one view of learning (increasingly nowadays a more socio-cultural one), recent evidence suggests that such a view may often not yet be reflected in classroom teaching and learning.

For example, a survey carried out in 2009 in 30 (mostly 'Western') OECD countries investigating 'Creating Effective Teaching and Learning Environments' suggests that socio-cultural views of learning are not yet widely established as the classroom norm in any of the educational contexts surveyed. The data gathered shows that classroom teachers in all participating countries continue to use what the survey calls 'structuring practices' (e.g. stating learning goals, summarising previous lessons, checking learners' homework and classroom exercises in exercise books) more frequently than more dialogic or 'student oriented practices' (such as task based group work and self evaluation) or 'enhanced activities' (like project work or debates). The report goes on to say that structuring practices are particularly frequent in foreign language classrooms (among others):

> in the mathematics, the foreign languages and the science classroom the predominance of structuring practices . . . is especially strong. (OECD 2009:100)

In this chapter, we focus on a socio-cultural view of learning within which language (LEC) plays a central role. We return to behaviourism to discuss its influence on language teaching in Chapter 4.

1.1 A Vygotskian socio-cultural view

If you have studied education you have probably heard of Piaget who was a biologist and saw child development as linked to individual physical maturation. Unlike Piaget, Lev Semonovich Vygotsky, a Russian working at about the same time (early twentieth century) understood child development to be the result of social interaction. His first major work *Thought and Language* was not published in Russia until after his death in 1934, and not published in the West until 1962, and his ideas only began to be widely influential at the end of the twentieth century.

So what are his ideas? For Vygotsky, the process of personal mental development in children cannot be separated from the process of acquiring culture. The main way in which this personal development (and culture learning) occurs is through the meanings a child derives from social interactions with his/her environment and the people within it. Although there are a variety of systems for communicating meanings, for example body language and pictures, the vast majority of the child's interactions are supported by language.

How does this development process work? In the culture acquisition or mental development processes of children, the mother tongue language begins as the language used in the world outside the child. The mother tongue then, over time, 'moves' to the inside of the child's head. In doing so, it becomes the child's principal tool for thinking about and making sense of their surrounding world. (In a sense, all academic education is about providing labels, a 'language', or tools for students to "think about and make sense of the surrounding world". This book, we hope, is an example!)

As an example of this process of the 'movement' of language from 'outside' the child to 'inside', those of you who have children may remember a stage when your child was about three or four, when you came across them at play and they were 'instructing' themselves, talking themselves through a particular sequence of actions, out loud. This was probably an example of what Vygotsky calls 'egocentric speech', and may have been one sign that the child's mother tongue language development would soon move 'underground' into the child's head and, through becoming 'inner speech', become the main tool for structuring the way that the child thinks.

This process of learning through interaction with people (parents, siblings, other children) and the environment (home, street, shops) via language is, in effect, the means through which children experience the primary socialisation we discussed in Chapter 2. Children therefore arrive at school with the cultural learning they have acquired through all their previous mother tongue language interactions. At school they have new cultural learning to do. They need to learn the culture of education in general, that of the school in which they study and, in particular, the culture of the classroom (or various subject classrooms) that they become part of. In the English language classroom (LAS), where the practices used for the teaching of English may be (more or less) different from those commonly used in their other subject classes, there may be further cultural learning to be done. Much of the responsibility for enabling all of this additional cultural learning lies with teachers.

1.2 The Zone of Proximal Development and scaffolding

For us, the most pedagogically useful concept arising from Vygotsky's work is connected to his idea of a Zone of Proximal Development (ZPD). This ZPD is an imaginary (notional) mental area, at a given point in time, between what a child can already do independently, and what she/he can do if helped by an adult, or by a more mentally developed (often older) peer. In other words, it is the mental area within which education needs to be working in order to be effective.

What then will such effective education actually be doing? We have said that in order to develop from what they can already do unassisted, learners need to be helped. Ideally, this help needs to be individualised, because no two individual ZPDs can ever be identical – different children will be at different points on their individual learning journeys. Teachers can provide appropriate assistance through what Wood, Bruner and Ross (1976) have called 'Scaffolding' – the help that the teacher offers to the learner, as she/he engages with the learning task. This help is again provided largely through talk and language and, if appropriately given, enables the learner to successfully complete a task that she/he could not have completed without the help.

For help to be able to scaffold a specific task it does however, need to be help of a particular kind. Wood et al. (1976) suggest that adults and helpers (who may or may not actually be formally called 'teachers') have six main functions available to use in the scaffolding process:

- Recruitment – getting the learner interested in and clear about the requirements of the task.
- Reduction of degrees of freedom – simplifying the task by, dividing the task into stages, and sometimes reducing the number of choices available to the learner at a particular stage of the task.
- Direction maintenance – keeping the learners on-task.
- Marking critical features – giving the learner clues about which features of the task are particularly relevant for success.
- Frustration control – helping to reduce the inevitable frustrations as a learner struggles to achieve something just above what they are actually capable of doing alone.
- Demonstration – demonstrating or modelling solutions to a task, or stage of a task.

What might this actually look like in a real situation?

Mercer (1995:73) provides an imaginary example of how a parent might scaffold a child to complete a jigsaw puzzle. Some of the ways which he suggests that the parent might intuitively use include some of the above functions as we outline below:

Scaffolding function	Parental scaffolding
Reduction of degrees of freedom	Doing the edges of the jigsaw for the child, so that it is clearer what the child needs to do next.
Direction Maintenance	Pointing out important pieces and where they fit keeps the child focused.
Marking critical features	Identifying the edges of the jigsaw or pointing to important central pieces may both be ways of providing clues about what aspects of the jigsaw it is important to recognise in order to complete it successfully.
Frustration control	Helping the child identify some of the central pieces of the jigsaw when they find it difficult, makes it less likely that they will get totally frustrated and give the whole task up.
Demonstration	Starting by doing the edges also provides the child with a model of how they might begin a similar task next time.

As we can see here, the same 'scaffolding' behaviour (e.g. identifying the edges of the puzzle) by the adult can in this case be placed in several different categories of function. Mercer emphasises that successful 'scaffolding' occurs when the adult recognises how much help the child needs, and hands responsibility over to the child as soon as the child is able to cope with a particular aspect of the task alone. The whole purpose of scaffolding is therefore to enable the child to develop.

The scaffolding functions above all assume one to one interaction. As the interaction proceeds, the helper chooses both which function to emphasise, and the extent to which any function is actually needed. In other words, while providing scaffolding, helpers are consciously monitoring the situation to see the current state of the learner's capabilities, and so assessing the extent to which the learner is now able to manage on their own. Scaffolding therefore only refers to help that is contingent (help that is actually needed) at the time. As soon as the helper senses that the learner is able to cope unassisted with some parts of (or all of) the task in hand, she/he hands over responsibility for completion to the child. This is what Bruner (1983:60) calls the 'handover principle'.

As we have said all of the ideas above to do with learning and 'scaffolding' assume a one-to-one, 'teacher'–learner interaction, in which a 'teacher' intervenes to help a learner successfully complete some task that she/he is engaged in and learning to do. While this may at times be possible in some classrooms in some places, it is unlikely to be common, since most teachers work with large numbers of learners simultaneously for much of the time, and are rarely able to tutor an individual student towards the successful achievement of a particular task. However, the principles for providing learners with appropriate support for their learning that underlie the term 'scaffolding', do also have relevance to classroom teaching and learning.

So, how could the ideas behind scaffolding be used in an ELT classroom? The following are just a few examples, ones which can be found in any book on methodology, even though the book may not make explicit links to the ways in which they support learning (for more on this see Chapter 6).

Scaffolding function	ELT 'scaffolding' examples
Recruitment	Ensuring that a learner-age-appropriate purpose for a task or activity is clear to all. Linking proposed tasks to pre-established learner-derived goals.
Reduction of degrees of freedom	Identifying the stages of the task for the learners and providing appropriate instructions for each stage. Eliciting and agreeing on the main language items/areas students will need to do the task successfully.
Direction Maintenance	Providing a time-limit for each (stage of the) task In group work – giving one student the role of 'task manager', whose job it is to keep everyone focused. Active teacher monitoring, in order to encourage on-task behaviour
Marking critical features	Teacher noticing if/when groups or individuals are stuck, and e.g. pointing, starting a sentence/phrase, writing on the board etc. Stopping the class to e.g. re-emphasise key language/part of text etc. or to e.g. suggest breaking one stage up into two stages etc.
Frustration control	See above + Celebrating success – helping students notice what they *have* done successfully.
Demonstration	Modelling – language and tasks (especially when introducing new language and/or new task-types)

Bearing in mind that the focus of this first section of the chapter is on the role of language as a tool for supporting learning, we hope you have noticed that in the right-hand column above, almost all the 'scaffolding' that the teacher provides occurs through their use of language. This highlights the importance of teacher talk in supporting learning – and how important it is that teachers understand why, when, and how to use what kind of language to do so. English teachers who are really intent upon supporting learning (as opposed to, say, finishing the chapter in the textbook or 'covering the syllabus') will also consider whether (and when) their particular learners need that particular scaffolding function to be expressed in English or in their mother tongue/LEC.

So far in this chapter we have described the crucial role of language in human learning; we have introduced one view of the relationship between language and learning and exemplified some of the practical classroom implications of such a view, particularly for the way the teacher uses language to support the learning process.

English teachers will vary in the extent to which they see the main purpose of what they do as being to support learning (rather than e.g. finish the book), as well as in their effectiveness in doing so. Similarly learners will be more or less easy to 'recruit'. The variations stem in large part from participants' interest in, attitudes towards or motivation for English teaching and learning. In the next part of this chapter, we look at one important contextual factor which may affect their attitudes. Some further factors affecting learners' and teachers' motivations are discussed in Chapter 6.

2. Languages in contexts

Before you read on, you might like to think about the following:

- *What languages (English, Hindi, Kiswahili, Arabic etc.) are used in your country?*
- *What are they used for?*
- *How important is English in your country? (e.g. what purposes is it used for?)*
- *How important is English to your country? (e.g. why is it used for these purposes?)*
- *Which second/foreign languages (apart from the medium of instruction) are taught in your schools? Why?*

- *Where is English used/taught in the education system in your country? Why do you think this is?*

From looking at the central role played by language throughout formal and informal education, we now consider how the particular languages used in particular contexts may affect learners' (and teachers') willingness to engage in learning English. Understanding how people feel about learning English, and why, is a key aspect in understanding any classroom context where English is being taught.

In this section, we discuss some types of relationships that may exist between languages and place, and some possible reasons that might account for these relationships. We then show why ELT professionals need to take these relationships into account when trying to understand their contexts better.

We start by considering each of the questions given above, using as examples some answers to these questions given by our former MA students (see Tables 3.1 and 3.2).

2.1 *What languages are used, and what for*

The world is multilingual. By this statement, we mean not only that there is no single language for humans, but also that in most countries there is more than one language of everyday communication in use (Trudgill 1995). In many countries, in fact, the languages used are so diverse that the majority of children in such countries grow up knowing and using more than one language.

In extreme cases, the language situation in a country or part of a country may be so complex (for some possible reasons, see Section 3.3 below), that children are not even clear which language is their 'mother tongue'. This can negatively influence their educational prospects if, as in the example in the quote below from Zululand in South Africa in the early 1990s, the medium of instruction for the first few years of primary school was supposed to be the child's mother tongue.

> A major problem with this strategy (of mother tongue education) is the artificiality of the concept of mother tongue. Young children living in urban townships may find themselves living next door to Nguni speakers, across the road from Sesotho, whilst their parents derive variously from Xhosa or other language groups . . . Such children when they enter school have a 'mother tongue' designated for them and have to spend three or four years learning through it, even though it may be as alien to them as English. (Street 1993:34)

Information about which particular languages are used in your particular part of the world, and the place and role(s) of English can help you better understand the attitudes – based on perceptions of the use and utility of languages in their context – that learners may bring to ELT classrooms in your context.

Different places have very different language profiles involving the use of different combinations of different languages. In Table 3.1, we show the responses to questions a and b above, given by three of our former MA students.

The first thing that we notice from Table 3.1 is just how different the three national language profiles appear to be, and how two of the three amply support our assertion above that most people in the world need to know more than one language. At this point, we need to point out that these data reflect our students' perceptions of the language situations in their country, which may in fact be even more complex than they appear. For example, the Korean respondent when replying to our subsequent oral question about 'what English is used for' stated that 'English is generally used for academic, business and educational purposes' and suggested that the reason might be because 'a great deal of information in the world is only available in English,

TABLE 3.1 Three students' responses to the question 'What languages are used in your country and what for?'

	What languages?	What for?
India	• 25 major regional languages • Hindi and English • Regional language, Hindi, English • Regional language or English • English • Regional language/Hindi	• Mother tongues used at home, (together with other, less widespread, languages) • Administration and nationwide communication • These three languages are subjects in all schools • Medium of instruction in schools at all levels • Main medium of instruction in higher education • Local internal administration and communication
Korea	• Korean	• All purposes
Azerbaijan	• Azerbaijani • Russian • English	• National and official language • Previously used for much official business but use now declining • Together with Azerbaijani, the language of official documents

on the Internet'. This shows that although in fact a second language does seem to be used for various quite common purposes within Korea, the perception (of our student at least) is of a single national language being used for everything.

At this point you might like to consider the following:

- *Which of the three countries in Table 3.1 does yours most resemble?*
- *What are the similarities?*
- *Why do you think they have occurred?*
- *In what ways is your country different from the other two in Table 3.1?*
- *Why do you think your country has developed differently?*

2.2 *Monolingual and multilingual societies*

For teachers it is not only just a question of understanding the language profile of their country, but also of knowing which of the languages are actually used or needed by individuals in their more local context of place.

A country may be officially multilingual, but not actually have very many multilingual citizens. For example, although four languages are officially used in Switzerland, three of the four are used by many of their speakers for almost every facet of life, (official business, education, media, family life, etc.), albeit with differences in pronunciation and vocabulary to reflect the formality of the function and/or the setting. So, many Swiss citizens, especially in the numerically dominant French and German speaking parts, may in fact be regarded as monolingual.

In contrast, in countries like India, completely different languages may be used for different societal functions. This very common phenomenon, where two or more languages (or two very different versions of the same language) are used by a single set of speakers for different social functions, is an example of what is broadly known as 'diglossia' (for further investigation of this concept, see Schiffman 1997). In classic diglossic situations there is usually one 'high' language, used for more official and/or formal situations and functions (often including secondary and, especially, higher education), and another 'low' language used for more domestic functions. People living in such a context, need to be competent in both languages (or different varieties of the language) if they wish to participate fully in all social situations in which they may find themselves.

If such countries are socially cohesive, everyone will, of necessity, need to be at least bilingual. Individuals without access to, or less proficient in, the 'official' or 'high' language, are clearly likely to be at a disadvantage within most formal spheres of social activity, including education. This may become a matter of particular educational concern if a country has a large number of disadvantaged individuals, without access to the 'high' language.

In quite a number of countries today, English seems to hold a kind of 'high' language status in terms of its perceived role as an enabler of national development. Where this is the case, a country may consider that it is disadvantaging itself if it continues to have only a limited proportion of its citizens with the linguistic skills in English needed for them to take on roles that may contribute to future national development. Policy-makers may consequently plan to try and widen access to educational opportunities by adjusting the national language policy in some way.

Would it be a serious disadvantage to be monolingual in your country/region/locality? Are most people monolingual or multilingual? What about you?

While there seems to be a widespread, although generally poorly evidenced, assumption that English contributes to national development, this assumption is beginning to be investigated. Coleman (2010) identifies four main ways in which knowledge of English may contribute to development within a particular context. It may:

1 Increase citizens' employability.
2 Facilitate international mobility (e.g. migration, tourism, studying abroad).
3 Enable access to crucial information or opportunities (e.g. to scientific studies relevant to the local context written in English and/or to training opportunities for which knowledge of English is a prerequisite).
4 Act as a 'neutral' national or official language for those living in contexts where other available languages would (for historical or political reasons) be unacceptable in this role.

However, discussions about the ways in which and/or the extent to which English does in fact contribute to 'national development' (itself a complex and variously understood concept) in any one context are ongoing (see e.g. Coleman 2011).

Do you or does your leadership think that English is important for the development of your country?

2.3 Reasons for countries' different language profiles

What causes countries to have such differing language profiles? We need to consider the context of time and look from a historical perspective to find answers. When we do, we discover that a limited number of frequently occurring historical themes/influences account for many of the differences.

2.3.1 Migration

The first more or less universal influence, which is very evident in many countries of the world even today, we can call 'migration' or the movement of people across language boundaries for political or economic reasons. To some extent, migration may be connected to geography. Some countries that are islands or peninsulas have historically been less frequently affected by large-scale migration. Korea, being a peninsula, for example, had not until the twentieth century been subject to large influxes of people from outside, and this may explain Korea's apparent or perceived monolingualism in Table 3.1.

2.3.2 Colonialism

A second related reason, a more recent and better-documented phenomenon, is that of colonialism. Here, through conquest and the forcible annexation of territory, a relatively small number of people from countries that were powerful in the world at the time, moved to, and assumed the government of, other places (e.g. Spain and Portugal in the sixteenth and seventeenth centuries, France, Britain, Holland and Russia in the sixteenth to nineteenth centuries). In the process, their language, inevitably of high status in the circumstances, began to be used for official business. English in India and Russian in Azerbaijan would be examples of this. In addition, the education systems, initially established for the families of the colonists themselves and later for the children of indigenous leaders, naturally used the colonisers' language as a medium of instruction and created the association of these languages (of which English was one) with high status and 'the elite'. This association holds true to the present and may help to account for why in certain contexts there is parental pressure on national governments to widen access to languages such as English, through making them the medium of instruction and/or increasing their presence in the curriculum.

2.3.3 Political divisions

Third, particularly since the early nineteenth century, the entire world has become politically divided up into discrete nation states. The borders between these states have often been drawn for political and economic reasons, rather than to reflect the geographical location of homogeneous language-speaking groups. In consequence, speakers of more than one language have frequently found themselves to be part of the same political unit and/or speakers of the same language are included in different units. Many African countries, for example Kenya, Zambia and Nigeria, or Belgium in Europe, find themselves in this position.

Do any of the above help explain the language profile of your context?

2.4 Language use and ELT

We are of course interested in how the above discussion relates to ELT contexts in schools and classrooms. We see three main connections. Firstly, for one or more of the reasons at (i) to (iii) above, the language situation in a country may mean English is the medium of instruction in some or all schools or colleges. Alternatively, for reasons to do with its increasing role as a global language, English may be a subject on the curriculum. Finally, in either case, people within a particular country and learners within a particular school will have a more or less positive attitude to the English language and to learning English, and this attitude will be a factor in the local ELT context. Below we look at each of these connections in turn.

2.4.1 Language and medium of instruction

Since schools are generally representative of the wider society, the major languages used in the society are likely to be used within the education system or schools. One of these major languages will usually be the medium of instruction for all subjects.

Which language is used as the medium of instruction at each level of the education system is likely to depend on:

- historical precedent: In the relatively few, long-standing, stable, nation states containing a clear linguistic majority speaking a single language (countries like China, Japan, United Kingdom, France, for example), there is unlikely to be much disagreement about which language should be the medium of instruction.
- conscious pragmatic decisions, taken voluntarily or through necessity, at some point in history, by countries that have in the past century undergone major political change (e.g. in the 1990s countries of the former Soviet Union like Azerbaijan, or in the

1940s to 1960s countries that were formerly colonies, like India. See Table 3.1).

It is sometimes the case that there is no single medium of instruction throughout the school system, with several languages taking that role, especially at primary level. This is particularly likely to be true in geographically large countries (with or without correspondingly large populations) or ones that have never historically been politically united for long enough for a single language to predominate. An example of the former is India. Here, for a combination of the above reasons, the ELT context is one where English, as well as having a formal role in the country at large, is the medium of instruction in some schools at all levels, and the main medium in Higher Education (see Table 3.1).

Where schools use a non-mother tongue language, often English, as the medium of instruction for some or all subjects, there is additional linguistic and cultural learning to be done, and the teacher's role, whatever their subject, will include assisting children in that further learning.

(i) Language and thought

We said above that children's first language becomes the principal tool for structuring the way they think. However, the extent to which language imposes structure on thought has been a subject of debate for linguists, amongst others, for much of the last century.

To what extent do you believe that your mother tongue/LEC influences or controls the way in which you think about the world?

(ii) The strong claim

This debate has centred on the extent to which any given language influences or controls what **can** be thought, and so how the world is conceptualised by its speakers. The Sapir-Whorf Hypothesis is named after Edward Sapir and Benjamin Whorf (two linguists who worked extensively on Native American languages). The hypothesis claims, in its strongest form, that the nature of any given language, for example how it represents time and space or how many lexical items it has for varieties of a particular phenomenon (e.g. sand, rain, wind) influences the way that a speaker of that language sees the world. 'Linguistic relativity', is the term often used to refer to the discussion about Sapir's (1929) strong claim that everybody's perception of the world is 'blinkered' by the language through which they 'see' it, and so we are 'at the mercy of the particular language' that we use. This strong claim is no longer generally accepted.

(iii) The weaker claim

A weaker claim is that *'people's behaviour tends to be guided by the linguistic categories of their languages under certain circumstances'* (Fasold 1990:53), in other words the nature of a given language only *predisposes* speakers of a language to view the world in a particular way. Those who oppose the idea that language determines thought altogether suggest that since different cultures give different significance and priorities to different features in society, so they develop language to reflect these priorities, but that every language system potentially can express anything that its speakers may need or want to think. Yule (1985:197), below seems to position himself somewhere between the weaker claim and opposition when he notes that:

> The notion that language determines thought may be partially correct, in some extremely limited way, but it fails to take into account the fact that users of a language do not inherit a fixed set of patterns to use. They inherit the ability to manipulate and create with a language, in order to express their perceptions.

The above argument around the Sapir-Whorf hypothesis was based largely on adult language use. Children are less skilled manipulators of language, and far less experienced perceivers of their world than adults. There may therefore be some basis for supposing that they will, especially when they first come to school, be more susceptible than adults to the influence of their particular language.

(iv) Relevance to education

So how is all this discussion of linguistic relativity relevant to the use of English as the medium of instruction (MOI) in places with other mother tongues? We'll give one example here from science, a subject that school systems in some contexts have recommended should be taught in English. Recent work in science education among mother tongue speakers of English (Scott 1998) seems to support a fairly strong view of linguistic relativity, in suggesting that children's commonsense and non-scientific ideas are significantly shaped by their English language. So, for example, in English we commonly say such things as 'shut the door to keep the cold out', 'the sun rises at eight o'clock' and that you 'suck liquid up' through a straw. These ways of expressing meanings in English might explain the difficulty that British children have with the fact that scientifically, you shut the door to keep the warmth *in*, it is the movement of the *earth* which creates day and night not that of the sun, and it is the air pressure pushing *down,* rather than the child sucking up, that moves liquid from bottle to mouth. However, although they may find the concepts difficult initially, most English children are able, despite their early different perceptions, to understand the scientific realities once these have been effectively introduced to them. In such situations 'effectively' means that teachers need to take their likely, first language (L1)/mother tongue/LEC-based preconceptions as the starting point for scaffolding processes.

If such language-based misconceptions (Scott calls them 'alternative conceptions') exist in a mother tongue educational setting, they will exist, and be complicated by, a setting in which the MOI is not the mother tongue. It is therefore crucial that teachers in such settings are fluent users of both the MOI and the students' LEC(s), and capable of predicting likely language (LEC) – influenced existing conceptions, to be able to understand learners' starting points, and so what needs scaffolding and how.

Linguistic relativity is thus not just an interesting academic debate. Some understanding of the fact that language can influence how learners think, and of what this might imply for how easy or difficult they find aspects of learning, can alert decision-makers to some of the additional complexities that may arise from using a language other than the mother tongue as the medium of instruction in schools.

2.4.2 Language as part of the school curriculum

The second potential link between a country's language profile and the language curriculum, requires us to consider which languages (other than the medium of instruction) are taught in schools as part of the school curriculum, and why. The world is full of different educational contexts in which different policies towards the teaching of 'other' languages in schools have changed over time. However, as we write this book in the early twenty-first century, existing national education policies suggest that in most countries in the world nowadays, for reasons to do with its global influence, English is regarded as the most important language to teach as a curriculum subject. How long this state of affairs will continue to be true remains to be seen (Graddol 2006).

3. The global importance of English

A number of authors have described their view of how English is now positioned among the languages of the world.

De Swaan (2001), for example, considers English to be at the centre of a hierarchy of world languages. His world linguistic system theory suggests that a single coherent global language system is now operating around the world and all known languages are connected in a strongly ordered, strongly connected, hierarchical, multi-tiered pattern. At the core of the system is hypercentral English, which is linked to a dozen supercentral languages (e.g. Arabic, Chinese, French, Hindi, Malay, Swahili) each of which in turn serves as a focal point for a cluster of peripheral languages. This world language system is held together by bilingual speakers and De Swann assumes that when speakers of a language learn an additional language, more often than not, they learn a language that is perceived to provide them with some kind of greater communication advantage. In other words, they choose to learn a language occupying a higher level than their L1 in the hierarchy. There is thus an attraction felt by the speakers of the peripheral languages towards the centre, which Calvet (2006) has described as a gravitational force. The fact that 'English is the hypercentral language that holds the entire world language system together' (2001:17) may help explain why so many mother tongue English speakers remain resolutely monolingual!

Others like Kachru (1985a) saw countries' relationships to the English Language more as a series of concentric circles. For him, native English speaking countries are in the Inner circle; countries (e.g. India, Nigeria) where English for historical or political reasons has had a more or less official presence for a long time inhabit the Outer circle and countries where English has until quite recently been a purely foreign language and not necessarily of much interest to most inhabitants (e.g. China, Brazil) as being members of the Expanding circle. Kachru (1998) uses the same system of circles to discuss English as an Asian language, using as examples for the Inner circle Australia, for the Outer circle Singapore and Malaysia and for the Expanding circle Indonesia and China.

Kachru and Nelson (2006) agree with De Swann (2001) that nowadays it is the perceived communicative advantage of knowing and being able to use English that drives the worldwide demand to learn the language. A recent study by Lin Pan and Block (2011) further supports this idea. In a survey of 53 teachers and 637 students at 6 Chinese universities, they asked participants to respond to prompts about why English is popular in China. The two statements with which the highest proportions of respondents in both groups agreed were: *It is more 'International' and 'global' than the other languages* (Ts: 74.1%; Ss: 72.7%) and *As the language for international business, English is necessary for China's economic development* (Ts: 63.0%; Ss: 68.5%).

This rapid spread of the worldwide study (and increasingly also use) of English in recent decades has itself given rise to two new developments. First, as English has become ever more widespread, local varieties of English have emerged. These exist mostly in Kachru's Outer circle countries, for example, Indian English or Nigerian English and differ from Standard British or American English in their pronunciation and/or lexical terms and/ or grammatical structures. Second, it is becoming clear that in many cases the primary purpose for learning English is not necessarily (only) to become able to communicate with native speakers, but rather (also) to be able to communicate with others for whom English is also a foreign or second language. In such cases, the role of English is that of a lingua franca (Seidlhofer 2005). Both these developments have led to questions being asked regarding which variety of English should be taught in classrooms. As yet, almost all national education systems continue to base their teaching on one of the established standard forms of English. However, the debate about whether 'native speaker norms' will remain appropriate for the uses that English will be put to in the future, is likely to continue.

What is the situation in your context?

- *Which variety of English is used as a model for English learners in your country? Why do you think this is?*
- *Are ELT materials in your country set in native speaker or local contexts?*
- *Is there any evidence of a local variety of English developing in your country?*

We now return to the questions we asked at the beginning of Section 2 and specifically to those relating to the importance of English in your context and to your context.

4. The Importance of English *in* and *to* your country

Despite the reservations of some (e.g. Pennycook 1994; Philippson 1992, 2010), the present reality in most parts of the world is that English is considered to be important for access to global economic and technological development, and so ought to have a role in the country and/or its education system. This came across very strongly in the answers three different former Masters students gave to questions c and d above. These can be seen in Table 3.2.

If you considered the questions at the beginning of this section, you may have noted down some of the main places where English is used and the uses that it is put to in your own country. You have probably realised that what learners see English as being used for, can directly affect individual motivation for learning English. **From Table 3.2 we can see** that if English is, at a macro level important **to** the politicians and decision- makers of a country for international business purposes and for access to academic and

TABLE 3.2 Three students' responses to the questions 'How important is English in and to your country and why'?

	Importance IN	Importance TO
Taiwan	• For international business communication	• 'It's like a bridge between other countries and our country for communication (culture, art), trading, business.'
Kazakhstan	• Before 1992 – in tourism, business, politics • After 1992, as above, plus in education, cultural exchanges, mass media	• 'Nowadays it is important as it helps to promote economic ties with other countries and contributes to restoring and "resurrection" of the economy of the country and to its science • technical progress.'
Japan	• Some international companies • For academic purposes	• 'We can live without knowing one English word. However, if you master English it may give you more chances of getting a better job, higher salary. If you want to enter university most of them have English entrance tests.'

technological information, it is then likely to become important **in** the country. If it is important **in** the country, it will become important **to** citizens of the country, usually for practical personal reasons, such as university entrance or career advancement. In such situations therefore, there is the potential for English learners to have clear instrumental reasons for learning the language, and to see, for example, the need for a good command of English in order to achieve their desired personal and/or professional goals.

And a few more questions for you to ponder:

- *Looking at the* **'importance to'** *column in Table 3.2: Have you ever used any of these, or any other similar arguments, to motivate your students?*
- *Where do you think our MA students got their answers from?*
- *What kind of further evidence or information would you need to check your opinions?*
- *Why do you think that the words* **'from Table 3.2 we can see'** *are in bold in the paragraph above?*

The answers given represent, we imagine, our students' 'educated opinion'. These opinions are likely to be based on some combination of 'common sense', experience and inside information resulting from educational policy documents that they have read, or training that they have received. If you wanted to check the accuracy of these opinions you would need to refer for example, to books like Graddol (1997, 2006) that examine the role of English in the world – to find some indication of reasons why countries regard their citizens' level of English as particularly important, or to national economic or education websites (which sometimes, for example in Japan, have their national educational aims stated in English). Such sources of information could help you to see how policy-makers officially view the role(s) of English in their context, and so whether English really is seen as the language of 'economic ties' or 'communication' or 'giving you more chances' and the extent to which statements such as those made above are supported by contextual reality.

Although we said we need more evidence than we presented above to become certain about what the role(s) of English in particular contexts actually are, we nonetheless believe that there is a connection between the importance of a language **to** and **in** a country and **in** a country and **to** an individual citizen of that country. We recognise, however, that such connections cannot be fully visible (since they include 'invisible' attitudes, for example). They therefore often need to be, at least partly, inferred through what is said or written (e.g. educational policy documents) or what is actually done (e.g. English teachers in the final year of secondary school exclusively focusing on preparing learners for national English university entrance exams).

Thinking about your answers to questions in this chapter, where might you find supporting evidence or official documents or statements of language-related policies in your context to check your personal opinions/thoughts against?

5. Where English is taught or used in the education system

The role of English in many countries' education systems, (although it may have historical roots), is increasingly influenced by pragmatic instrumental factors. These, as students' comments in Table 3.2 suggest, include the need to be able to communicate with business partners, participate in international political affairs and gain access to the large proportion of publications worldwide. (In 1997, Graddol suggested that 28% of books and 95% of articles cited by Science Direct were written in English.)

It is not therefore surprising to see that in Japan, for example, English proficiency is an entry requirement for most universities, or that in India, English is the medium of instruction in higher education. In order to enable potential undergraduates to access scientific/academic literature written in English, many countries require, and most offer, the study of English at secondary level. A strong trend, now, at the beginning of the twenty-first century, seems to be the introduction of English to primary curricula, and/or the desire of parents in an increasing number of countries to send young children to private 'cram' schools to learn English. This trend, to begin the study of English ever earlier, both formally within state education systems and informally through private tuition, suggests a popular perception that existing secondary school-based provision does not enable English learners to achieve what they want or need to achieve. Reasons, real or imagined, for such a perception might include, the quality of the teachers, the appropriacy of teaching methods and/or materials, the facilities available, the format of the examinations or the number of hours devoted to language learning in the curriculum.

Whatever reasons national planners and/or individuals see for problems in language education, will influence the kinds of decisions that are made to try and solve them. For example, if it is thought that lack of success is due to too few hours of instruction, then countries will seek ways to provide more learning opportunities, by for example, beginning the teaching of English at primary level, or encouraging the expansion of private language schools. On the other hand, if the reason is seen as being to do with the quality of teaching, then this may result in an increase in in-service provision, or in changes to the curriculum in initial teacher preparation programmes for language teachers.

As an aside here (but see Chapter 9), it is our view that few of the proposed solutions consider existing contextual factors sufficiently completely, when planning how to effectively manage the huge (and expensive!) educational changes that such responses involve.

6. Summary and task

In this chapter we have discussed language from a number of different points of view.

- The role of language in learning, and the fact that children arrive at school with cultural learning already acquired through their L1.
- Language as the main vehicle for the scaffolding that teachers provide as they guide learners of any subject, including English, in the classroom.

We then went on to look at languages in different national and local contexts and saw

- varied the language situation seems to be in different countries, with fully monolingual countries being a minority;
- the language situation in any particular country is usually a result of historical and/or political processes, which also affect the roles played by, and learners' attitudes towards, English and other languages within the school curriculum;
- and extent to which the language that we speak may affect how we perceive the world in which we live, and the importance of this when considering the MOI.

Next we considered the global importance of English and what effect this might have on ELT contexts.

- We saw that at present English seems to be regarded as important in most countries.
- Despite the global role of English, the importance ascribed to learning English within education systems varies.
- Changing perceptions of the importance of English in and to a country, may lead to dissatisfaction with current ELT provision, and attempts by national educational planners or individual learners (or their parents) to remedy the situation.

One of the adjustments to the language learning and teaching process that is most commonly made in response to dissatisfaction with the status quo, is a change to the language teaching method (and/or language syllabus and language learning materials) recommended for use in the language classroom. In the next two chapters, we look at some of the changes in how people have thought about language teaching over the last half-century. Underlying the changing ideas over time have been new insights into the nature of language and language learning, and the realisation that there cannot be 'one best method' suitable for all contexts.

Task:

This has been a chapter with lots of questions. We hope we have given you some ideas of ways to think about how you might answer them for your context, and we conclude with a few final questions:

a) *In your country what do ELT teachers and other educators consider to be the main lacks in the current provision of foreign/second language education?*

b) *Do you have any evidence to support your/their feelings?*

c) *What could be done to bring about an improvement to whatever you identified at (a)? (When you finish the book, you may find it interesting to come back to look at whatever you have concluded here, to consider whether you want to adjust or add to any of your ideas)*

References and further reading

Bruner, J. S. 1983. *Child's Talk: Learning to Use Language.* New York: Norton.

Calvet, L. J. (A. Brown, trans.) 2006. *Towards an Ecology of World Languages.* Cambridge: Polity Press.

Coleman, H. 2010. *The English Language in Development.* London: British Council.

Coleman, H., ed. 2011. *Dreams and Realities: Developing Countries and the English Language.* London: British Council.

Coulmas, F. 1997. *The Handbook of Sociolinguistics.* Oxford: Blackwell.

De Swaan, A. 2001. *Words of the World: The Global Language System.* Cambridge: Polity Press.

Fasold, R. 1990. *The Sociolinguistics of Language.* Oxford: Blackwell.

Graddol, D. 1997. *The Future of English.* London: British Council.

— 2006. *English Next.* London: British Council.

Kachru, B. B. 1985a. 'The power and politics of English'. *World Englishes*, 5/3, pp. 121–40.

— 1998. 'English as an Asian language'. *Links and Letters*, 5, pp. 89–108

Kachru, Y. and C. L. Nelson. 2006. *World Englishes in Asian Contexts.* Hong Kong: Hong Kong University Press.

Lantolf, J. P. and G. Appel, eds. 1994. *Vygotskian Approaches to Second Language Research.* Norwood, NJ: Ablex Pub. Corp.

Lin Pan and D. Block. 2011. 'English as a "global language" in China: an investigation into learners' and teachers' language beliefs'. *System*, 39, pp. 391–402

Mercer, N. 1995. *The Guided Construction of Knowledge.* Clevedon: Multilingual Matters.

Pennycook, A. 1994. *The Cultural Politics of English as an International Language.* Harlow: Longman.

Phillipson, R. 1992. *Linguistic Imperialism.* Oxford: Oxford University Press.

— 2010. *Linguistic Imperialism Continued.* London: Routledge.

Sapir, E. 1929. *The Status of Linguistics as a Science. Language*, 5, pp. 207–14

Schiffman, H. F. 1997. Diglossia as a Sociolinguistic Situation. In: F. Coulmas, ed., *The Handbook of Sociolinguistics.* Oxford: Blackwell,pp. 205–16.

Scott, P. H. 1998. 'Teacher talk and meaning making in science classrooms: a Vygotskian analysis and review'. *Studies in Science Education*, 32, pp. 45–80.

Seidlhofer, B. 2005. 'English as a Lingua Franca'. ELT Journal Volume 59/4: 339–341.

Street, B. 1993. 'Culture is a verb'. In: *Language and Culture British Studies in Applied Linguistics*. Clevedon: Multilingual Matters.

Trudgill, P. 1995. *Sociolinguistics: An Introduction to Language and Society.* Harmondsworth: Penguin.

Vygotsky, L. S. 1978. *Mind in Society: The Development of Higher Psychological Processes.* Cambridge, MA: Harvard University Press.

Wertsch, J. V., ed. 1985. *Culture, Communication and Cognition: Vygotskyan Perspectives.* Cambridge: Cambridge University Press.

Wertsch, J. V. 1991 *Voices of the Mind: A Sociocultural Approach to Mediated Action.* New York: Harvester Wheatsheaf.

Wood, D., J. S. Bruner and G. Ross. 1976. 'The role of tutoring in problem solving'. *Journal of Child Psychology,* 17, pp. 89–100.

Yule, G. 1985. *The Study of Language.* Cambridge: Cambridge University Press

4

From cultures to methods

Introduction

In the previous chapter, we considered the use and role(s) of language, languages and particularly English, at various layers of the context of *place.* In Chapters 4 and 5, we are particularly concerned with the context of *time,* and how ideas about language and the practices that are thought to support language-learning change differently over time in different contexts.

There are three terms that we use frequently throughout these chapters to express particular ideas. We define them here.

Method: *a prescribed set of procedures thought to be most effective for teaching and learning language.*

Methodology: *What teachers actually do – the practices and behaviours that can be seen happening in a teacher's classroom.*

Approach: *A set of more or less consciously held (or explicitly stated) beliefs about the nature of language and the language learning process that influence how language is taught in a particular language learning context.*

The history of language teaching methods is well documented (see, e.g. Howatt 2004; Richards and Rodgers 2001) and you may wonder why we spend time on it here. In Chapter 3, we pointed out that changes in the roles and perceived importance of English have resulted in frequent changes to ELT provision in school systems. Later in the book (Chapter 9) we say that when considering and planning changes to such provision it is important to understand the contextual starting point, what typically happens in classrooms 'now', before making plans to implement change. Our purpose for describing methods here is therefore only to provide you with fairly broad descriptions, which, when matched with features of your own context, will help you identify the practices, explicit method(s) and/or underlying approach(es) to ELT that are most usual in your context now (at whatever layer of place you are concerned with, your own classroom, an institution or the country as a whole).

For the majority of formal state ELT contexts the most immediately visible evidence of current practices is provided by the more or less officially and explicitly advocated teaching method or approach. However, understanding what really happens in classrooms in any context usually requires more than just a quick look at official documents. Although these documents will usually affect how teachers behave and what they do, teachers everywhere also develop their own methodology. Teachers' decisions about which behaviours and practices they choose to make part of their methodology, are influenced by their own, largely invisible, approach. In almost any given context therefore, teachers' methodologies will differ to some degree from the officially advocated method or approach.

Changes to language teaching methods (or approaches) may be the result of changes in thinking or of contextual changes in the wider world. We open this chapter with a discussion of two main reasons which we believe have influenced method change in ELT. The remainder of the chapter then considers two methods and one group of methods that illustrate some of the ideas about language teaching that were most influential during the twentieth century. In Section 2, we consider the Grammar Translation method, in Section 3 the Audio-Lingual Method (ALM), and in Section 4 the group of methods that emerged in the 1960s and 1970s and that together are usually known as Humanistic methods. Because all of these methods, or some of the strategies and practices associated with them, are still in use, more or less modified, somewhere in the world today, we describe their main visible characteristics as well as the main thinking behind them.

1. Why do methods change?

Although language teaching methods have almost always in fact been implemented in classrooms as teachers' individual methodologies, throughout much of the twentieth century there was a more or less explicitly stated assumption among educational experts and decision makers that it was possible to find 'one best method' – one universal set of procedures – for the teaching and learning of languages. Ideas of what this 'best method' might be for ELT changed considerably over time. Which changes occurred where, at what point in time, and the reasons for such changes, were of course affected by many of the influential contextual features discussed in chapters 1 to 3. However we believe that two further interconnected 'macro-reasons' underlie changes in ELT methods or approaches. These are discussed below.

1.1 A changing understanding of how we may look at the world

The first reason is that over the past 50 years attitudes to what may constitute valid and/or reliable research have been changing in academic circles. The changes began in the United States and Europe but continue to spread more widely worldwide. They have been most evident in the slow, but steadily growing move away from belief in the unique ability of the *positivist scientific method* to help us explain the world in which we live.

By *positivist scientific research method* we mean the belief that

- it is possible to discover truths about phenomena in the world, that can be universally 'applied' regardless of context.
- the only way to find such 'truths' is through research in which a detached researcher objectively records and interprets the results of empirical tests.

This very singular view of how we may come to understand the world, has been increasingly challenged, in terms of what it is thought possible to discover, the methods used for discovery, and the feasibility of 'objectivity'. As Johnson (2009:8) points out below, there is little evidence that the use of such positivist methods in educational research has done much to improve what happens in classrooms.

> . . . the most damaging critique of this perspective is how little influence it appears to have had on improving classroom teaching and learning.

The view that the positivist method is the only way in which we may reliably and validly find out about the world in which we live is now increasingly challenged (e.g. Lincoln and Guba 2005; Cresswell 2007; Holliday 2007; Johnson 2009). Researchers assert that where research concerns investigation of the complex interrelationships and reciprocal influences that determine much human behaviour (e.g. behaviour in language classrooms), a different set of research principles is required, one in which researchers

> no longer ignore the fact that teachers' prior experiences, their interpretations of the activities they engage in, and **most importantly the**

> **contexts in which they work** are extremely influential in shaping how and why teachers do what they do. (Johnson 2009:9; our emphasis)

In contrast to the bullet points above, those who question the universal applicability of positivist research methods believe (in simplified summary) that:

- some (particularly human) phenomena in the world cannot be studied without reference to context, and consequently findings may have something that is 'transferable' but are extremely unlikely to be universally 'applicable', and
- researchers cannot help being a part of the research (e.g. what you notice is influenced by who you are) and can only endeavour to make their 'subjectivity' explicit in their research decisions, and provide 'trustworthy' accounts.

The positivist paradigm however remains very influential in research of all kinds. Policy-makers (and the media/the public) still seem to be more impressed by research which provides the 'numbers' and 'statistics' (typically used in positivist designs) than with detailed narrative reports of case studies, for example. One reason may be because in the context of a world in which people seem to be increasingly pressed for time, the results of statistical tests summarised in one or two pages can be read quickly and, if the numbers referred to are large 'enough', they give an impression of general relevance. Another reason may have something to do with the fact that most people find prose easier to understand than statistics, and so research results based on numbers have an air of authority and *seem* more objective – even though human beings will inevitably have made subjective decisions as they worked with the numbers, chose the statistical tests and generated the results and interpretations!

As people who have produced numbers and statistics as well as findings expressed in prose, we are not suggesting here that one method of generating and presenting research findings is superior to the other – simply that the limits of both need to be clearly understood.

The challenge to positivist research paradigms has resulted in (and from) a move away from an assumption that there must be a universal right answer to every question or a universal best way of carrying out each human endeavour. This has been underpinned by a growing recognition of the importance of context, in every field of human behaviour. In education, the teaching method thought appropriate in a given context at a point in time usually broadly reflects cultural beliefs about knowledge, teaching and learning. If these beliefs begin to be questioned, then questioning of existing assumptions about appropriate teaching and learning, and so appropriate methods, is likely to follow. ELT researchers have played a prominent role in this questioning process.

1.2. Research resulting from the growing influence of English

The second reason for changes in ELT methods has to do with the role of English in the world (see Chapter 3). It is questionable whether either the English teaching profession, or the academic study of the English language and the language learning process, would have become so widespread without the influence of the United States, and the consequent development of English as a world language during the second half of the twentieth century.

However, as the LEC in the United States and increasingly the lingua franca for the world, research into the English language and the teaching and learning of English has been particularly well funded for many years. Linguists' increasing understanding of the nature of language has revolutionised our understanding about relationships between the forms of any language and the meanings they express, and so about what it is that needs to be described if we wish to fully understand the way in which a language system works. Applied Linguistics, a research area which barely existed 50 years ago, has tried to work with linguists' insights, to consider what they can tell us about the language learning process, appropriate teaching methods, and about the design of language syllabuses, teaching materials and tests (see Chapter 5).

The growing status of English as a world language, has created a huge demand for English lessons and consequently for Language Schools. The private English language school sector, is now represented in virtually any city of any size throughout the world, and has been one of the most influential channels for the spread of new methods across the world. This spread has brought problems, where methods and materials that were originally developed in the United Kingdom, Australia or the United States (Holliday's BANA countries) for use with small classes of highly motivated learners in language schools, have been introduced with little or no adjustment into the very different contexts of state education systems (Holliday's TESEP). The disappointing educational outcomes and the demoralisation of state school teachers that have often resulted, have further highlighted the importance of matching methods to contexts, and weakened belief in the possibility of one 'best' method.

The remainder of this chapter considers two methods and one group of methods that have been and continue to be, influential in language teaching in most parts of the world.

2. A brief history of methods: The Grammar Translation Method (GTM)

GTM (and/or practices associated with it) remains probably the most widely used language teaching method in the world today. In Europe, it developed in the late eighteenth and early nineteenth century at the point where modern foreign languages (e.g. English, French and German) were beginning to be taught more widely in schools. Up to that time the main languages taught in European schools were the classical languages, Greek and Latin. These, having been taught for many centuries, had evolved a teaching method, which teachers of the 'new' languages inherited and systematised yet further. Below we consider certain features of this method one at a time.

2.1 The view of language and language proficiency

Since Latin and classical Greek were 'dead' languages, in the sense that they were no longer used as a language of everyday communication (LEC) by any community, it is not at all surprising that the teaching of languages using the GTM focussed on the written language. It was assumed that through knowledge of the written grammar system of the language, and the written vocabulary lists, it would be possible to understand the literature, and so the culture, of the language to be learned. To be proficient in the language was to be able to read the literature of the language in the original, although proficiency was often tested by written translation tasks, marked for their accuracy of form.

2.2 The view of language learning

Learning a language was perceived as a useful mental discipline and as a means of learning about the European cultural heritage. Language was taught through the explicit teaching of grammatical structures and a one-to-one correspondence of vocabulary items in the language of everyday classroom communication (L1) and the target language being learnt (L2). Both structures and vocabulary items were generally linked to an example text in the L2, and could therefore be seen in linguistic context, and be practised by the process of translating the text sentence by sentence. Insofar as there was much explicit thought about the learning process, learners were expected to memorise the grammatical structures and vocabulary items for use with later texts. There was great emphasis given to error-free accurate written reproduction of the L2.

2.3 *Syllabus*

The language syllabus was the grammar of the language, as described and recorded in grammar books. These, in turn, tended to be the products of scholars' analysis of written language. Vocabulary lists were provided with each example text. There was little attempt to differentiate between more or less frequently occurring items. Compared with today's grammar books based around language corpora containing millions of items from a huge number of different spoken and written sources, the grammar books of even 50 years ago were based on very limited evidence of how (the written form of) language is actually used.

2.4 *Materials*

These consisted of books whose units or chapters contained L2 texts and practice exercises. There was very little variation from one chapter to the next. Each text either introduced or gave further practice in one or more grammar structures together with a list of 'useful words and expressions'. Since texts and practice sentences were closely tied to the practise of particular grammar structures and vocabulary items, sentences sometimes sounded rather strange ('the philosopher pulled the lower jaw of the hen' (Sweet 1964:73)) as they were stretched to include examples of appropriate items. Any of you who have ever studied in, or taught, a class entitled something like 'Intensive Reading', will probably have come across more recent versions of these sorts of materials.

2.5 *The teachers' and learners' roles in the classroom*

The teacher used the L1 to manage learning in the classroom. Use of L2, beyond the reading out or repetition of text extracts, was rare, and not necessary since the focus was on the understanding of written language. The teachers' task was relatively easy since they usually followed a text book with a very regular format, where what needed to be taught was perfectly clear, where the range of teaching techniques was extremely limited and where there was little or no ambiguity about what constituted a right or a wrong answer. Since teachers were not required to be able to speak in the L2 to any great extent, they could feel confident about their book-supported knowledge of the language. Confidence was further enhanced by the fact that from one year to the next little changed, in either the content of what was taught or in the manner of its teaching.

All learners were assumed to need to learn the same content, and to learn it in the same way. They were expected to learn the grammar rules and vocabulary items off by heart outside the class. Within the class they were expected to follow the teachers' instructions, participate in the translation of the text, answer comprehension questions or complete exercises. They were not usually expected to learn to speak the L2 fluently.

How similar is the above to what was (and maybe still is) 'traditional' language teaching in your context?

2.6 Strengths and weaknesses

GTM allows 'language' to be taught even where most English teachers' own language proficiency is limited and where there are few chances to have either direct face-to-face, or indirect (through the aural, visual or written media) contact with the L2 outside the classroom. Those successfully learning a language using this method are likely to have a good knowledge of the grammar of the language and of a wide range of vocabulary items. For those whose main aim is a reading knowledge of the L2, it may be helpful. However, even for these, the method does not train learners to develop a variety of normal reading skills, (in which the manner of reading is linked to the purpose for reading) because of its tendency to insist on word-by-word translation.

Since GTM assumes all learners require exactly the same knowledge and can be taught in exactly the same way, it fails to explicitly encourage teachers to recognise that learners are individuals, with differing attitudes, learning styles and purposes for learning the L2. Where language 'knowledge' is presented as being made up of facts that can be said to be right or wrong, and is then tested by means of exercises requiring accurate reproduction of correct language facts, there is bound to be a tendency to memorise facts for the exam. This may result in students who appear to be successful learners and can pass exams, but are in fact unable to use what they appear to know once the examination is over. Language lessons taught using this method are also, nowadays at least, often viewed as dull, and since the tangible result of many years language learning is frequently only an examination pass, such lessons do little to motivate learners for whom such a pass is not the only or the primary goal.

Since GTM treats language learning as learning a finite body of knowledge, just like learning any other subject, it fits easily into an educational culture in which the teacher's role is to be the 'knower', the one who defines and transmits what is to be known, while the learner is purely the receiver of the teacher's knowledge. In such educational cultures, secondary school and university teachers are specialists in a particular subject, there are clearly defined subject boundaries, and each subject has a finite body of content to be learned. Learners are seen as a mass rather than as individuals, as people who lack relevant knowledge on their arrival in school, and so need to be filled with subject knowledge by the experts, the teachers. Knowledge in such a culture is then a body of, mostly factual, subject information, common to and needed by all learners which can be transmitted. Educational cultures with the above view of teacher and learner roles and the nature of knowledge have been called 'Transmission based' by Young and Lee (1987), and as mentioned in Chapter 3 (the 2009 OECD TALIS survey) language classroom activities today still tend to be based around versions of the 'structuring practices' associated with transmission-based cultures.

Is or was your educational culture 'transmission-based'? Again, what makes you think so?

3. A brief history of methods: The Audio-Lingual method (ALM)

The Audio-Lingual Method was developed during and after the Second World War, initially to help American servicemen learn to speak the languages they needed to know in order to communicate with their many allies and enemies in the parts of the world in which they were fighting. It represented collaboration between two fields: Linguistics and Psychology. Based on what was then thought to be a scientific description of language and view of how learning occurs, it was, for a time, thought to represent a 'best' method of language teaching and learning. During the 1950s and 1960s, the ALM spread from its original base in the United States to influence language teaching in many other parts of the world. If you were ever taught in a 'language laboratory' or a classroom in which you spent much of your time repeating drills of various kinds, this suggests that it influenced your context also.

3.1 The view of language and language proficiency

The ALM claimed to be able to provide a scientific description of a language system, based on samples of real native speaker speech. However, these were the days before corpora enabled us to have access to literally millions of samples of language in use, and so we would want to ask linguists questions like the following.

- How many samples of speech from how many different speakers do you need to take to get sufficient data for an accurate structural description?
- What do you do about accents or dialects in your description?
- What sort of speakers should be represented, only the educated or a cross-section?
- What range of types of speech (e.g. formal or informal) would be needed to get a full picture of how the language system worked?

The samples that were collected were transcribed phonetically and analysed according to their levels of structural organisation. It was therefore immediately significantly different from GTM in the sense that it viewed spoken rather than written language as the basis from which to begin its study.

As a result of their analyses, structural linguists perceived each language as consisting of an orderly set of systems which it was their job to describe. At the base of the structure was a sound system which had rules about how sounds (phonemes) could be combined in certain ways to form meaning units (morphemes) which could then again be combined according to certain rules to form words, phrases and sentences. Language proficiency could therefore be measured by the extent to which a learner could accurately produce the L2, according to the rules at each level of the system.

Researchers at this time recognised that the systems of different languages differed from each other to varying extents, and saw errors in language learning as being influenced by differences between L1 and L2 systems, causing the learner's L1 system to '*interfere*' with their learning of the L2 system. They believed that through *contrastive analysis* in which major areas of difference (and so of potential interference) between the L1 and L2 systems were identified, they could help anticipate and minimise the effects of such interference. A huge amount of work was done by linguists in the United States and elsewhere, to provide scientific descriptions of language structure. One of the languages most carefully analysed and described was English.

3.2 View of language learning

Just as structural linguists claimed to be able to provide a scientific description of how any language was structured, provided they had the empirical data, so Behaviourist Psychologists claimed to have scientifically identified how humans learn. They acknowledged that humans are capable of a wide range of behaviours. Whether these behaviours occur or not depends on the development of appropriate habits, through repeated cycles of three crucial elements – *Stimulus-Response-Reinforcement* (for more on this, read Richards and Rodgers 2001). Behaviourists transferred this theory of learning as habit formation to language learning. They stated that what was desired from learners was verbal behaviour in the L2. Such L2 behaviour could be achieved by the development of L2 habits through repeated cycles in which the teacher provided plenty of language *Stimuli*, which allowed learners to make correct *Responses* which the teacher would then *Reinforce* through praise and encouragement to carry on further.

They believed that new language habits would be learned most effectively if in the L2, as in the L1, items were first presented in their spoken forms. ALM teaching was therefore based around the development of learners' aural-oral skills, with new 'habits' or structure rules introduced one at a time, and thoroughly practised orally in a variety of contexts, before the patterns for their formation were formally presented. Any errors (which ideally should not be allowed to occur) would be immediately corrected at the *reinforcement* stage of the cycle, in order to avoid the development of incorrect habits. It was recognised that language patterns always express meanings related to particular situations and that they should therefore as far as possible be presented to learners in typical situations.

Thinking about what we have just described, do you think that you consciously learned your L1 through repetition of correct utterances, or if you have children, do you think this is how they have learned theirs? Do you feel the L1 learning experience is similar to or different from the behaviourist view above?

3.3 Syllabus

Like GTM, in ALM it was assumed that all learners needed to learn the same components of the language system. Using structural linguists' descriptions, syllabuses were written which listed the key structure items at each level of the system. Early on in the syllabus there was an emphasis on aural discrimination of sounds and oral imitation and repetition of sounds, words and sentences. Reading and writing were introduced later and dealt only with language that had already been encountered in oral form.

3.4 Materials

Many ALM materials were based around dialogues of varying lengths which aimed to place the particular structure being taught into a L2 situation in which it might normally be found. The dialogues were repeated until memorised and then the grammar pattern which it introduced was drilled. The aim was to *overlearn* or *automatise* the new verbal behaviour so that thereafter it would be part of a set of new L2 habits. Here again the influence context of *Time* becomes apparent as the technological development of the 1960s and 1970s saw the first emergence of Computer-Assisted Language Learning (CALL) materials to promote such 'overlearning'. At this point the role of computers was just to act as a means of providing the learners with a range of (usually) drill based practice materials. They were not seen as a means of enabling learners to play a role in choosing what or how to learn.

Are oral drills used in your context? If so, why, what are they used for?

3.5 Teachers' and learners' roles in the classroom

Teachers in the ALM classroom are even more central than in the GTM class. They are crucial throughout any language lesson since they often represent the correct model of the L2 needed to provide learners with stimuli to respond to, and are also providers of reinforcement for accurate responses, or of correct forms if, unfortunately, errors are made. They are needed as conductors (almost literally) of a variety of repetition and substitution drills and as controllers of the tape recorder or the language laboratory. They have books and tapes to support them, so they do not necessarily have to be imaginative, but they do have to be very active and need to be able to speak the L2 far better than their GTM colleagues, since the use of L1 in the classroom is strongly discouraged in order to minimise interference.

Once again learners are seen as identical: as human organisms who need to be directed to react to stimuli with correct responses. They are very dependent on the teacher and have very little control over the pace, style or content of the class. They are not encouraged to initiate interaction in L2 in case this results in error, which, since it is incorrect behaviour, is clearly undesirable.

3.6 Strengths and weaknesses

Like GTM, ALM represents a Transmission-based educational culture. Teacher and learner roles in relation to one another are unchanged, there is still a finite body of knowledge to be learned, and it is the job of the teacher to pass it on to the learners and monitor the extent to which they know it.

The aim of this method is to produce learners with L2 habits that are available for use in especially spoken, but also written forms, in the L2 environment outside the language classroom. Compared to GTM, learners' being taught using ALM do hear the language used in a limited number of more or less typical situations, and get a great deal of very controlled oral practice. Through memorisation of dialogues, repeated drilling and immediate correction of all errors, it is assumed that they will develop the correct habits of the L2 system.

However, over time it became clear that frequently when learners tried to use their L2 habits in natural interaction with L2 speakers outside the classroom, they were unable to transfer what they had memorised in a dialogue representing one situation, into other situations in the real world. Despite teaching based on the most scientific available descriptions of language and a teaching method based on a scientific theory of learning, in terms of its aim of producing skilled users of the L2, ALM disappointed many.

In retrospect it is easy to criticise the belief in the supremacy of 'science' which characterised this method. It is also possible to question just how 'scientific' the description of language actually was, or how applicable theories about animal learning (on which behaviourism was based) could be to human language learning.

What differences and similarities did you think of between the behaviourist view of language learning and your experience/memory of L1 learning?

Ours include:
Similarities

- Children do sometimes imitate and repeat what others say when learning their L1.
- Children do repeat things to themselves and try them out in different linguistic contexts.
- Language is closely tied to situations.

Differences

- Most children grow up in an environment in which there is a lot of interaction between them and those around them.
- Children do not just respond but initiate interactions, using combinations of language items that they have never heard used, to express real meanings.

- Children usually get instant feedback about whether their meaning has been understood (rather than whether their language was accurate).
- Children's language is only very rarely either 'practised', or corrected for its formal accuracy.

The Behaviourist theory of language learning as habit formation was expressed most fully in the psychologist Skinner's book, 'Verbal Behaviour' (1957). However, two years after the book was published, the theory was discredited once and for all when the linguist Chomsky (1959) published his review of Skinner's book. In this, he pointed out a fundamental flaw in the Behaviourist theory. The theory stated that new verbal behaviour could only be a result of the formation of a new language habit through a series of Stimulus, Response and Reinforcement cycles. Chomsky pointed out that (as mentioned above) if this was so, how did Behaviourists account for the many children learning their L1, who frequently utter sentences that they have never heard before, and indeed the fact that all of us as adults constantly create unique, never-before-uttered, sentences in both our L1 and in any other languages that we know. Major changes in ELT lay ahead.

4. A brief history of methods: Humanistic methods

In chronological terms, these methods overlap with communicative approaches, but because they remain Methods, *(a prescribed set of procedures thought to be most effective for the teaching of language),* we discuss them in this chapter. The four methods that we shall touch on here are Total Physical Response (TPR), Community Language Learning (CLL), Suggestopaedia (SP) and the Silent Way (SW). We will not look in detail at exactly what each method requires the teacher to do. Further information can be found in Richards and Rodgers (2001), and Larsen-Freeman (2000). All the methods developed in the United States, apart from SP which began in Bulgaria. None of them have ever had a very wide following, but they are worth looking at because, although they all retain an implicit belief in 'one best way', they represent a break with some fundamental assumptions about teachers, learners and the learning process that were inherent in GTM and ALM. In this sense they have strongly influenced aspects of the implementation of communicative approaches, as we will see in Chapter 5.

4.1 Language learning as an active cognitive process, rather than habit formation

Humanistic methods contrast strongly with the ALM in that they explicitly recognise that learning the L2 structure system requires autonomous active mental effort on the part of the learner. They all emphasise the fact that L2 learning is not a matter of mimicking what you hear. Instead, individual learners build up their own mental picture of the L2 rule system. They do this through active and creative use of the L2 in meaningful practice (SW), through communication via varied tasks and peripheral learning using L2 cultural artefacts (SP) or by themselves deciding what they want to communicate about or what they want to practice (CLL).

4.2 A new view of error

Whereas GTM and ALM stressed the need for accuracy in all learner output, the Humanistic methods took a different view and interpreted error as a sign of active mental effort towards the construction of a personal mental picture of the L2 system. As such, they stressed the importance of teachers tolerating error, correcting it unobtrusively, repeating the correct form, or correcting it later so that learners hear the correct form. All methods stressed that in order to encourage a positive classroom atmosphere (see Section 4.4 below) whatever form error correction took it should be as unthreatening as possible to the learners.

4.3 Learners as individuals

All these Humanistic methods recognised that language learners are individuals and that therefore their language learning success will vary according to the extent that they are willing or able to take part in activities in the L2, make the effort to think about what they are doing with the L2, and so build up a more or less explicit personal picture of the L2 rule system. They also agreed that learners were actively responsible for their own learning, although they differed as to when such responsibilities begin. While SP and TPR believed that to begin with learners should rely absolutely on the teacher, SW and CLL insisted that learners should take full responsibility for what they do from the very start of their L2 learning programme. All methods, though, agreed that the ultimate aim was for learners to become independent learners, actively participating and co-operating with their classmates to make the most of all language learning opportunities inside and outside the classroom.

4.4 The importance of the learning environment

These methods agree on the important role played by the language-learning environment in influencing the extent to which learners are able to become the active participants in their own development outlined above. For this to happen, learners need to feel relaxed and confident in their own abilities. Language classrooms therefore need to minimise the fear of failure by providing learners with language based tasks and activities at a level that learners can usually carry out successfully, and avoid stress by not forcing learners to speak before they feel ready to. A further common theme is the need for a co-operative, rather than a competitive examination-focused atmosphere in the classroom, an atmosphere in which learners are encouraged to recognise that they have a lot to offer each other. This parallels the emergence of a more interactive, socio-cultural view of learning more generally.

4.5 The multiple roles of the teacher

Teachers in GTM and ALM language classrooms were the undoubted authority, the controller of all activities, the provider of all knowledge and the assessor of all performance. Humanistic methods, although differing as to the role of the teacher in the early stages of the learning process, all agreed that as soon as possible, learners should be encouraged to move from dependence on the teacher to independence from the teacher. Thus, while all the methods viewed certain responsibilities of the teacher as constant (for example maintenance of a relaxed classroom atmosphere) they also all expected that the role of the teacher would change as learners became more able and willing to take responsibility for their own learning. This reminds us of one of the main principles of 'scaffolding' (Chapter 3), the 'handover principle'.

4.6 Closing comments

The above sections aim only to identify some of the ways in which Humanistic methods set some of the parameters for ELT principles which would later be further developed by communicative approaches. Humanistic methods represent a move away from a purely transmission-based educational culture in which language is a subject with a certain number of facts to be learned, these facts to be passed from the teachers to learners, who show their learning by accurately retrieving the facts from their memories when asked to do so by teachers or examinations. Instead they represent examples of what Fullan and Hargreaves (1992) call 'co-operative' and Young and Lee (1987) 'interpretation based' ELT educational cultures. Such cultures recognise that subject boundaries are fuzzy and often overlap and that learning subject content alone is insufficient, and needs to be paralleled by developing the skills that will enable the content to be used for practical purposes. Teachers' responsibilities in such a culture are to organise learning opportunities and to encourage learners to develop their own learning and thinking strategies. They recognise that learners are individuals who learn in many different ways (see Chapter 7), and who may need to learn different skills and information, and so acknowledge the need for different teaching content and techniques.

5. Summary and task

In this chapter, we have looked at the way in which ELT methods have developed from a method deriving directly from the teaching of classical languages, via a method that claimed to be completely 'scientific', towards a number of methods which, though never very widespread, have strongly influenced current 'communicative' ELT teaching practices and approaches which we will discuss in Chapter 5.

It is clear that one of the reasons why ELT has been so very fully researched has to do with the role of English as a world language and the United States as an economically powerful English-speaking country. However, we have also been able to notice that trends in ELT methods have shadowed, or perhaps even led, the growing trend in many parts of the world for education systems more generally to at least advocate a move from a strictly transmission-based to a more co-operative/interpretation based educational culture.

In the following chapter we will bring the discussion of Methods and Approaches more up to date, by looking at currently influential approaches underlying common ELT practices.

Task:

This task asks you to investigate the effects of TIME on ELT practices in your context. Consider what changes have taken place, why these have happened, and compare what you discover with what we have written here. Have the trends been similar?

In order to carry out this task, you will need to think about what you can do to find the information you need.

Some people you could ask include: older people with language learning experiences, yourself – your own experiences as a learner, teachers from as many generations as possible.

Some texts you could consult include: textbooks, syllabuses, exam papers and curriculum documents from different eras.

Depending (of course!) on the time you have available we would suggest you consult as many of the above sources (and any others you can find/think of) as possible. Try not to rely just on one source.

References and further reading

Brown, H. D. 2006. *Principles of Language Learning and Teaching* (5th edn). White Plains, New York: Pearson Education.

Chomsky, N. 1959. 'A review of B.F. Skinner's "Verbal Behaviour"'. *Language*, 35/1, pp. 26–58.

Cresswell, J. W. 2007. *Qualitative Inquiry and Research Design*. Thousand Oaks, CA: Sage.

Denzin, N. K. and Y. S. Lincoln, eds. 2005. *The Handbook of Qualitative Research* (3rd edn). Thousand Oaks, CA: Sage.

Fullan, M. and A. Hargreaves, eds. 1992. *Teacher Development and Educational Change*. London: Falmer Press.

Holliday, A. 2007. *Doing and Writing Qualitative Research* (2nd edn). London: Sage.

Howatt, A. 2004. *A History of English Language Teaching* (2nd edn). Oxford: Oxford University Press.

Johnson, K. E. 2009. *Second Language Teacher Education: A Socio-Cultural Perspective*. New York: Routledge.

Larsen-Freeman, D. 2000. *Techniques and Principles in Language Teaching* (2nd edn). Oxford: Oxford University Press.

Medgyes, P. 1986. 'Queries from a communicative teacher'. *English Language Teaching Journal*, 40/2, pp. 107–112

Moskowitz, G. 1978. *Caring and Sharing in the Foreign Language Classroom: A Sourcebook on Humanistic Techniques*. Rowley Mass: Newbury House.

Richards, J. C. and T. Rodgers. 2001. *Approaches and Methods in Language Teaching* (2nd edn). Cambridge: Cambridge University Press.

Rivers, W. 1983. *Communicating Naturally in a Second Language: Theory and Practice in Language Teaching*. Cambridge: Cambridge University Press.

Skinner, B. F. 1957. *Verbal Behaviour*. Acton, MA: Copley Publishing Group.

Stevick, E. W. 1980. *Teaching Languages: A Way and Ways*. Rowley Mass: Newbury House.

— 1986. *Images and Options in the Language Classroom*. New York: Cambridge University Press.

— 1990. *Humanism in Language Teaching*. Oxford: Oxford University Press.

Sweet, H. 1899. *The Practical Study of Languages. A Guide for Teachers and Learners*. London: Dent. Republished by Oxford University Press in 1964.

Young, R. and S. Lee. 1987. 'EFL curriculum innovation and teachers' attitudes'. In: R. Lord and N. H. L. Cheng, eds., *Language and Education in Hong Kong*. Hong Kong: Chinese University Press, pp.83–97.

5

From methods to approaches

Introduction

Following on from Chapter 4, this chapter continues our brief overview of the evolution of ideas and practices in ELT. In Chapter 4, we looked at Methods. We noted that by the end of the period under consideration, researchers into and practitioners of Humanistic methods had already begun to question the idea, implicit in methods such as Grammar Translation and Audio-Lingualism, that learners all learned in the same way and had the same language needs. There had not, however, yet been much explicit change in professional understanding of what language is, and so of what a proficient user of any language needs to know and be able to do.

This chapter looks mainly at changes in how 'language' has been understood in ELT since the 1960s – changes in answer to the question: 'what is language?' These changes have been very influential in helping the profession recognise that in (English) language teaching and learning it is no longer possible to believe that all contexts can use a single method. We here therefore, try to explain some of the main reasons why the ELT profession has moved from one that, up to the 1960s at least, professed to be using a limited number of more or less uniform methods, to a profession that today recognises (in principle at least) that it is natural for teachers to base their classroom decision-making on their own understandings of a shared approach, and so natural for there to be a wide variety of context-dependent classroom practices.

You will notice that many of the references in this chapter are to texts from the 1970s and 1980s. This is not because we have not looked at any books or articles since then! Instead, it is a sign of a relative lack of new developments in the understanding of what language is in the intervening years. Research from the 1960s to the 1980s began to demonstrate that viewing language as a tool for communication and expression made its description much more complex. Since then, the focus of much research has turned to trying to understand what such complexity implies for language teaching and learning.

In this chapter, we do not discuss second language acquisition (SLA) – or the ranges of possible answers to the seemingly equally important question 'how is language learnt?' This is in part because an understanding of what language is, is a prerequisite for any discussion of SLA. It is also a very complex field with an enormous literature. However, we do make a few general comments now on some current ideas.

Very broadly, much recent research into the manner in which learners build up a mental picture of the L2 linguistic system emphasises the need for learners to be provided with sufficient comprehensible input for them begin to notice and *make sense* of form-meaning regularities and so develop mental maps about how the L2 system works. Equally important, if learners are to develop an ability to *use* their knowledge effectively and appropriately for their own purposes, is that they are provided with sufficient opportunities to try out language. These opportunities need to be of the kind which demand that they interact and express themselves (whether orally or in writing) in the L2. Through participating in these interactions, the reactions of those they are communicating with can help them see whether their ways of using the language do in fact 'work' to express intended meanings or to understand enough for their purposes. Where an effort at communication does not achieve its purpose, this might mean that the learners either (need to) adjust their 'mental maps' or, for example, adjust their pronunciation or learn some new vocabulary. (For an accessible introduction to SLA, see Lightbown and Spada 2006.)

In terms of teaching (supporting language learning), as became apparent when we looked at Humanistic methods in Chapter 4, an important trend in ideas about language learning since the 1960s has been firmly away from the purely Behaviourist beliefs of the Audiolingual method. Instead, it is now fully accepted that learners are *individuals,* who come to the classroom with previous experience of their L1, who have different learning styles and are capable of using different learning strategies (see Chapters 6 and 7) to take an *active* role in their own learning. These trends have contributed to the development of some of the ideas which influence ELT today – consider buzzwords such as 'learner autonomy', 'student-centred classrooms', 'multiple intelligences', 'differentiation' and similar terms.

Section 1 below reintroduces the term Approach in the sense that we use it in this chapter. Section 2 looks in detail at the changes in our understanding of the nature of language that have led us to a view of language as a tool for communication and so to a different perception of what a competent communicator in any language needs to know and be able to do. In Section 3, we consider some of the potential implications of such a view of language for what should be taught and learned (syllabus) and how proficiency may be assessed (language testing). The final section discusses how the practical implications of a view of 'language as a tool for communication' have led to an ELT profession in which teachers across the world use a range of contextually influenced methodologies.

1. Communicative approaches

Very many ELT contexts today would probably claim to be following a broadly 'communicative' approach, but what do we mean by the terms 'communicative' and 'approach'?

'Communicative' refers to a particular view of language, what it is and what it is for. Such a view, as we shall see in this chapter, answers the question '*what is language?*' by saying that it is both *a body of knowledge and a set of abilities or skills that use that knowledge.* It sees the principle function or purpose of language as something used by human beings to communicate, through appropriately expressing and understanding interactional (social or affective feeling-related) and transactional (information obtaining or providing) functions. A communicative view of language would therefore, answer the question '*what is language for?*' by saying something like:

> to enable humans to communicate with each other: that is to express and comprehend whatever interactional or transactional meanings they need for whatever purpose, in ways that are appropriate to whatever social or cultural context they find themselves in.

This uniquely human ability to communicate/interact through the use of language is, as we have seen in Chapters 2 and 3, thought to be fundamental to the development of individuals and cultures.

We have defined an Approach (see Chapter 4) as a set of more or less consciously held **beliefs** about the nature of language and the language learning process that influence the manner in which language is taught in a particular language learning context.

People holding similar sets of beliefs may be said to be following a similar Approach. We say '*similar*' rather than the '*same*' because even where people use the same language to talk about their beliefs, they will inevitably understand this language slightly differently – from their own perspective, based on their own prior experience – and anyway, not all their beliefs will be conscious ones.

Our definition of Communicative Approaches however, needs to incorporate not only shared beliefs about language, but also beliefs about the language learning process. We will draw these from our very brief discussion in the Introduction.

Teachers in a context can be said to be following a broadly Communicative Approach if their teaching is based on a contextually appropriate interpretation of the following set of beliefs about language and language learning.

Language is

- both a body of knowledge and a set of abilities or skills which use that knowledge
- used to enable humans to communicate with each other, to express and comprehend whatever functions they find that they need and want to express in their particular living context.

Language learning is

- an interactive process requiring active mental participation, in which learners work to develop the skills and sensitivities needed to use the language for their own communicative purposes. Over time, and at least partly through repeated experiences of *using* the language, they also make sense of a new body of language knowledge.

In Section 2 of the chapter especially, we point out some other beliefs that we feel are particularly typical of communicative approaches.

2. Changing perceptions of language

Some decades ago, Tarone and Yule outlined some of the main shifts in thinking regarding what it was that language teachers should teach:

> In recent years there has been a major shift in perspective within the language teaching profession concerning the nature of what is to be taught. In relatively simple terms, there has been a change of emphasis from presenting language as a set of forms . . . which have to be learned and practised, to presenting language as a functional system which is used to fulfil a range of communicative purposes. This shift in emphasis has largely taken place as a result of . . . arguments, mainly from ethnographers and others who study language and its context of use, that the ability to use a language should be described as 'communicative competence'. (1989:17)

The biggest shift was perhaps the shift in views of the goal of language learning from 'linguistic competence' to 'communicative competence'. In this section, we are going to look a little more closely at how the idea of communicative competence developed and what it is thought to mean.

In Chapter 4, we mentioned that Chomsky (1959) had effectively demonstrated that Skinner's Behaviourist view of the language learning process could not *alone* account for how either first or subsequent languages were learned. In the years that followed, increasing attention was focused on the structural linguists' claim that any language was purely an orderly, finite, fully describable set of rule systems applied by language users to express their meanings.

If this was true, then L1 speakers' ability in any language, to express whatever meanings they wished to in the real world, must be based on their underlying knowledge of the L1 rule system at all levels. If this was what competence in a language involved, then in language-learning it followed that a thorough knowledge of the rules of the language system ought to equip L2 language-learners also to express and understand whatever meanings they might need, outside the classroom. Yet it was increasingly clear by the mid to late 1960s that this was not the case for the majority of language learners emerging after years of language study in Audiolingual or Grammar Translation Method classrooms.

2.1 Hymes's communicative competence

One of the most influential insights into the nature of language has been the recognition by the American sociolinguist, Hymes (1970), that 'Competence' in a language involves more than what Chomsky called Linguistic competence, or the system-based knowledge of how to produce grammatically correct sentences. (From this point on we are going to use the term *Sentences* to mean only 'grammatically complete units regarded purely formally in isolation from their context and their function' (Cook 1989:24).)

Hymes pointed out that in addition to the knowledge needed to produce such *sentences,* any user of a language needs to be able to produce *utterances* that are in every sense acceptable in the context in which they are used. We define *utterances,* again following Cook (cited above, p. 24) as 'a unit of language used by somebody in context to do something – to communicate.'

This awareness that competent language users are able to form utterances that may or may not be grammatically correct but are appropriate to the particular situation in which they are used, was behind Hymes's famous statement that 'There are rules of use, without which the rules of grammar would be useless.' (Hymes 1970, cited in Brumfit and Johnson 1979:15).

For Hymes it is necessary to know both sets of rules to be 'Communicatively Competent', since while it is enough to know the rules of grammar to be able to produce sentences, to produce utterances it is also necessary to know the rules of use.

If we think about ourselves as communicatively competent users of our L1, we can see at once that this is true. For example, we as UK L1 English-speakers and relatively competent communicators in that language, understand the phrase 'kick the bucket' and know when, where and with whom it would effectively communicate our meaning. (For those from different contexts, in the United Kingdom, it is most often used for its metaphorical meaning, which is 'to die'. We would not use it at a funeral, especially if talking to the bereaved family. However, in informal chat and jokes it is not uncommon and not offensive/an accepted euphemism.)

Without knowledge of our L1 rules of use, we would be unable to produce the utterances needed to communicate effectively in our daily lives and be unable accurately to interpret many of the utterances addressed to us by our fellow L1 speakers. Without communicative competence we would not be able to function as members of our L1 cultures, since, as we saw in Chapters 2 and 3, many cultural rules and norms depend on language for their transmission. Any full model of language must therefore recognise its role at the centre of human communication, as the fundamental human tool for social interaction, and strongly influenced in its use by the spoken and unspoken social rules of the L1 user culture.

The implications of this for the existing, purely grammatical-rule-governed model of language were enormous. If competence in a language involved knowing how to use the rules to express the desired meaning in a given situation, this suggested that different situations might require the rules to be used differently. It became clear that of course this is exactly what happens in any language.

In normal use of English for example, grammatically identical sentences can be used to express different functions (to do different things – for example the phrase '*Let's close that door*' could, depending on the context, be a suggestion, an order or a warning), and grammatically different sentences can be used to express the same functions (to do identical things, for example, again depending on context, both '*Pass the butter*' and '*Would you be kind enough to pass me the butter*' are ways of making the same request). Competence in English and any other language is then not just a matter of being able to form grammatically correct sentences. It also involves the ability to choose *which* grammatically correct forms of a sentence it is appropriate to use in utterances which will communicate a particular meaning to particular people, in a particular place, at a particular time. In English, choices marking appropriacy may be made at all levels of the language system, from differences in intonation, to different choices of vocabulary items (as illustrated by our 'kick the bucket' example above) and different sentence structures.

As you can probably see, this idea of 'communicative competence' as the sign of a proficient language user has enormous implications for language-learning and teaching. However, it is one thing to know that this is true, and quite another to work out how to actually use this realisation in the language classroom.

Before we look at how people have tried to use this view of language in the learning-teaching process, we need first to look at a further set of insights that resulted from a view of 'language as communication'.

2.2 Discourse and the idea that language has structure above the utterance level

Hymes's insight into communicative competence enabled us to realise that there is more to knowing a language than only knowing its grammar rules, vocabulary items and sound system. Soon thereafter came a further development, when British linguists such as Widdowson (1972, 1978), and Sinclair and Coulthard (1975) pointed out that when we use spoken and written language, we almost always use several utterances, not just one, and that the way that we order and combine these utterances is not purely random. Just as word order can affect the meaning expressed within an utterance, so utterances used in longer stretches of spoken or written language are combined in ways that 'hang together and have unity' (Cook 1989:14) and that enable the intended meaning to be clear. Longer stretches of both spoken and written language are therefore structured at discourse level. Discourse is made up of sequences of spoken or written utterances, used in communication, and the study of how discourse is structured is called Discourse Analysis. We outline two main features of discourse below.

2.2.1 Discourse has coherence

Rules of discourse structure are of two main groups. First, a piece of language may hang together as a result of situational factors. If we

> look at the features outside the language, the situation, the people involved, what they know and what they are doing . . . these facts enable us to construct stretches of language as discourse having meaning and unity for us. (Cook, cited above: 14).

Here then, in addition to the meanings being expressed by the language itself, it is features of the context outside the language that help to unify the utterances. Such discourse is said to have *coherence.* As is true for most rules of use, there are as yet few generalisable rules regarding what makes discourse coherent. However, aspects of some types of the most typically occurring social purposes for which language is used like, for example, conversations, have been quite carefully studied by discourse analysts. This research shows that, in certain situations, sequences of utterances expressing particular communicative functions often occur in a fairly predictable order. A simple example of how spoken discourse might be structured is given below.

You have planned to go to see a film this evening. You meet a friend you know well in the street in the morning on your way to work, and invite her/him to come with you.

A. (You) (B) friend

A. greeting
B. greeting
A. explanation of where you plan to go this evening
invitation
B. accept
reject + excuse
A. (if accepted)- express enthusiasm + arrangements for meeting
(if rejected)- express sadness + possibility of another time
MOVE TO ANOTHER TOPIC OR
A & B. farewells

Conversations like the above do have a structure. The speakers take turns. The turns are often short. The turns build on what the previous speaker has said. There are points in the conversation where either the topic changes or the conversation ends. While the actual grammatical forms and vocabulary items used would vary according to situational factors such as the exact relationship between you and your friend, your age and how much of a hurry you were both in, the functions expressed would in our culture usually be most of those listed above. They would also appear in more or less the order listed. If they were expressed in a very different order, or conveyed very different meanings, it would upset the *coherence* of the Discourse, the thread of shared meaning that gives the discourse unity for the two speakers would be broken and they would need to work to restore it.

> The key to the concept of coherence is not something that exists in words or structures, but something that exists in people. It is people who 'make sense' of what they read and hear. They try and arrive at an interpretation which is in line with their experience of the way the world is. (Yule 2005:126)

If your L1 is not English:

- *Try and construct a similar sequence of functions for the same social situation in your own language.*
- *What kinds of predictable structures does discourse have in your language? Do you notice any differences in functions used, between your example and the one given above?*
- *What do any differences suggest that a communicatively competent user of your language needs to know?*

If your L1 is English

- *Do you agree that the example given represents a likely sequence of L1 utterances?*

What contextual factors would most strongly influence the lexical/structural choices that you made in such a situation?

2.2.2 Discourse has cohesion

We said that there were two main features of discourse structure. The second is more formally marked by specific language items and so is more visible. It can most easily be seen in written texts, but it is a feature of spoken language also.

Whether you write a quick note, a personal or formal letter, or an academic essay, there are (more or less clearly defined) rules governing the order in which you present the meanings that you wish to express. This ordering is of course partly a result of your desire to present your meanings in a way that hangs together (see *Coherence* above). But it is also linguistically marked by *cohesive devices* which explicitly show '. . . the ties and connections that exist in texts' (Yule 1985:105). Some of the most frequently occurring cohesive devices in English are what Cook (1989:16) calls 'Referring Expressions', like third person expressions, (he, she, it, his, hers. . . and so on).

An important aspect of communicative competence is therefore knowledge of the manner in which, in a given situation, it is appropriate to present the meanings that you express in your spoken or written utterances. Once again it is clear that there are rules, even though they have so far only been described for a few of the most frequently occurring human interactional situations, and for certain types of written texts. Communicatively competent users of any language (unconsciously) know these discourse rules. In their day-to-day interactions with other people they can both produce coherent and cohesive spoken and written utterances, and interpret other people's as intended. If discourse rules are not followed, the discourse breaks down and comprehension becomes difficult. If, at that point, speakers or writers do not 'repair' the discourse structure, it is likely that the meanings that they wish to express will not be successfully communicated. Just as with rules of use, discourse rules are culture bound, a further marker of shared knowledge and behaviour between competent speakers of the same language.

Communicative approaches recognise that language has 'structure' above the sentence level.

2.3 The components of communicative competence

You may well be asking by now, so what, what does this actually mean in practice? What is it that teachers need to do, what is it that learners should be learning so that they can apply rules of use and discourse rules and so become competent communicators? If you are asking these questions you are in good company. Linguists since Hymes, such as Canale, and Savignon (both 1983), syllabus designers such as Wilkins (1974) and Nunan (1989) and language testers such as Morrow (1979, 1986), Weir (1990) and Bachman and Palmer (1996) have all worked to try and define more fully what communicative competence involves.

Canale (1983) has one of the most well known and frequently cited definitions of communicative competence. He viewed it as being made up of four components. The first three of these relate directly to what we have already discussed.

- Linguistic competence – the *knowledge* of the structure rules of the language at each level and the *ability* to use these to form grammatically correct spoken and written utterances in the language.
- Sociolinguistic competence – the *ability* to produce and understand language appropriately in different situations. This involves both *knowledge* of what it is appropriate to say and write in a given situation (appropriate content), and the *ability* to choose the appropriate vocabulary items and grammatical structure to express it (appropriate form).
- Discourse competence – the *knowledge* of the conventions associated with the production of longer stretches of written or spoken language in different situations. The *abilities* to follow these conventions and so to combine the utterances needed to express

the desired meaning appropriately for the situation or understand others' meanings when they do so.

Canale also introduced a fourth category here. This he called Strategic Competence. We will here combine Canale's view of this competence with that of Bachman and Palmer (1996), who regard it as being at the very heart of communicative competence. They see it thus:

- Strategic competence – the global *ability* to combine all the above knowledge and abilities as well as the general background knowledge gained through experience of life, to create and interpret utterances appropriately for any given situation. This global ability also involves *knowledge* of the appropriate verbal and non-verbal strategies for dealing with any situation in which communication breaks down and the *ability* to use them to restore effective communication.

Hopefully you will have noticed that this description of communicative competence in all cases views competence as being made up both of certain conscious or unconscious knowledge, and of the ability to use the knowledge in an appropriate manner to express or understand a desired meaning and maintain effective communication.

Communicative approaches see language proficiency as consisting of a combination of language knowledge and abilities to use such knowledge to 'communicate'. Canale however, points out that for almost everyone there is sometimes a gap between communicative competence, the underlying language knowledge and skills, and actual communication, the use of that underlying knowledge and skill in real life communication. This mismatch had been noted, in terms of linguistic competence only, by Chomsky in 1965, who pointed out that even in our L1, most of us find that sometimes, because of the pressures of the situation in which we are trying to express our meaning, we are unable to exactly reflect our underlying linguistic competence in our actual spoken performance. Grammatically imperfect spoken performance in real-time interaction is therefore not at all unusual among fluent speakers of any language. This recognition of the presence of formal errors as a normal feature of much fluent, native speaker spoken language has meant that communicative approaches tend to be more accepting than earlier methods of L2 oral errors that do not interfere with communication.

Communicative approaches recognise that there are differences between spoken and written language, for example, in the degree of consistent formal accuracy that it is reasonable to expect most learners to produce orally.

2.4 *Communicative competence and language description*

Ever since it has become clear that communicative competence involves more than knowledge of the grammatical system, linguists have struggled with the complexity of the task posed by the need for a full description of any language to also state its discourse rules and rules of use. As we have seen above these rules are intimately connected to the culture within which the language is used. Any attempt to fully describe such rules therefore requires linguists to become ethnographers, since much of what needs to be described is culture specific. For example to begin to be able to describe the rules of use it is necessary to answer questions such as those below for any situation in which language is commonly used:

- Which meanings may appropriately be expressed this situation?
- What factors within the situation govern the choices of how the meaning is expressed?
- What vocabulary items are used, what grammatical structures, what combination of functions?
- In what order would the meanings (functions) expressed by the chosen utterances normally be expected to come?
- What is it appropriate to do if, for some reason, communication breaks down?

Since the development of these insights in the 1970s and 1980s, the expansion of English as an international language complicates matters further. Today, most English learners will often, or perhaps always, be using their English with others who are also using English as their second (or third or fourth) language. Therefore, the value of learning the cultural norms implicit in descriptions of native speakers' rules of use is being questioned. For example, we, as British people (with English as our first language) would never ask a stranger on a train in England how much they earn (considered rude), nor tell someone that they are 'fat and fair' (also considered rude). We have encountered both situations elsewhere in the world (the first as an ice-breaker, the second as a compliment) when interacting with people using English, which they have learnt as a foreign language, according to their own cultural rules of use. Their use of language would previously have been understood as demonstrating their failure to learn 'native-speaker' rules of use. However, in today's context a different way of understanding communicative competence is needed. Alptekin (2002) has suggested that the target for most English learners and users today should be the development of 'intercultural communicative competence' (ICC). (We must have developed some ICC, since we understood the intent behind the above remarks and were not, in fact, offended!)

Not only is the task of describing the rules of use of all languages impossibly huge, but also there is no fixed repertoire of situations for any one culture, and probably never will be. In addition new language use situations are emerging all the time. For example, the use of mobile phones and the continuously changing forms of internet communication for banking, shopping and chat generate new rules. These same technological advances, of course also enable the collection of examples of real language in use, in quantities and of a variety that structural linguists could never have dreamt of. Corpora such as the CoBuild Corpus at the University of Birmingham, United Kingdom, now exist in many parts of the world, containing huge stores of authentic spoken and written language, sampled from a wide range of sources and discourse situations, representing a range of normally English L1 speaker interaction. Corpora have already served as valuable sources of reference for writers of communicative grammars and modern dictionaries who wish to exemplify their explanations of the meanings carried by grammatical forms and lexical items. At some time in the future, further advances in technology may allow even larger stores of naturally occurring language data (including samples from interactions between second language users of English) to be collected. These might then enable the constantly developing rules of use and /or discourse rules of English and all other languages to be sketched out in ways that will be helpful to language-learners and teachers. Until then language teaching has to cope without such full descriptions.

In rare teaching contexts, such as those following the Dogme approach discussed below, the lack of a full description of rules to be passed on to learners is not seen as posing a problem for classroom teaching. After all, as seen in Chapter 4, methods which emphasise the transmission of 'rules' have not proved successful for helping learners to use language. Instead, it is expected that teachers in such contexts will feel comfortable and confident about using the descriptions that do exist to guide them in providing learners with what Chapter 3 (referring to L1) suggested as fundamental conditions needed for communicative competence to develop: exposure to the target language, opportunities to use the language and motivation to do so and learn.

Few contexts exist which encourage and enable English teachers to feel confident and comfortable with such limited guidelines. Instead, as Celce-Murcia, Dornyei and Thurrel suggested in 1995, and as remains largely true today, most of those involved in influencing the conditions in which language teachers work (and we believe most language teachers also) are still looking for more concrete descriptions.

> Language teaching methodologists, materials writers and language testers badly need a comprehensive and accessible description of the components of communicative competence in order to have more concrete pieces of language to work with. (p. 29)

Attempts to work through the practical implications of notion of communicative competence as a goal for learners in English classrooms and to try and create some 'ordered' framework for communicative language teaching have most often been made by syllabus and test designers. We turn to their work next.

3. Language syllabuses and language exams

A language syllabus is a means of organising the content and sequence of the language-learning experience. A language-proficiency test (like TOEFL or IELTS that you may have taken at some time yourself) is supposed to show learners' current level of language ability. As long as language proficiency was considered to involve mostly linguistic competence, the syllabus designer could refer to grammar books for help in deciding language content and how it should be ordered, and language testers could test learners' ability to accurately recognise and reproduce a sample of items from the syllabus.

In a situation where language proficiency is understood to demand communicative competence, but where many features of such competence have not been described, the syllabus designers' and language testers' job became far more complex. Many attempts continue to be made to try and devise language syllabuses that will help develop learners' communicative ability in a systematic way and language tests that are able, reliably and validly, to measure such ability. There are though others within the profession who see too much adherence to organised syllabuses as unhelpful for developing an ability to communicate and/or who feel that the enormous changes in what technology can offer should be utilised more fully, especially to provide learners with opportunities to use the language that they know in genuinely interactive ways. This part of the chapter briefly mentions examples of all of these.

3.1 Language syllabuses

Earlier language teaching methods, based around linguistic competence, were able to follow a clear route through a structural syllabus to achieve language-learning goals which may nowadays seem rather unclear to us. Communicative language teaching (CLT) from the very beginning had a clear goal (that learners should achieve communicate competence in English), but no clear route to follow to achieve it. While this initial goal was phrased as above, Coulthard, bearing in mind many of the insights from Humanistic methods, wrote:

> the aim is not to produce someone who is communicatively competent but rather someone who is a competent communicator, and there is an enormous difference. (1984:103)

The shift here is from the 'what' is to be learnt (communicative competence) to the 'who', the learner (as 'communicator'). If the aim of language learning is to enable learners to become competent communicators, it follows that language syllabuses needed to be designed to enable learners to develop the knowledge and abilities outlined in Section 2.3 above. It also follows that different learners who want to use the language for different purposes in different situations, will probably need to develop their communicative competence differently, in ways which will be supportive of their personal purposes.

Communicative approaches believe that the language syllabus should, as far as possible, be based around learners' needs.

One influential syllabus type initially emerging from a view of language as communication (and so based around meaning) was the notional functional (or functional-notional) syllabus devised by Wilkins (1974, 1976). This tried to apply the principle that syllabus content should be appropriate to the likely purposes for which learners would need to use the language. It therefore presented language as lists of language notions and language functions.

Notions according to Wilkins were semantico-grammatical categories – that is categories of meaning that are usually represented in a language system by particular grammatical forms, for example:

- Time, direction, cause, frequency, existence, ownership

Functions were categories which (as we have seen earlier) represent the purposes for which language is used, for example:

- Identifying, agreeing, offering, enquiring, greeting, ordering, advising

From these lists of notions and functions, Wilkins suggested, one ought to be able, if one knew the learners future language needs, to design a syllabus that would enable them to achieve their communicative purposes.

Communicative syllabuses often see functions (what the learners need to become able to 'do' with language) as one of their organising principles.

3.2 The common European Framework of Reference for languages

The notional-functional view of syllabus was the starting point for a project which remains one of the most ambitious attempts ever undertaken to develop a framework that could be used to develop 'communicative' syllabuses that could meet different learners' needs. This is the Council of Europe's Common European Framework of Reference for Languages (CEFR) which, aims to systematically describe 'what language learners have to learn to do in order to use a language for communication and what knowledge and skills they have to develop so as to be able to act effectively' (CEFR, p. 1). The project represents an interesting example of how the macro context of *time* and *place* implicitly influenced an ELT project. The establishment of the Council of Europe, like the European Union, was a response to the many political mistakes that had contributed to the two World Wars in the European region in the first half of the twentieth century. The motivation behind the CEFR was thus at least partly political – to provide a framework for developing language curricula and syllabuses that would enable European citizens to more easily learn each others' languages, and thereby increase interaction and mutual understanding between European nations.

This project started more than 30 years ago, and is still ongoing. It has so far resulted in a detailed six-level scale describing communicative language proficiency, from Basic user (levels A1 and A2) via Independent user (levels B1 and B2) to Proficient user (levels C1 and C2). At each level, the framework outlines the competencies (what learners ought to be able to 'do') in each of the 'traditional' four skills, together with suggested communicative situations in which learners might be expected to show their competence, and functions that a competent learner would need to know how to perform in such situations. For English, there are now also quite detailed lists of the linguistic structures and vocabulary items that might need to be taught for at least four of the six levels. In principle, by using the framework as a guide, and making appropriate choices from the lists of competencies, situations, functions and linguistic items provided, it ought to be possible to develop a language syllabus that reflects the communicative needs of groups of learners of different ages and/or learning for different purposes, and so begin to develop competent communicators.

The above represents only a very brief summary of the Council of Europe's work in communicative syllabus development. The CEFR represents a rich resource of, for example, language use situations, activities that people might want to carry out in those situations and the functions and notions that might be needed to do so. These have the potential to provide helpful guidance for curriculum planners, syllabus designers, materials writers and language testers in any context. The full CEFR document is available free at the website shown in the references at the end of this chapter. We regard it as a valuable resource.

Despite our enthusiasm, anyone trying to use it to develop a communicative syllabus for any particular group of learners will still need to make many decisions. Some of these are illustrated in the next section which details the first phase of the CFER project, which aimed to develop a syllabus outline to enable a fairly general group of learners to develop proficiency at level B1 (then called the Threshold level).

3.3 *The Threshold level*

The first step for the Threshold level project was to identify who the learners would be. They agreed that they wished to design a syllabus for

> people who want to prepare themselves in a general way to be able to communicate socially on straightforward everyday matters with people from other countries . . . and to be able to get around and lead a reasonably normal social life when they visit another country. (Van Ek and Alexander 1975:x)

The syllabus aimed to provide those completing it with 'a general social communicative ability' (cited above: xi).

The next step was a needs analysis ' . . . to find out as exactly as possible what they will need to do with a foreign language' (Van Ek 1975 in Brumfit and Johnson 1979:103). First of all a needs analysis had to identify:

- The situations in which learners would be likely to need the language, and within these situations:
- The roles that they were likely to play, for example, stranger, guest, colleague . . .
- The topics that they would need to communicate about
- The settings in which they would be most likely to find themselves, for example familiar, unknown, formal . . .

Next it was next necessary to try and define what learners would want to be able to do with the language in each situation.

- What language activities might the learners want to carry out? From fairly easy activities like listening to and understanding airport announcements, or reading menus, to higher level activities like summarising a L1 report orally in the L2 . . .
- What functions might the learner want to be able to perform, for example, thanking, apologising, suggesting, introducing . . .
- What notions will learners need to be able to speak and/or write about? This of course would depend greatly on what situations were identified earlier, but the Threshold syllabus tried to identify a core of general notions relevant to all situations, for example; existence, present, past, future, spatial relations . . .

Having agreed on activities, functions and notions, appropriate for the situations, the next step was to identify:

- what language forms and vocabulary items would be needed to carry out the activities, perform the functions and express the notions, and additionally
- to what degree of skill learners would need to be able to do all the above, at what speed, to what degree of accuracy and in what range of contexts

All of the above had to happen before they could begin to think about compiling a syllabus that organised the above information into a logical sequence for classroom learning and teaching.

Apart from the time and cost of carrying out such a process, two further difficulties remain for communicative syllabus designers. First, how does one decide on the relative difficulty of different functions and notions once they have been identified, and so on how to order them in the syllabus? Second, since most functions and also many notions can be expressed in a number of a different ways, how does one decide which exponents of each function to include and which to ignore.

Despite the complexity outlined above, the work of the Council of Europe and numerous smaller projects has produced many detailed lists of situations, topics, roles, activities, functions, notions and structure and vocabulary items that are now available for other syllabus designers to use. These are especially useful for those working in contexts, such as academic (English for Academic Purposes-EAP) or occupational settings (English for Specific Purposes-ESP) where learners have clear instrumental purposes for learning the language.

All of the above refers only to the **Language** needs of the learners. It does not take the **Learning** needs of particular learners in particular pedagogic settings into account. Some of these are mentioned in Chapters 6 and 7.

3.4 Syllabus design today

Syllabus designers today continue to try and match syllabus content to learners needs. Syllabuses tend to be strongly influenced by the ideas about language represented above and by developing ideas about the language learning process (which were briefly outlined in the introduction to this chapter).

Most current syllabus designers broadly agree that learners need both linguistic competence and the ability to use it appropriately and skilfully in communication. However, if you consider what *places* most *people* are learning English in during the second decade of the twenty-first century (*time*), you find that they are studying at various levels in their national state education systems. Such learners often do not have clearly defined 'needs' (other than to pass the exams). For such general learners, it remains difficult to design a syllabus that can express the content to be taught in a language classroom in ways that clearly lead to the development of competent communicators in that language.

One result of this difficulty in many contexts is to, more or less explicitly, adopt the syllabus of the, or a, textbook. While many of these 'textbook syllabuses' continue to have a sequence of language structures at their core, they may also be organised in terms of the skills that they expect learners to develop, and /or the topics around which comprehension and interaction activities will be based.

Other contexts in the world today claim that their learners are following task based syllabuses. These claim to be organised not around communicative situations that learners might find themselves in or topics that they might want to communicate about, but instead around tasks. Different people define 'task' in more or less different ways. Bachman and Palmer drawing from a survey of applied linguists' definitions suggest that a task is:

> An activity that involves individuals in using language for the purpose of achieving a particular goal or objective in a particular situation. (1996:44)

This suggests that the focus of the activity is on achieving the goal rather than on practising any particular structural feature of the language. However, Nunan points out that the types of goals that most classroom based learners will experience are those set by pedagogic tasks rather than real-world tasks. He defines a pedagogic task as:

> a piece of classroom work that involves learners in comprehending, manipulating, producing or interacting in the target language while their attention is focussed on mobilising their grammatical knowledge in order to express meaning, and in which the purpose is to convey meaning rather than manipulate form. The task should also have a sense of completeness being able to stand alone as a communicative act in its own right with a beginning, a middle and an end. (2004:4)

He suggests, like Bachman and Palmer, that a task based syllabus would promote the use of language to complete the task, rather than to practise a structure, or use particular vocabulary items. The focus would be on providing opportunities for learners to engage in activities (tasks) which required them use their existing grammatical knowledge to interact with one other through expressing and comprehending the meanings (functions and notions) needed to complete the task. In so doing it is suggested, learners are helped to notice the extent to which their existing grammatical knowledge is adequate for conveying whatever meanings are needed to complete the task, and the teacher can identify which grammatical or lexical features of the language might need further explicit work once the task had been completed. Although there are national language education systems which claim to have adopted a task-based syllabus, there is so far little evidence that this has resulted in the majority of learners becoming competent communicators. (This may not be a problem with the syllabus itself, but rather a sign that the other aspects of the context are not congruent with such an approach.)

A move even further away from the idea of a predetermined language-based syllabus is represented by the Dogme movement in language teaching. This movement currently remains largely a BANA, private language school based, phenomenon. Its three principles are that:

- teaching should be conversation driven. Conversation is the fundamental form of language and tends to be as much interactional (feeling driven) as transactional (information driven). Communication in language learning should not therefore be based purely around the many types of communicative activity that ask learners to find or exchange information, but should rather encourage learners to use language to express their personal ideas and feelings.
- since many published language learning materials and textbooks still tend to focus on grammar more than on developing competent communicators,

> lessons should be materials light, conversation driven and focused on the English students need rather than what the coursebook deems we should be teaching them today. (Thornbury 2005:3)

- language learning is a process whereby language emerges through collaborative classroom communication among the learners, and it is not therefore necessary to follow an externally set syllabus.

Whatever the label that is given to the syllabus (or the underlying teaching-learning approach) that is followed in a particular context, one trend is clear. Evolving answers to the questions '*What is language*'? and '*How are languages learned*'? point to 'syllabus' content that will enable learners to develop both their knowledge of the L2 language system and skills at using the L2, similar to those they already have in their L1. Current theories of second language learning suggest that for this to occur, learners need to have access to as much comprehensible language input and as many opportunities to try out their existing knowledge of the language system through communicating with others, in conditions which make them want to do so, as possible. Most English language syllabuses today, whether based around the interests of a particular group of classroom learners, a textbook or a formal, nationally designed, syllabus document, would claim to be trying to provide such input and interaction opportunities. These will often still retain a structural syllabus as the main guiding thread, reflecting perhaps the practical challenges in almost all contexts of moving entirely away from transmission-based teaching – however much educational leaders say, can argue and may claim it is important to do so.

Communicative approaches do not follow syllabuses whose content is expressed PURELY in terms of language structures.

3.5 Technology in language teaching

Chapter 4 mentioned that the use of computers to support language learning began in the 1960s and 1970s, when the first computer programs were developed to provide further opportunities for learners to practise drills, undergo 'programmed learning' and so develop correct language habits.

As language teaching moved into the 'communicative' era, technology has developed in ways that enable learners to have access to an ever wider range of more interesting and interactive language practice and language use opportunities. The development of language-learning resources on CD ROMs in the 1990s provided access to text, graphics, sound and video, with which learners could, to varying degrees, interact in their own ways. The worldwide adoption of the internet in the twenty-first century has enabled a range of new and ever more interactive possibilities through use of online resources. Very broadly these include information resources, virtual 'worlds' of various kinds (e.g. Second Life, or games) and computer-mediated communication (CMC) in various forms of 'social media'. These potentially enable learners to be exposed to and communicate in English directly with each other and /or with speakers of English elsewhere at more or less any time. This communication can either be asynchronous through, for example emails, or synchronous during games or through using the wide range of chat rooms that now exist on every continent. In more and more contexts today language classrooms have access to the internet, interactive whiteboards and the ubiquitous PowerPoint. These ought to make it ever more possible for imaginative teachers to provide learners with interaction opportunities within the classroom and to encourage them to look for their own opportunities online outside the classroom.

In the past decade especially, there has been massive investment in some parts of the world in 'bringing technology into the language classroom' through the provision of large computer labs for language learning and /or linking classrooms to the internet. Whether such investment has the hoped for impact on language learning in any context depends on how (or even whether!) the technology is used. This in turn depends on, for example, whether teachers have been helped to become aware of what technology can offer to the language learning process and to feel confident in using it, and whether technicians exist to help with hardware problems when these arise. Our experience (supported by the large number of teachers we have seen – inappropriately – 'lecturing' with PowerPoint slides) is that policy makers and institutional leaders are 'better at' buying the hardware, than at helping its expected users to understand its possibilities for language-teaching and learning. A danger is that the use of technology in the classroom can give an illusion of a different or current approach, when in fact the way it is used represents the old transmission-based teaching 'dressed in new clothes'.

3.6 Language testing

A general expectation in most educational cultures is that teachers/national education systems ought to be able to discover (through testing) whether/the extent to which, learners have achieved the expected curriculum goals. Once again, this did not seem to be a problem when linguistic competence was considered to be all that the language learner needed to know.

However, if being a competent communicator is the goal, a by-now-familiar problem arises. If the syllabus does not define exactly what a learner is supposed to learn, how can the tester know what exactly the language tests should be testing? This lack of clarity in testing is particularly important since traditionally, school or university tests of all subjects in many educational cultures all over the world aim to be as objective as possible.

As long as language tests limited themselves to the paper and pencil testing of objectively correct or incorrect vocabulary items or grammatical structures and/or factually right or wrong answers to reading or listening comprehension questions, language testing could continue to be treated like the testing of any other subject. As soon as it became clear that communicative competence involved more than this, testers began to consider how they might develop more integrated test items involving more open responses to reading and listening inputs and examples of actual spoken and written language performance as it might typically be used in situations that the learners might encounter. Testers now needed to answer a number of questions that had never been particularly difficult before. A few of these are:

- What should the content of the tests be?
- What should the weighting of the test be?
- How can test items be designed that:
  - allow learners to show a valid sample of their spoken and/or written ability in natural circumstances?
  - minimise subjectivity in the assessment of that ability?
  - can be administered by local testers who may themselves not always be proficient users of the language?

These in turn give rise to practical, resource-based questions such as

- Can we find the extra money needed to pay for the extra staff time and extra space that will be needed if we are to test performance?
- Do we have the expertise needed, or can we afford to buy it, to train the necessary test writers and markers, to design, administer and mark tests of learners' (especially oral) performance?

Most of the above are extremely difficult to answer for a syllabus that may not explicitly define what it is that the learners' should know and be able to do. A consequence has been that, as with syllabuses, testing practices in ELT contexts continue to vary enormously. In some countries decades of research into communicative testing has meant that important national-level language tests at least, are based around attempts to assess learners' ability to produce and understand naturally occurring examples of English. At the other extreme, there are many contexts where tests are still limited to the assessment of linguistic competence and other aspects of language that can be objectively answered and marked.

If important school tests continue to emphasise linguistic competence, this will affect attitudes towards any attempts to change language learning and teaching approaches.

> If people in a change context (parents, learners, teachers, institutional leaders) see an obvious lack of harmony between the behaviours/practices underlying the proposed changes and those that are perceived to help learners pass high-stakes exams, it is the practices that support success in assessment that will 'win'. (Wedell 2009:25)

This is not surprising since in most school contexts teachers and learners are both judged by their test results and therefore if the test demands particular sets of knowledge and/or skills, these are what will be focused on in classrooms. This is especially true where the tests to be taken, such as university entrance tests, will make a difference to learners' future prospects.

The '. . . effect of testing on teaching and learning.' is commonly called the *backwash* or washback effect of test content and format (Hughes 2002:1). At its simplest the washback effect of a tests refers to the fact that if a test does not try to assess certain language knowledge or skills, they are unlikely to be learned or taught. A more developed view suggests that test washback can, through its influence on the content and process of English teaching, also have wider impact on for example, how teachers and learners understand their roles and how they should behave in the classroom, and so potentially on the manner in which or speed at which changes in the wider educational culture are able to occur (Shohamy 2001).

4. Communicative approaches in different contexts

We have seen that it has proved very difficult to act in a systematic way to develop syllabuses and tests that fully reflect the very different perception of what a language-learner needs to know to become a competent communicator in that language. As a result in many ELT contexts, syllabuses and tests have continued to use linguistic competence as their organising principle. In some contexts the effects of any changes brought to the language classroom by so-called communicative syllabuses or textbooks, have been minimised by the lack of appropriate language teacher preparation programmes or support for in-service teacher development, or by the practical need for learners to pass existing tests that continue to view language proficiency in a narrow, but easily understandable way.

School systems in most countries, together with most teachers and learners, like to be as clear as possible about what is to be learned and how teachers and learners should work together to ensure learning occurs. There was therefore, and to varying extents still is, a tendency to try and mould the changes brought about by new understandings of language and language proficiency into a single set of procedures that represent a prescriptive communicative Method.

Evidence for this tendency is the rise of various models for organising any language learning sequence or lesson, with a more or less limited range of practices deemed appropriate at each stage. These sequences include P-P-P (Presentation-Practice-Production), CRA (Clarification of language point, Restricted practice, Authentic use); ESA (Engage, Study Activate) (see, e.g. Harmer 2007; Scrivener 2005). These have again emerged from BANA language schools' developing understandings of what teaching towards communicative competence might mean, and were formalised into a kind of method to serve as the basis for the training of new language teachers for private language schools. Teachers in such language schools, with access to a wide variety of materials often found that using these 'communicative methods' to organise their teaching worked well in their context of small classes of 10–15 highly motivated, fee-paying learners. When exported without adaptation to very different state classroom contexts in other parts of the world, they have often been found to be inappropriate.

A parallel tendency, again arising in response to the lack of clarity about what the teaching principles and practices emerging from a communicative approach actually are, has been to assume that teachers and learners using a communicative approach must behave in certain prescribed ways. This has given rise to what Holliday (1994) calls the 'myths' of teaching 'communicatively'. Some examples he gives (cited above: 165) include:

- 'Communicative' teaching equals oral work
- 'Communicative' teaching equals group work
- 'Communicative' teaching equals getting rid of the teacher as the major focus in the classroom.

Another myth, noted by Nunan (1989), is that explicit grammar teaching is never appropriate. This seems to have resulted from a familiar human tendency at times of radical change to veer from one extreme (an excessive focus on teaching grammar), to the other (a belief that grammar teaching could be ignored).

Such 'myths' are not only 'wrong', but also, in many contexts will almost certainly cause discomfort and stress for both teachers and learners. This is especially so in those (many) educational cultures which continue to emphasise the rule-learning view of language learning, and/or in which teachers are expected to remain central authority figures throughout each lesson and/or in which there is no tradition of learners initiating classroom language or moving around the classroom. In such contexts it is likely, especially if learners clearly feel uncomfortable about the demands for more active involvement that a communicative approach entails, that teachers will decide to modify new teaching practices, or even ignore them altogether. The quote below from Shamim (in Coleman 1996:109) exemplifies this.

> As examinations approached and learners began to show signs of panic, I had to make other compromises, such as increasing teacher talking time during discussion sessions. I gradually found myself assuming more and more authority in the classroom, and this seemed to make the learners happy and relaxed. It was indeed ironic that the techniques I had been trying to use to create, supposedly, a non-threatening and relaxed atmosphere in the classroom had, in fact, become a potential source of tension and conflict.

We have already mentioned that the manner in which a communicative approach has been interpreted in syllabuses and tests around the world remains very varied. The same is true of the extent to which 'communicative' classroom procedures have been adopted and the manner in which teachers interpret them. So, in English classrooms today there are many interpretations of 'communicative' teaching, which although they may broadly share an approach (broadly similar sets of beliefs about language and learning), vary considerably from one another in terms of classroom practice.

Communicative language teaching (CLT) is not a systematic method. This is partly because it is not yet practically possible to describe the content of communicative competence or the exact nature of the language-learning process, and so is impossible to define exactly what learners need to know to be able to communicate competently, or therefore, how they should be taught. There is, in addition, also the widespread recognition (in principle even if not always in practice) that since language exists to enable us to communicate, and learners are all individuals who learn in different ways and for different purposes, they will have different language and learning needs if they are to become competent communicators. As a result there cannot logically be a single set of language knowledge taught to all learners using a single language-teaching method. Instead, there is a need for a variety of combinations of practices that can be adapted as appropriate for learners' needs and the contextual reality in which they are studying. These ideas suggest that ELT is now in an era of (more or less principled and informed) eclecticism or 'post-method pedagogy' (Kumaravadivelu 2003, 2006).

Teaching which is 'communicative' (supports particular learners in becoming competent communicators) will inevitably look different in different classrooms (even in the 'same context').

However, since within ELT there is a broadly agreed rhetoric about language, language- learning and teacher and learner roles, many contexts worldwide have (officially at least) adopted curricula which are based on a communicative approach.

5. Conclusion

In this and the previous chapter we have attempted a brief summary of major changes in ELT approaches and methods over time. We summarise these changes over time (left to right) in Table 5.1. Items below the line refer to approaches or more or less invisible ways of thinking (and answering the three questions: 1. What is language?, 2. What is language learning? and 3. What is learning more generally?), and items above the line to visible classroom

TABLE 5.1 ELT timeline

	G-Translation	ALM	Humanistic methods	Communicative approaches Post-method principled eclecticism
1. Language	Body of factual knowledge	Systems	Systems and skills	Tool for communication (appropriate use of systems and skills)
2. Language learning	Memorisation	Habit formation	Active cognitive effort	Input/output, interaction, meaningful appropriate use
3. Learning	Memorisation	Behaviourism	(Beginnings of) constructivism	Social constructivism/ socio-cultural views

methods or practices. The final right-hand column represents what we have called communicative approaches.

6. Summary and task

This chapter has looked at the manner in which our current understandings about language and (very superficially) the language learning process now make it impossible to believe that there can be a single prescribed language teaching method appropriate to all contexts. Instead, we find an ELT world in which the official language of ELT shares a broadly similar 'communicative' view of language and language learning. However, since 'Language' is so central to human communication, interaction, learning and development, and since contexts vary so much in how people understand these terms, teachers (and others) are bound to interpret this language differently. What actually happens in 'communicative' classrooms in different contexts of PLACE around the world can therefore look very different.

In the next two chapters we consider the context of PEOPLE in the micro-context of PLACE, by looking in more detail at teachers and learners in ELT classrooms, and how they may contribute to developing a variety of classroom cultures.

Tasks:

As we said in the introduction to Chapter 4, the main purpose of Chapters 4 and 5 has been to help you identify the existing situation in your context in terms of the prevailing approaches, methods or methodologies. The following are tasks to help you do this.

Look at Table 5.1. Where are you below the line? And where are you above the line? (You may not be 'at the same place'). And where do you think ELT more broadly in your context is? Again consider both above and below the line.

We made the following seven summary statements about CLT in the text above. If you are in a context which states that it follows a communicative approach, consider how far they are true in your context. What evidence do you have for your decisions? (You might find this evidence in for example, the textbook, past exam papers, various official documents and your own and colleague's classrooms.)

1. *Communicative approaches recognise that language has 'structure' above the sentence level*

2. *Communicative approaches see language proficiency as consisting of a combination of language knowledge and abilities to use such knowledge to 'communicate'.*
3. *Communicative approaches recognise that there is a difference between spoken and written language, and, for example, in the degree of consistent formal accuracy that it is reasonable to expect most learners to produce orally.*
4. *Communicative approaches believe that the language syllabus should, as far as possible, be based around learners' needs*
5. *Communicative syllabuses often see functions (what the learners need to become able to 'do' with language) as one of their key organising principles.*
6. *Communicative approaches do not follow syllabuses whose content is expressed PURELY in terms of language structures.*
7. *Teaching which is 'communicative' (supports particular learners in becoming competent communicators) will inevitably look different in different classrooms (even in the 'same context').*

POSSIBLE MINI-PROJECT

(If you teach at secondary school or above)

- Choose five of your most mature and thoughtful learners.
- Ask them to list the three situations in which they expect to use English most frequently outside school.
- Ask them what they think they will need to be able to do in English in those situations.

List their needs.

Does the syllabus you follow cater for these learners' needs?

Can you see any problems that may arise in trying to design a language syllabus that matches these learners' individual needs?

(If you teach primary school level learners)

- Ask three of your colleagues the same questions as those above for their pupils.

List the needs that their answers suggest.

Does the syllabus you follow cater for these learners' needs?

Can you see any problems in designing a syllabus to match these needs?

References and further reading

Alderson, J. C. and D. Wall. 1993. 'Does washback exist?' *Applied Linguistics*, 14, pp.115–29.

Alptekin, C. 2002. 'Towards intercultural communicative competence in ELT'. *English Language Teaching Journal*, 56(1), pp. 57–64.

Bachman, L. and A. Palmer. 1996. *Language Testing in Practice*. Oxford: Oxford University Press.

Brumfit, C. and K. Johnson, eds.1979. *The Communicative Approach to Language Teaching*. Oxford: Oxford University Press.

Canale, M. 1983. 'From communicative competence to communicative language pedagogy'. In: J. Richards and R. Schmidt, eds. *Language and Communication*. London: Longman, pp. 2–27.

Celce-Murcia, M., Dornyei, Z. and Thurrel, S. 1995. 'Communicative competence: a pedagogically motivated model with content specifications'. *Issues in Applied Linguistics*, 6(2), pp. 5–35.

Chomsky, N. 1959. 'A review of B.F. Skinner's "Verbal Behaviour"'. *Language*, 35 (1), pp. 26–58.

Common European Framework of Reference for Languages. 2001. Cambridge: Cambridge University Press [accessed 1 July 2012]. Available from: www.coe.int/t/dg4/linguistic/Source/Framework_en.pdf.

Cook, G. 1989. *Discourse*. Oxford: Oxford University Press.

Coulthard, M., ed. 1984. 'Discourse analysis and language teaching'. In: *Ilha do Desterro Special Issue dedicated to Discourse Analysis*. Brazil: Florianopolis SC, pp. 93–106.

Coulthard, M. 1985. *An Introduction to Discourse Analysis*. London: Longman.

Crookes, G. and S. M. Gass, eds. 1993. *Tasks and Language Learning: Integrating Theory and Practice*. Clevedon: Multilingual Matters.

Dubin, F. and E. Olshtain. 1986. *Course Design: Developing Programs and Materials for Language Learning*. Cambridge: Cambridge University Press.

Harmer, J. 2007. *How to Teach English* (2nd edn). Harlow: Longman.

Hughes, A. 2002. *Testing for Language Teachers* (2nd edn). Cambridge: Cambridge University Press.

Holliday, A. 1994. *Appropriate Methodology and Social Context*. Cambridge: Cambridge University Press.

Hymes, D. 1970. 'On communicative competence'. In: C. Brumfit and K. Johnson, eds, *The Communicative Approach to Language Teaching*. Oxford: Oxford University Press, pp. 5–26.

Kumaravadivelu, B. 2003. *Beyond Methods: Macrostrategies for Language Teaching*. New Haven and London: Yale University Press.

— 2006. *Understanding Language Teaching: From Method to Post-Method*. Mahwah, NJ: Lawrence Erlbaum Associates.

Lightbown, P. and N. Spada. 2006. *How Languages are Learned* (3rd edn). Oxford: Oxford University Press

Morrow, K. 1979. 'Communicative language testing: revolution or evolution'. In: C. Brumfit and K. Johnson, eds, *The Communicative Approach to Language Teaching*. Oxford: Oxford University Press, pp. 143–57.

Morrow, K. 1986. *Innovations in Language Testing*. Windsor England: NFER/Nelson

Nunan, D. 1989. *Designing Tasks for the Communicative Classroom*. Cambridge: Cambridge University Press.

— 2004. *Task Based Language Teaching*. Cambridge: Cambridge University Press.

Savignon, S. J. 1983. *Communicative Competence: Theory and Classroom Competence*. Reading, MA: Addison-Wesley.

Scrivener, J. 2005. *Learning Teaching* (2nd edn). Basingstoke: Macmillan ELT.

Shamim, F. 1996. 'Learners resistance to innovation in classroom methodology'. In: P. H. Coleman, ed., *Society and the Language Classroom*. Cambridge: Cambridge University Press, pp. 105–21.

Shohamy, E. 2001. *The Power of Tests: a Critical Perspective of the Uses of Language Tests*. Harlow: Longman.

Tarone, E and G. Yule. 1989. *Focus on the Language Learner*. Oxford: Oxford University Press.

Thornbury, S. 2005. 'Dogme: dancing in the dark'. *Folio*, 9(2), pp. 3–5.

Van Ek, J. 1975. *The Threshold Level in a European Unit/Credit System for Modern Language Learning by Adults*. Strasbourg: Council of Europe.

Van Ek, J. and L. G. Alexander. 1975. *Threshold Level English*. Oxford: Pergamon Press.

Wedell, M. 2009. *Planning for Educational Change: Putting People and Their Contexts First*. London: Continuum.

Weir, C. 1990. *Communicative Language Testing*. New York & London: Prentice Hall.

Widdowson, H. G. 1978. 'Directions in the teaching of discourse'. In: C. Brumfit and K. Johnson, eds, *The Communicative Approach to Language Teaching*. Oxford: Oxford University Press.

Wilkins, D. A. 1974. *Second Language Learning and Teaching*. London: Edward Arnold.

— 1976. *Notional Syllabuses*. Oxford: Oxford University Press.

Yule, G. 2005. *The Study of Language* (3rd edn). Cambridge: Cambridge University Press.

— 1985. *The Study of Language*. Cambridge: Cambridge University Press.

6

Teachers and learners: As part of and creators of their context

Introduction

The main focus of this and the following chapter is on the *people* in the micro context of place – the language classroom. We have suggested before that it is the people involved in teaching and learning who are central to an understanding of the relationships between contexts and cultures, and between these and decisions about ELT approaches. We therefore need to spend some time looking more closely at these central actors and how the classroom context may be experienced and understood from their perspective. We hope that the ideas discussed in these two chapters will not only support the development of a better understanding of any context, but also suggest further ideas for the types of conditions that will be needed if changes are desired.

The chapter starts by exploring the idea that the relationship between teachers and learners and context is complex, and that as well as being *influenced* by context (see Chapter 7), the people can be thought of both as *part* of or even *creating* their (classroom) context. One fundamental starting point for deciding what may be possible in any classroom context is an understanding of what teachers and learners already know. We consider what teachers and learners may know from two points of view, the knowledge that exists 'inside' individuals and the knowledge that can be constructed 'between' people. We discuss what knowledge they might bring to the classroom, and then look at how the interactions between the people in the classroom can play an important part in the development of knowledge. The final section looks briefly at the role that the feelings and emotions of the people in a classroom may play in the teaching and learning process – again from the two perspectives of 'inside' and 'between'.

1. Teachers and learners and contexts

You will all have memories of how different classes had different 'atmospheres' when you were students. If you are a teacher, you will also doubtless have experienced the differences between classes – the 'difficult class', or the 'good' class. What, at first sight, seems to be fundamentally important or make the difference is in the first case probably the particular teacher, and in the second the particular group of learners. If you think about it a little further however, you might remember, for instance, that not all teachers in a school consider the same classes to be difficult in the same way, nor do all learners have the same reactions to the same class atmosphere or the same teacher. So, it wasn't simply 'those learners' or 'that teacher' that caused those feelings and judgements, it had **'something'** to do with you too, 'you' *in relation* to 'them'-'you and that group' or 'you and that teacher'.

The individual teachers and learners and the relationships between them can therefore be seen as being 'part of', and being 'creators of' classroom contexts, as well as 'products' of that context. This is the main idea of these two chapters. We will discuss this main idea here in general terms. In subsequent sections and the next chapter, we will try to identify features of the **'something'** that make the difference.

> *Take a few moments to imagine some teaching and learning in action in an English class you have experienced . . . really try to see this . . . as if you were watching and listening to a video. You might like to put the book down or make a cup of tea as you do this.*

You will probably have pictured a classroom with people in it – typically one teacher and a number of learners. (We will discuss aspects of this physical presence of people in classrooms – numbers of learners in any one class, for example – in Chapter 8.) Perhaps you found yourself visualising, even perhaps naming or remembering details about particular people when you ran your mental video. In this chapter, we are concerned with the idea that 'who people are' makes a difference to what happens in language classrooms through how they behave and interact. This suggests that people, as well as being *part of* the micro-context through occupying physical classroom space in a particular environment, also to a large extent, *create* the context of teaching and learning through what they do (including their language use), and through their mental or behavioural responses to their feelings about what happens.

In order to understand 'who the people are' we will need to consider various factors such as age, or previous learning experiences or personal histories. Yet in considering such individual factors, it soon becomes apparent that broader, influencing, macro-contextual factors will come into the discussion. How can discussions on personal histories, for example, avoid reference to culture at macro, institutional or disciplinary level? In this sense, then, teachers and learners can also be considered to be the results, or '*products*' of their cultural contexts, including the classroom culture (see Chapter 2). The behaviour and thinking of participants in a class occurs in response to what happens, to what is offered, expected or allowed. All of these are influenced (perhaps even determined) by elements of all other layers of the context (see, e.g. Coleman 1996).

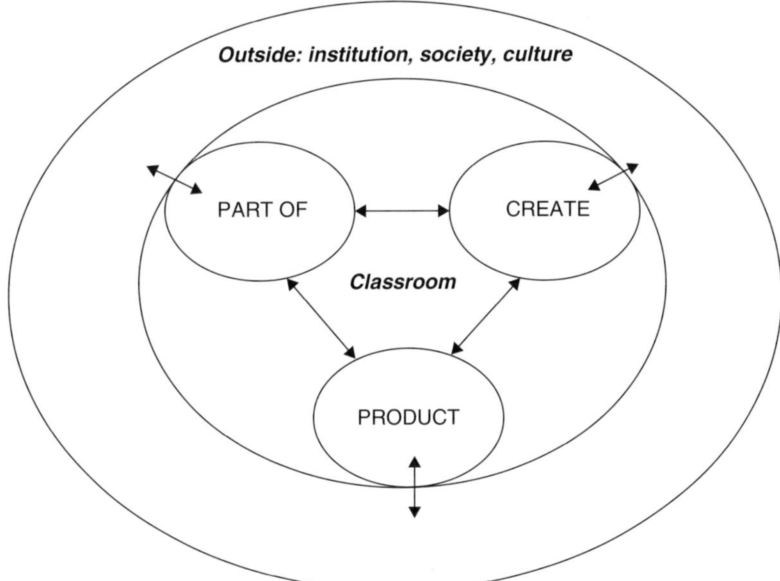

FIGURE 6.1 *Roles of teachers and learners in contexts.*

The diagram above is an attempt to represent some of these relationships. The inner oval represents the classroom, and just by being there participants become *part of* the context. As they are *part of* the context, they can be involved in the interactions which in part *create* it. Through those interactions, they can learn and so emerge, changed, as *products* of that classroom context. This cycle continues – and it continues at every layer. For example, any classroom is set in the wider context and so is itself also '*part of*', '*creating*' and '*a product of*' that wider context (see Figure 6.1).

As an ELT teacher how free do you feel to create your own classroom context? How much does the fact that you are, of course, a product of your wider (institutional educational) context consciously affect what you do? Think about some concrete examples from your own teaching experience.

For example, what factors influence the types of interactions that you have with learners (or encourage learners to have with each other) in the classroom, and where do these come from? What is the relationship between your wider context and the teaching materials that you (have to) use?

2. On people creating contexts of and for learning

Several decades ago, Earl Stevick wrote about language learning 'Success depends less on linguistic analyses, materials and methods and more on what goes on inside and between people in a language classroom' (1980:4). There is now an increasing amount of research support for this statement and we will be considering some of this here.

We will consider the notions of '*inside and between people*' in classrooms, first from the perspective of '**what people know**', and then from the perspective of '**what people feel**'. Much discussion in applied linguistics and educational psychology is concerned with these themes. Here however, we will look at some current ideas which have proved practically useful to us but which have been, at least until recently, less commonly cited or written about. If we do not discuss an area here (e.g. Motivation), this does not mean we think it is irrelevant, but rather that there is already a great deal of available ELT literature on the subject. Sometimes, we will indicate when we think you could usefully consult this.

2.1 What people know

2.1.1 Inside

The 'content of heads', what teachers (and learners) already know, ought to make a difference to what teachers do, and will affect what they and their students can learn and how quickly they can do or learn it. In addition, there are different 'kinds' of knowing, which will affect whether and /or how teachers and learners want or are able to use what they know. We illustrate what we mean for teachers below.

For example, imagine a teacher working with class of young learners who have already learnt and shown that they understand and can use 'adjective + noun' word order in English, the nouns 'orange' (the fruit) and 'book', and the words for primary colours. Imagine now the learners are meeting the word 'orange' used as an adjective for the first time in the following line from a simple illustrated textbook dialogue: 'I want the orange book not the blue book'. If as a teacher you do not know what learners already know, and therefore cannot take this into account, you will probably use some kind of explanatory technique (using visuals perhaps, or L1) if they need help understanding the meaning.

If, on the other hand, you do know what learners already know, and feel it is important to build on this, you may decide this is a good opportunity to 'scaffold' (see Chapter 3) the development of 'strategic competence' (see Chapter 5), or 'learning to learn' strategies or 'guessing from context' (whether or not you are consciously thinking in these exact terms). If so, you will want to support the learners in 'doing it themselves' and not 'do it for them'. What you do next will be very different from the explanatory techniques mentioned above. It might involve helping students to notice the similarity of the patterns 'the orange book' and 'the blue book', asking the learners where in their vocabulary books they already have these words (under 'colours' and 'fruit') and suggesting they should write one of these words again and asking which one and where ('orange' rewritten also under 'colours').

Of course, even if you do know what the students know, if you as a teacher do not consciously know *about* 'strategic competence', or 'learning to learn' or 'guessing from context', you may not be aware of any practical ways of promoting the development of these skills, or that these are ideas and techniques you need to learn about.

We purposely use '**may**' in the paragraph above, as work on skill-learning as applied to learning- teaching suggests that as well as consciously learning (some of) what they are formally taught, teachers 'pick up' or absorb teaching techniques and strategies, by osmosis, as it were, from 'exposure to others' teaching'. This kind of learning is called implicit learning (Claxton 1997; Lortie 1975) and teachers may learn in this way without consciously intending to, and without having read anything about, or having heard anyone talk explicitly about the techniques in question.

If we think about it some more it is not really surprising that so much implicit learning takes place for teachers. Teachers have all spent years exposed to others' teaching as learners. This is different from other professionals whose professional learning only begins when they make their career choice. This length of exposure to teaching (which Lortie, cited above, has called 'the Apprenticeship of Observation' for teachers), will have provided plenty of opportunities for the implicit (more or less conscious) learning of teaching behaviours and attitudes. In addition, some initial teacher preparation and in-service programmes also explicitly try to provide chances for participants to expand on this 'apprenticeship of observation', through the provision of further opportunities to observe others teaching.

If you are a practising teacher, you almost certainly use various practical techniques spontaneously in your classroom which have been implicitly learnt from your own prior experience. Depending on your context, and the range of your experiences as a learner/observer, these techniques will be more or less supportive of your learners' learning. However, when you have 'spontaneously' used implicitly learnt techniques in a lesson, you will not find it easy to explain why you used them, other than perhaps noting that 'it felt right'. Neither is it easy to *plan* to use such techniques, because planning requires making conscious choices which in turn depends on consciously 'knowing what you know'. So, all teachers know (in this sense) and use techniques that they don't know they know!

Given the 'right' experiences, the teacher in the above classroom context, may through such implicit learning therefore have been able to intuitively 'scaffold' the learners without ever consciously planning to do so. Alternatively, the teacher may never have seen or experienced any examples of such 'scaffolding' techniques during their time as a pupil or a learner-teacher. If in addition, their formal initial teacher preparation never mentioned such ideas, then they will not have had a chance to learn them, even intuitively, and their choices for action to support learning (in a scaffolding sense) are more limited. They will have to act using what they do explicitly or implicitly know (however learnt), which, in the above example might mean that they 'do it for them', by explaining, showing or translating for the learners.

These are not the only possible relationships between what teachers know and what they do. There are teachers who appear to know the theoretical reasons for acting in a particular way (e.g. scaffolding learners) and can talk about these reasons, but do not actually use any related practical techniques or procedures in the classroom. There are three possible explanations for why this might be so. First, they may have made a considered and conscious rationally argued decision to reject a particular reason or the bigger theory from which it stems. For example, we have met teachers who understand the need to provide opportunities for learners to interact in their classrooms, but in fact do so only rarely, and who can clearly explain why they do not do so (often in terms of what learners need to know in order to pass important language tests at the end of the year). Second, it may be that teachers 'know the words but do not understand the concept'; in other words they can use words like 'communicative' or 'scaffolding' when talking to colleagues, supervisors or school leaders, or can write them in exams in their initial teacher preparation programmes, but have never really understood or owned the underlying concepts. In this sense the words are, as it were 'laminated' or 'stuck on' without making any real difference to what is underneath. Finally, a teacher may be the type of learner (someone who approaches learning anything, including teaching, by reading about it first) who does understand the reasons, but needs time to identify, practice and develop the use of related teaching techniques which suit them and their context, and has not yet been able to do so.

Anyone considering introducing changes to what teachers need to understand/ be able to do, and wanting to discover what teachers really 'know' already, might choose to observe and/or interview and/or test them. However, if observers or interviewers wish to obtain a true picture of what teachers know and do (so that they can understand what sorts of challenges any proposed changes might entail) they need to be aware that various possible relationships may exist between what they see teachers do in classrooms and what the teachers can and do talk about (what they consciously know).

We think there are four main different possibilities and describe them below using the example of a teacher's knowledge of 'discourse competence'. This term could be replaced below by many of the other terms that are or have been commonly used in ELT, for example, 'group-work', 'task-based learning', 'learner autonomy', 'writing skill development', 'peer assessment' and many, many others.

1 The teacher talks about discourse competence, but does not use any related strategies with learners to support its development.

2 The teacher talks about discourse competence and plans and uses related strategies with learners to support its development.

3 The teacher uses some strategies which support learners in the development of discourse competence but is not able to talk about why she/he does so.

4 The teacher does not use any strategies which support the development of discourse competence, does not know about it, and is unaware that she/he doesn't know about it.

Table 6.1 summarises these possibilities, and adds some comments/possible reasons for each.

It can be argued that language learners too, in the business of *learning,* have similar possibilities. Let us take the 'blue' and 'orange' example above, and consider vocabulary learning. One way of helping learners remember vocabulary is through the development of semantic networks (or working with and creating 'lexical sets'). One strategy for doing this is for them to build their vocabulary notebooks (or flash card sets etc.) in such terms. Ideally, if you as a teacher believe this is useful (and your conscious 'beliefs' are always worth re-examining from time to time) you would want your learners to be in state 2 or 3 in the chart above. While the use of appropriate strategies (3) is arguably the most important, if older learners were also able to consider

TABLE 6.1 Teacher knowledge of, and *use* or non-use of, particular techniques or procedures, and the explicit or implicit *reasons* for this

	Can talk about reason	Uses related procedures	Comment
1	✓	x	• Rejected • 'Laminated' learning – not really understood • Newly understood – practical procedures not yet developed
2	✓	✓	• Integrated in thinking and action – can be planned
3	x	✓	• Intuitively used, implicitly learnt, cannot be planned
4	x	x	• Unaware

learning strategies consciously (2), they might also, for example, decide to look for, find, and plan to use other strategies for organising and remembering vocabulary which they felt would work better for them (e.g. mind-maps).

Table 6.1 can also help you think about the ways your learners 'know' language. 'Laminated learning' in situation 1, in the table, for example, seems very similar to a language learner who can talk *about* grammar rules and can get the correct answer in discrete item grammar tests, but cannot *use* the grammar rules they 'know' to produce language for meaningful, spontaneous communication. In almost all contexts, we have frequently heard people saying that learners already 'know' for example, the present perfect, because it has been covered in the textbook. In this case, many learners may in fact not 'know' the present perfect at all. Even when those same learners have been able to demonstrate a knowledge of the grammatical form of the tense in a test question, this will still not provide any evidence that they 'know' 'the present perfect' in the sense of being able to use it appropriately to communicate or understand meanings. Indeed this tendency to equate what has been 'covered' and tested (in the above sense) with what has been learnt shows how powerful and entrenched pre-communicative approaches remain (see Chapters 4 and 5). So finding out what learners' starting points are requires more than, for example, looking at where they have 'got to' in the syllabus or textbook, and more than looking at results of pen and paper tests. It requires a diagnostic approach over time, backed up by careful focused noticing.

To return to the main point, then, **the content of people's heads**, what the people (teachers and learners), already 'know' and 'don't know' (however we understand that) is an important starting point for thinking about people and the context of any learning.

As a teacher, honestly considering what you do and do not know is as important for your own professional development as it is for the language learning of your students. In other words, 'knowing what you don't know is the first step to learning it'. Teachers supporting learning need to know what learners already know in order to make appropriate judgements about what to do, or how to do things or how long to continue doing them. It is vital, then, to consider what the learners already know before planning learning opportunities. For any individual teacher planning classes and courses the main message here is: '*You can't put down stepping stones for someone to find without first knowing where they are*' (Claxton 1997). We see a connection here with the importance of understanding learners' ZPDs in order to provide appropriate 'scaffolding' (see Chapter 3) – impossible to do if teachers do not know where learners are.

While a teacher's concern must be to discover where the particular learners are, the same principle also applies to curriculum and materials designers. They, and all other educational professionals in the wider context, whose decisions affect what happens in classrooms, need to take where teachers are 'now', (what they know, how they think and how this affects how they act in classrooms) carefully into account, if they wish to introduce changes to teachers' existing patterns of thought and action, (see Chapter 9). In other words, knowledge of starting points is relevant and important at every level of the educational context.

Time for some questions! Consider one class you teach, and ask yourself how well you knew your learners' starting points, what they knew at the start of the last lesson you taught them. Try to recall something that happened in the lesson that would support your assessment that you did or did not know their starting points (as individuals). How did you come to know whatever you did know about your learners' starting points? More generally, what could you do to know more?

Thinking about yourself, and what you as a teacher (or other education professional) know or do not know, can you think of anything specific you could do to move out of situations 1 or 4 in Table 6.1 with regard to any or all aspects of your work? (In general we would say to teachers that observing teaching, talking to other teachers about what they do and why, and reading about ELT could all be helpful).

2.1.2 Between

Above we considered what people know from the 'inside' in terms of 'what is in their heads'. We continue the theme of knowledge here. In Chapter 3, we suggested that there is a sense in which 'what people know' is created through interactions **between** people in societies. This is true at the classroom level too and so we now consider this idea from the perspective of the classroom.

In Chapter 3, we also talked about Bruner's notion of 'scaffolding' based on the work of Vygotsky. This can be said to describe the fundamental role of a teacher. In essence this, as the metaphor suggests, is about providing sufficient (but not too much, and not for longer than required) support for the learner to 'build' new meanings or skills (that is, to learn). Put another way, scaffolding is about providing an appropriate context to enable learning. Part of that 'appropriate context' may involve provision of such 'scaffolding material' as textbooks, pencils, test tubes or computers for example. However, as discussed in Chapter 3, a major item of 'scaffolding material' is a teacher's use of language. (The word 'con-text' has 'text, or language, embedded in it!). Teachers, then, ideally support and guide (scaffold) learners to complete classroom learning tasks and activities successfully, through using language to provide demonstrations, instructions, explanations, or to ask or reply to questions, in ways that are responsive to the learner's actual needs.

'**What the learner needs**' at any given moment in a classroom must be gauged by the teacher from what the learner says or does. In other words, identifying needs occurs via a two-way interaction between teacher and learner. The process of interaction in a 'scaffolding' mode enables learning for both learners and teacher. For the learner, this learning is about how the task is to be carried out, as well as about the intended 'language learning' that it is hoped the task will support. Teachers, through repeated interaction with their learners over time, can understand more about their learners (what they know, and how they learn, and what their difficulties are and how they see things) and so be in a better position to determine their needs. They can also, potentially, learn more about their own existing skills as supporters and scaffolders of learning and through such learning develop their scaffolding skills further.

We return to a detailed examination of scaffolding here, because whether or not its principles are enacted in any classroom will play an important role in determining the classroom culture. Let us take an example of effective scaffolding from everyday life. Typical examples of scaffolding are often drawn from parent-child dialogues – with the parent in 'teacher' or 'scaffolder' role, as we saw in Chapter 3. Here is an example however of roles reversed. This is an exchange between a mother and her son (recorded decades ago) who is teaching the mother how to use the new video player/recorder (VCR) the family has just acquired (Malderez and Wedell 2007).

Son:	So what am I showing you?
Mother:	How do I get this thing to work?
S:	Press the 'standby' button
	(M presses)
S:	Put the video in
	(M puts video cassette in slot)
S:	get the video remote
	(M reaches for TV remote)
S:	No, the *video* remote
M:	(looking around) Which one's that?
S:	You know which one it is! (looking towards coffee table)
	(M 'finds' right one on coffee table, and nods, looking from the other, TV remote, to the one in her hand)
S:	Press 'play'
	(M presses button on remote marked 'play', looks at TV – content of video cassette not visible on screen)
M:	See! It's not on!
S:	(patient explanatory tone) We're on TV not the video channel. Find the TV-slash-Video button
	(M looks at video remote in her hand & presses button marked TV/VCR – looks at screen where the contents of video cassette are now playing)
S:	Yes, that's it! See? You can do it!

Let's see what the son actually did.

- He checked they both understood the goal of the exercise.
- He broke the process down into steps.
- He let the mother press the buttons, put the cassette in, and find the remote herself: he didn't do it for her.
- He reminded her of what she already knew which would be useful in the present learning situation (in saying 'You know which one it is' he reminded her, in fact, that she knew which the TV remote was, and could use this knowledge to 'work out' that the other one in the room must be the video remote).
- He didn't give unnecessary information when he could see it wasn't needed (e.g. say exactly where the TV/Video button was).

- He ensured the learner recognised her achievements ('See you can do it'!) through directing attention to the successful outcome (reactions, 'feedback'): video playing on TV screen.

What scaffolding functions introduced in Chapter 3 could you match with some of the above moves?

One thing the son does in the dialogue, which has not yet been mentioned in connection with scaffolding, is 'correct' the mother ('No, the *video* remote'). The motivation for this, we assume, is to ensure that the mother is successful. If this is an accurate interpretation, and because (unusually) this is a case where there *is* one right way of doing the task, we consider this a scaffolding move (although one with a much more limited potential for use in a language classroom).

Corrections are very common in classrooms. Are 'corrections' in language classrooms in your context used to enable learners to be successful in achieving their communicative purposes, or do they have other functions?

The learning context (place, time and people) in the example here was also important to the meaning created beyond and between the words. As the dialogue took place in the living room where the VCR would actually be used, the place context was full of things or apparatus that would be needed for the learning as well as similar apparatus that was not needed for this particular task. Other kinds of context were also helpful to support the learning. It was a family joke that the mother was 'hopeless' with all things technical, although she could and did use the TV remote. In other words, behind and between this exchange is the shared knowledge of what the mother does already know and know how to do, and how she was likely to be feeling. It was this 'given' knowledge of 'starting points' that enabled the son to be an efficient 'scaffolder' of the mother's learning, as he could remind her of knowledge she had ('You know which one it is') which would be useful in the present situation (to distinguish which piece of apparatus in the room was required). The dialogue itself too was important as information went both ways. The son 'talks the mother through' the process – *informs* her of the steps. In the other direction, through the mother's talk ('Which one's that?' 'It's not on!'), the son 'learnt' where the problematic phases of the process were for the mother, and was able to respond explicitly to those.

The broader view of teaching and learning to which 'scaffolding' can be said to belong is often called 'dialogic', and although currently much discussed (Alexander 2008; Mercer et al. 2009), it can in fact be considered to be as old as Socrates. 'Dialogic' teaching and learning is also often contrasted with a 'transmission' view of teaching and learning, meaning a one-way flow of knowledge from a 'teacher-knower' to an 'ignorant learner'. However, there is always also 'transmission' of knowledge within any dialogue, or interaction. The difference is that this knowledge flows in both directions (as we have seen above), and so knowledge is created and resides in the spaces *in between* people-in-dialogue.

Just as dialogic does not mean with no transmission (but rather something which emerges from responsive two-way transmission), neither does it, as some might think, (and unlike in Bruner's term 'scaffolding') necessarily mean one-to-one teaching. Although some definitions of the word 'dialogue' involve a notion of between two people, this is not what is meant here. In the Greek origin of the word, 'dia' does not mean 'two' but 'through' and 'logos' can be understood as 'the meaning of the word'. Bohm (1996:6) has suggested therefore that

- 'dialogue can be among any number of people'

and also that it

- 'makes possible a flow of meaning in the whole group out of which may emerge some new understanding'

and finally that

- 'this shared meaning is the 'glue' or 'cement' which holds people and societies together'

Dialogue in this sense then collaboratively creates 'new' meaning or knowledge. In addition, over time, between people who interact frequently, as teachers and learners have the opportunity to do in classrooms, it also helps to create (classroom) cultures, since 'shared meanings' are one of the features of any culture (see Chapter 2).

3. What people feel

The second part of this chapter discusses the feelings that exist within and between people in any language- classroom context, and considers some ideas about how such feelings may contribute to the creation of a classroom culture which is more or less supportive of learning. We begin by discussing the difficulty in separating knowledge from feelings.

In the discussion above, we found it difficult to write about 'knowledge' in a consistent way. You may have been surprised we did not give a definition or that, when considering teachers' knowledge of teaching, we seemed to talk about (at least) two different *kinds* of knowledge, according to how it was learnt (explicitly, through language, or implicitly through exposure to teaching). Others (e.g. Johnson 1996) distinguish between these two types of knowledge. The first type refers to what teachers 'know about' and can talk about, called 'declarative knowledge'. The second, 'procedural knowledge' includes 'know-how' (explicitly learnt teaching skills), together with the implicitly learnt (or automatised) knowledge which prompts those gut feelings, or intuitions that lead teachers to 'know to' do the 'right' thing at a particular moment in a lesson to support the learners' learning. It is this last type of 'knowing to' knowledge that is particularly difficult to disentangle from feelings (Malderez and Wedell 2007).

Therefore in considering the 'inside' of people identifying the distinction between what they know and what they are able to do (or even what they actually do do), is not the only problem we have. Other researchers have grappled with the difficulty in differentiating not only between knowledge and feelings but also between these and, for example, 'assumptions' 'beliefs', 'values' and 'attitudes'. Woods (1996), for example, finding this differentiation impossible, coined the acronym BAK, (Beliefs, Assumptions, Knowledge) to represent a model of the 'thinking' of teachers. Borg (2006) on the other hand, uses BPK, (Belief, Practice, Knowledge), placing practice at the centre as the main focus for research into teacher knowledge, and acknowledging that much of this knowledge can only be seen in and learnt through practice.

Other models of teacher knowledge and thinking have tried to accommodate the affective dimension also, for example 'the teacher iceberg' in Malderez and Bodoczky (1999). Therefore, although we have suggested above that it may be difficult to disentangle knowledge and feelings from one another, we do feel that it is both possible and useful to explore what goes on inside and between the people, from the angle of the affect (Arnold 1999). It is after all the feelings inside and between people that constitute the emotional or affective context of teaching and learning, and it is this affective context which contributes a lot to the different 'atmospheres' that classes can have.

3.1 *Inside*

Here we will briefly consider various research areas which may help us understand how individual's feelings and emotional states may make a difference to what happens in classrooms. We will first consider existing emotional states, before considering changes in feelings and any patterns to those changes.

3.1.1 Emotional states

In language learning, Krashen (1982, 1985) introduced the idea of the affective filter to explain why there are times when learning proceeds more smoothly, or more easily than others. Thinking about emotions, we might want to group them into the 'negative' (bad feelings) states, such as fear, worry anxiety and so on, and the 'positive' (good feelings) states, such as excitement and happiness. You will doubtless remember times when you were particularly worried or anxious, and will no doubt also know that during those times you did not usually do your best work. It will come as no surprise to learn then that researchers have confirmed that when people are experiencing negative emotional states such as anxiety, their ability to learn is hindered (Eysenk 1979; Gardner and McIntyre 1993; Horwitz and Young 1991; Oxford 1999).

What about the positive states? What about happiness, for example? It would seem that, although preferable, this is not an ideal state for learning either. Indeed most of you can again probably remember times when moments of great happiness have also taken your attention away from your work. What state is it then that you need to be in, if you are to be able to learn most effectively?

Csikszentmihalyi, a psychologist, studied this question in terms of what it takes to 'live well', and so achieve the general background state of 'well-being', which is likely to be the most helpful to the learning process. He found that those people who considered themselves (and were considered by others) to live well, were those who most often engaged in activities which created a state he has called 'flow'. The notion of flow is different from 'happiness' because to experience happiness you have to focus on and be conscious of your inner states and that takes your attention away from whatever you are engaged in. One essential characteristic of an activity which produces 'flow' is involvement – you are totally absorbed in it, so that your perception of time is distorted in the sense that you 'don't notice it passing'. (You will of course be happy to have had the flow experience, but you will only become conscious of this after the experience is over.)

Ideally, all teachers aim to provide an environment in which learners are as focused on whatever tasks they are given as this state of 'flow' describes. What then are the characteristics of activities that enable 'flow'? Csikszentmihalyi describes these as ones that:

> allow the person to focus on goals that are clear and compatible . . . [and] provide immediate feedback [and] . . . make it clear how well you are doing [and during which] a person's skills are fully involved in overcoming a challenge that is just about manageable. (Csikszentmihalyi 1997:28)

It is this last point that most clearly links learning with emotions. A *'challenge'*, doing something new, is what anyone needs to do in order to take them one step further or to learn. Ensuring that challenges are '*just about manageable*' can be linked with notions of the Zone of Proximal Development (Vygotsky, see Chapter 3 and above), or Krashen's 'i + 1' (1982). (Krashen believed that, for optimal language learning, the language that learners were exposed to needed to be comprehensible, but just above the level a learner was at – the 'i' for input at the learner's level, the '+1' for the 'just above'. In other words it needed to be 'just about manageable'). Csikszentmihalyi identified that people feel negative emotional states when there is an unbalanced relationship between their skills and a challenge they have set themselves (or which has been set by others).

> If challenges are too low relative to one's skills one gets relaxed, then bored. If both challenges and skills are perceived to be low, one gets to feel apathetic. (Csikszentmihalyi 1997:29)

Conversely if the challenge is high and the skills to cope with the challenge are also high, then a person can move from arousal or control into a state of '*flow*'. These relationships are illustrated in the diagram below.

The characteristics of activities producing *'flow'* states resemble checklists we have seen of characteristics for good language practice activities (see, e.g. Ur 1996).

Figure 6.2 is also useful for considering which aspects of what happens in classrooms might be responsible for learners' less positive states. For

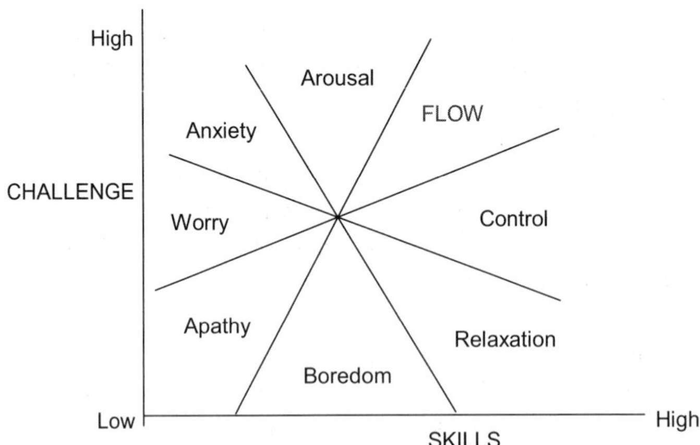

FIGURE 6.2 *The quality of experience as a function of the relationship between challenges and skills (Csikszentmihalyi 1997:30).*

example, if you think your learners are bored, perhaps the work was too easy for them.

There are other possible ways of understanding the causes of various emotional states which hinder learning, such as a problem of a 'need not met' in Maslow's 'hierarchy of needs' or a motivational problem, or teachers' lack of sensitivity to individuals' learning styles for example. All of these are often discussed in ELT literature (see, e.g. Arnold 1999; Williams and Burden 1997), so we do not explore the first two any further here (and for a discussion of learning styles, see Chapter 7).

The emotional state of the teacher also matters. If the teacher is rarely in 'flow' (i.e. totally engaged in the complexities of supporting learning) the learners are unlikely to be able to be so either. A dialogic, 'scaffolding' approach to teaching is a way of making it more likely that the teachers will be faced with challenges from which they too can learn. If the teachers have frequent moments of 'flow' in their classrooms, they are likely to feel job satisfaction (a sense of well-being) and so avoid becoming cynical, stuck or burnt out (and education systems will be more likely to retain expensively trained teachers). For a scholarly summary of work relating to the emotions of teachers, see Day (2004).

Think back to the last time you 'didn't notice time passing'. What were you doing? Was it an activity which involved a 'challenge that was just about manageable'? How did you feel afterwards? (We have had quite a few 'flow' moments writing this book – even writing parts of this 'challenging' – for us – chapter!)

3.1.2 Emotions of change and predictable sequences

You, like us, will certainly have had the experience of emotions that come and go, and may attribute these changes to yourselves (your personality, level of tiredness or health, for example) or to external situational factors (what happened or what was said). Generally, of course, it is our individual perception of events which will determine our mood and emotion. This perception will result from interplay between our personality and events, mediated also by our current internal physical context (tiredness, hormones, hunger). This makes it very difficult in general for teachers to predict emotions – for themselves or the learners – and therefore to prepare strategies to minimise any negative effects of emotions on learning.

However, researchers have identified certain series of likely emotional responses over periods of planned change. These have been called the 'emotions of change'. These seem relevant to our discussion since any learning can be seen as a form of change, (whether this is the demanding cultural change that many education reform projects require, or the changes in knowledge and behaviours any language learning requires).

Think about any project you have embarked upon (making something perhaps, or some transformation to your home).
How did you feel at the beginning? After a while? At the end? If you didn't reach the end – or haven't yet – why not?

Figure 6.3 broadly illustrates emotions of change over the time of any change process. It shows the movement from the initial positive feelings associated with optimism and the excitement of the new, via more uncertain feelings as the potential difficulty of the changes begin to become clearer, and then back up gradually to more positive feelings, as confidence in the ability to cope with the changes increases, all ideally culminating with the satisfaction that comes from successfully completing a project.

If, as we believe, the principles underlying Figure 6.3 can also describe changing feelings through a language learning process, then teachers can *expect* to need to deal with certain changes in learners' emotional states if learning is to occur. Teachers will have to create the 'optimism' of the start of the learning process ('recruitment' in scaffolding terms), which encourages learners to engage with it in the first place. Thereafter they will need to look out for signs of 'informed pessimism' in their learners and be ready to provide all the types of scaffolding and encouragement necessary to keep the learner going through this phase, and so ultimately regain the more optimistic emotions that come with confidence and feelings of success.

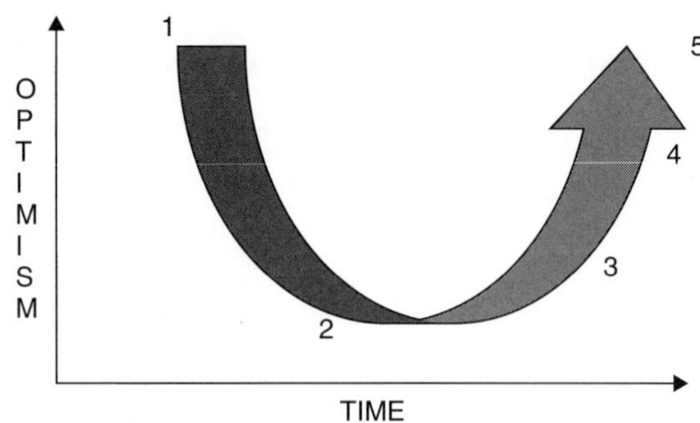

<u>The Emotions of Change</u>

1. Uninformed optimism; 2. Informed pessimism (doubt); 3. Realism (hope);
4. Informed optimism (confidence); 5. Reward (satisfaction).
(Adapted from Brandes, D. & P. Ginnis 1990)

FIGURE 6.3 *The emotions of change.*

3.2. *Between*

Classrooms contain groups of people. The people in many classrooms, however, are either simply collections of individuals or 'groups-with (or against)- the- teacher'. Groups, in the socio-psychological sense, can support teaching and learning through providing both a safe affective background as well as a resource for learning in the dialogic sense. For people together in classrooms to constitute a group in this sense, they must, as a minimum, firstly make an explicit effort to develop and agree shared goals and ways of working, and then interact with each other more than with outsiders with respect to achieving their goals.

As with the Emotions of Change above, Groups too have predictable 'lives' or phases, which generate certain group emotions at different stages. These have been variously described, but we will use terms from Erhman and Dornyei (1998).

- **Formation**

  The group formation phase is the one during which shared goals and norms are established and inter-member relationships created. This stage brings a certain anxiety with it as group members, meeting for what may be the first time, worry about how they will be perceived by others.

- **Transition**

  The transition phase often involves a certain 'storming' (period of tensions or arguments) as, now that group members know each other better, people feel more confident and so differences of opinions and stances emerge and people jostle for roles and positions.

- **Performing**

  The performing stage is the phase when the group can get down to the task for which it was constituted, and should involve no intrusive emotions (when the group is 'in flow').

- **Dissolution**

  The dissolution phase is likely to be accompanied by feelings of sadness.

Groups constituted for long periods (like classes of learners together for a term or a year or more) are likely to go through recurring 'transition' and 'performing' phases throughout their lifetime.

Teachers wanting 'dialogic groups' will need to be aware of these broad group phases and the likely emotions associated with them, as well as of strategies for managing group processes so as to obtain the longest 'performing' phases possible. There is a certain literature now in ELT which suggests practical ways for teachers to manage the group processes in a language learning classroom (e.g. Dornyei and Malderez 1999; Dornyei and Murphey 2003; Hadfield 1992). Whether a particular class actually exists as a group in the sense we are discussing here, or whether a group is in a 'transition' phase, may again partly explain differences in the atmospheresof classes that we referred to in the introduction.

4. Summary and task

Both this and the following chapter focus on the people in the classroom context.

This chapter has looked at ways in which the people in a classroom create its culture and the context of learning.

The first section of this chapter explored the different ways teachers 'know' things, which affects what they do and don't bring to their practice in classrooms. Next it considered the importance of teachers starting from 'where learners are' through understanding what learners already know. Then it looked at how knowledge (new meaning) is created between people through dialogue, and how it is this interaction which both enables individuals to learn and creates cultures.

The second part of the chapter considered how people's feelings, in particular the different feelings generated by different stages in learning, different tasks, different degrees of group cohesion and different stages of group processes can affect learners learning. In doing so, we considered some ways of thinking which can provide a means of interpreting manifestations of emotional states and acting on the affective context to make it more supportive of learning.

The next chapter continues this focus on people, this time looking at the way they are influenced by the context (at whatever layer of place or time), and are in this sense 'products' of it.

Task:

Think about the way you teach. What is unique about your style? In other words, what might strike/interest a colleague about your way of teaching? (You could invite someone into your class to tell you). If they asked you 'why' you do what you do, could you explain and give reasons that go beyond 'that's just what I do/teachers do' or 'it just feels right'? If not, why not? Where does your 'knowing to do this' come from, do you think?

If you have more time, or if you are not a teacher, observe a teacher teaching. What strikes you? (This is likely to be something that you would do differently, if you were the teacher, or something you have never seen before). After the lesson, talk briefly to the teacher to thank them and to find out (if they are able to explain to you) why they did what they did. We suggest you prompt the teacher by saying something like: 'I was interested when you X-ed/ in X. Can you tell me a bit more about it?' – and stop there, because if the teacher can give you a reason, that prompt should be enough, and if they can't (because it was learnt implicitly) you are not making them feel that they ought to 'make up' an answer.

After your brief chat, think about what the teacher said.

If the teacher gave you a reason for their actions:

If you are a teacher: did the reason convince you? Do you agree with the reason given- why/why not? Is this a strategy you might want to adopt yourself? Do you do different things for the same kinds of reasons?

If you are not a teacher: Does the teacher's answer tell you anything about what teachers in your context have been taught or have had the opportunity to learn?

If the teacher did not explain why they did what they did.

What kinds of experiences that teachers are exposed to in your context might account for the teacher doing what they did?

References and further reading

Alexander, R. 2008. *Towards Dialogic Teaching* (4th edn). Thirsk, UK: Dialogos.

Arnold, J., ed. 1999. *Affect in Language Learning*. Cambridge: Cambridge University Press

Brandes, D. and P. Ginnis. 1990. *The Student-Centred School*. Oxford: Blackwell.

Bohm, D. 1996. In:L. Nicol, ed., *David Bohm On Dialogue*. London: Routledge.

Borg, S. 2006. *Teacher Cognition and Language Education*. London: Continuum

Claxton, G. 1997. *Hare Brain, Tortoise Mind*. London: Fourth Estate/Harper Collins

Csikszentmihaly, M. 1990. *Flow: The Psychology of Optimal Experience*. New York: Harper and Row

— 1997. *Living Well: The Psychology of Everyday Life.* London: Weidenfeld & Nicolson.

Day, C. 2004. *A Passion for Teaching.* London: Routledge-Falmer.

Dörnyei, Z., and A. Malderez (1999). 'The role of group dynamics in foreign language learning and teaching'. In: J. Arnold, ed., *Affect in Language Learning.* Cambridge: Cambridge University Press, pp. 155–69.

Dörnyei, Z. and T. Murphey. 2003. *Group Dynamics in the Language Classroom.* Cambridge: Cambridge University Press.

Ehrman, M. and Z. Dornyei. 1998. *Interpersonal Dynamics in Second Language Education: The Visible and Invisible Classroom:* London: Sage

Eysenck, M. W. 1979. 'Anxiety, learning and memory: a reconceptualization'. *Journal of Research in Personality*, 13, pp. 363–85.

Gardner, R.C. and P. D. Macintyre. 1993. 'On the measurement of affective variables in Second Language Learning'. *Language Learning*, 43, pp. 157–94.

Hadfield, J. 1992. *Classroom Dynamics.* Oxford: Oxford University Press.

Horwitz, E.K. and D.Young, eds. 1991. *Language Anxiety: From Theory and Research to Classroom Implications.* Englewood Cliffs, NJ: Prentice Hall.

Johnson, K. 1996. *Language Teaching and Skill Learning.* Oxford: Blackwell.

— 1999. *Understanding Language teaching.* New York: Newbury House.

— 2009. *Second Language Teacher Education: A Socio-cultural Perspective.* New York: Routledge.

Krashen, S. 1982. *Principles and Practice in Second Language Acquisition.* Oxford: Pergamon Press.

— 1985. *The Input Hypothesis: Issues and Implications.* London: Longman.

Lortie, D. 1975. *Schoolteacher: A Sociological Study.* Chicago: University of Chicago Press.

Malderez, A. and C. Bodoczky. 1999. *Mentor Courses: A Resource Book for Trainer Trainers.* Cambridge: Cambridge University Press.

Malderez, A. and M. Wedell. 2007 *Teaching Teachers: Processes and Practices.* London: Continuum.

Mercer, N., L. Dawes and J. K, Staarman 2009. Dialogic Teaching in the Primary Science Classroom. *Language and Education,* 23(4), pp. 353–369.

Oxford, R. L. 1999. 'Anxiety and the language learner: new insights'. In: J. Arnold, ed., *Affect in Language Learning.* Cambridge: Cambridge University Press, pp. 58–67.

Stevick, E. 1980. *Teaching Languages: A Way and Ways.* Rowley, MA: Newbury House.

Ur, P. 1996. *A Course in Language Teaching: Practice and Theory.* Cambridge: Cambridge University Press.

Wertsch, J. V. 1991. *Voices of the Mind: A Sociocultural Approach to Mediated Action.* Cambridge, MA: Harvard University Press.

Wertsch, J. V. 1995. *Sociocultural Studies of Mind.* Cambridge: Cambridge University Press.

Wertsch, J. V. 1998. *Mind as Action.* Oxford: Oxford University Press.

Williams, M. and R. L. Burden. 1997. *Psychology for Language Teachers.* Cambridge: Cambridge University Press

Woods, D. 1996. *Teacher Cognition in Language Teaching: Beliefs, Decision Making and Classroom Practice.* Cambridge: Cambridge University Press.

7

Teachers and learners: As 'products' of their context

Introduction

In Chapter 6, we looked at some ways in which what the people in an English classroom know and feel and how the behaviour that results may 'create' a more or less supportive classroom context in which to work. In this chapter, we look at this relationship from the other way around. We consider the ways in which the individuals within the classroom (teacher and learners) may be different as a result of their prior experiences. We discuss how they may have been influenced by (and in this sense are 'products' of) the various contexts they have experienced over time and how such differences may affect the current classroom context. It is important for teachers to be clear about the types of differences that might exist in order to be able to decide which prior experiences are useful and worth building on, and which are not. Finally we briefly explore how the coming together of different people, as individuals and 'types' can produce very different affective and cognitive contexts for learning – for both learners and teachers. All the above, in combination, contribute in important ways to any given classroom context, particularly to the classroom culture.

1. People as products of contexts: Factors distinguishing individual teachers

We will look first at some macro-contextual differences between teachers before considering factors that will influence differences at an individual level.

1.1 Contextual differences

The range of possible differences between teachers often appears to be enormous. The reasons for such differences can be interpreted in different ways. If we think about context as place, teachers can be seen as different according to *where* they teach. Teachers in different institutions in different parts of the world may look different and behave differently. However, looking at the invisible context, or culture, we might see aspects of these 'place' differences as originating from the particular cultural or disciplinary group the teachers belong to (see Chapters 1 and 2). Alternatively, we could look at differences in terms of the methods and approaches used in different places. As we saw in Chapter 4, in the past many language teachers needed little language proficiency (one-step ahead of the learners) and a very narrow range of classroom management skills. Current approaches require language teachers to be more fluent and confident in the language, and able to develop their own language and teaching skills and abilities independently. This makes the demands on them all much, much greater (Chapter 5). Thus, some of the most obvious behaviours associated with the ELT approach or method followed may, as illustrated in Table 7.1, also make teachers (and learners) in one context 'look' very different from those in another.

TABLE 7.1 Some likely visible differences between 'traditional' and 'communicative' classrooms

'Traditional' teacher transmitting knowledge about English	'Communicative'/'learner centred' teacher helping learners to develop as 'competent communicators'
Teachers and learners in the classroom use English to a limited extent for limited purposes.	Teacher and learners use English in the classroom most of the time for all purposes.
Teacher and learners use a limited range of materials (usually a textbook) which follow a fairly predictable sequence of knowledge inputs/exercises and activities.	Teacher and learners use teaching-learning materials from a wider range of sources, chosen to meet learners' needs and interests and contextual realities.
Teacher uses a predictable and limited range of largely whole-class teaching procedures and classroom management skills.	Teacher uses a range of flexible and complex classroom management skills to scaffold learners as they participate in (or even initiate) a range of tasks and activities, involving varied patterns of classroom interaction, and varying degrees of focus on form.

However, let's pause for a moment, in this discussion of differences to remind ourselves of what unites us. Teachers in any context have, as far as we know, rarely, if ever been mistaken for plumbers! Teachers in any context can still usually be found in schools and classrooms with learners (although thanks to technology and e-learning some teachers may now work at a distance from their learners in a wide variety of physical locations). Teachers are accorded the status appropriate to their context, they behave in ways that are accepted as appropriate for teachers working in that time and place with those learners. What unites us all therefore, is our common need (whether conscious or not), to fit in with the norms, values and expectations of 'teachers in our context'.

1.2 *Personal differences*

Two major areas influence personal differences between teachers whatever their macro-context. These can be described as relating to experience and personality. However, again there is overlap between the two. Just as 'experience' cannot easily be separated from the macro-context, so 'personality' affects how new experience is received. In addition, previous experience will have, to some extent at least, influenced any teacher's current 'personality'.

1.2.1 Experience

The three main factors we see as responsible for most differences between teachers with regard to prior experience are:

- The nature and extent of formal initial teacher preparation and in-service support provision received.
- The nature and extent of informal learning of teaching.
- The career stage, or stage in teacher learning.

(i) The nature and extent of formal opportunities for teacher learning received.

Throughout the world, at any one time, there are a huge range of very different models of initial teacher preparation and support for ongoing, in-service teacher development. At one extreme, there are language teacher preparation programmes that emphasise the learning of *teaching*, and aim to produce 'reflective practitioners' (Schön 1987). Such teachers have the capacities both to manage their own lifelong learning of the particular language and of teaching it (that is they have 'learnacy' [Claxton 2004]), and to scaffold the learning of their pupils in well-managed learning groups (that is they have 'adaptive expertise' [Johnson 2009]). At the other extreme, we find programmes for teachers that give little recognition to the idea that teaching itself needs to be learnt, and so focus almost exclusively on ensuring that future language teachers have knowledge about and proficiency in the language to be taught (see, e.g. Freeman and Richards 1993; Richards 2008; Roberts 1998; Wallace 1991). Teachers emerging from such different programmes are likely to view their work very differently. In a gross oversimplification, for example, those who graduate from the first kind of programme are more likely to work 'dialogically' and those from the second in 'transmission' mode (see Chapter 6).

(ii) The nature and extent of informal learning of teaching

Many initial teacher preparation programmes, of whatever type, involve students in spending some time observing teachers in school classrooms. There will however, be differences between teachers not only in the kinds of teaching that they observed during their programmes or afterwards, and the purposes of such observations. There will also be differences in what was done both during and after such observations, or how such observation opportunities were 'processed'. In other words, what matters is not just the length of 'exposure' to teaching, or even the nature of that teaching. Also important is the extent to which teachers are skilled at both noticing salient features and analysing their findings, as well as the extent to which they see the value of continuing to do so in their own classrooms throughout their professional lives.

(iii) The career stage or stage in teacher learning

The point teachers have reached in their careers may also create differences between teachers. It is not as simple as saying that the more experienced a teacher is the 'better', since, depending of course on an individual's career history and personality (see, e.g. Huberman 1993), cynicism, complacency and other 'negative' attitudes may also accompany being an 'old-hand' in a career.

There are differences between teachers not only according to their career stage but also according to where they are on a teacher-learning continuum. There has been some attempt to identify stages in beginner teachers' learning and these seem to progress, adding stages over time, as follows (Campbell and Wheatley 1983; Feiman-Nemser 2003; Kagan 1992):

- through an initial concern with 'self' (do I look like a teacher, behave like a teacher, how should I be? etc.)
- to a focus on activity in the classroom (what are the learners doing? how are they behaving? what activities shall I give them? how can I control them?)

- to finally a focus on the learners' learning (what do they know? how do they learn? are they learning? what can I do to help them learn better?)

Which stage teachers are at is not always necessarily directly related to the number of years spent in teaching, but may also be influenced by a number of other factors, including, for example, whether or not the teacher has developed 'learnacy' and how familiar the teacher is with the context of teaching. For example, most teachers return to a certain 'concern with self' (how should I be?) every time they stand in front of a new class, especially if it is in a new broader context, and unfortunately there are some 'old hands' who have never really added the third stage.

Johnson (1999) suggests that well prepared teachers will have learnt, during their initial teacher preparation, the value of developing 'robust reasoning' and of continuing its development throughout their careers. She proposes a core set of questions which teachers can usefully, and repeatedly ask themselves, developing increasingly strong arguments to support their answers over time. For her, this process of developing ever more robust reasoning in answering these questions is a basis for continuing to learn as a teacher. Her questions are:

- Who am I as a teacher?
- Who are my students? How do they experience my teaching?
- What do I know about my teaching context?
- What do I know about the subject matter content that I teach?
- Why do I teach the way I do?
- What are the consequences of my teaching practices for my students?
- How do I make sense of theoretical knowledge?
- Who is my professional community?
- What sort of change do I see fit for my own teaching? (Johnson 1999:139)

Different teachers will answer the above questions differently, and their answers will be more or less 'robust'. Therefore how a teacher answers, and how complex or strong an argument a teacher can make in his/her response to such questions, might provide some indication of 'where they are', how they are likely to behave, and what they are likely to do in a classroom.

1.2.2 Personality

Although many different personality types can make 'good teachers' (which, of course, will be variously defined in different contexts) students do, in our experience, frequently identify certain personality features as helpful. These are such qualities as being fair, having enthusiasm for the subject and an ability to relate to them or being empathic (Borg 2006). Given the discussions in the previous chapter on scaffolding and affective issues, we clearly agree. However, we feel that much of what tends to be called 'personality' results from learning of one kind or another. For example, 'enthusing', 'motivating' learners or 'relating' to students might also be considered as skills (and therefore 'learnable'). Having said that, our experience of initial teacher preparation suggests that there are some people who come to teaching with more of such 'soft' skills already learnt, or with a more positive disposition to learn them, than others. This may have given rise to the old adage that teachers are born, not made. While we disagree with this, as long as it remains rare for time to be allocated on formal teacher learning programmes for the development of such soft skills, it is inevitable that, given individual differences, some teachers will appear more 'born' than others.

2. People as products of contexts: Factors distinguishing individual learners

Before you begin this section, we suggest you work through part a) of the following task:

> *Think carefully about two different English learners you know well. Consider the similarities and differences between them. Then a) for each similarity and difference, generate possible explanations, and b) as you read through this next section, add further possible explanations.*

2.1 Contextual differences

Macro-contextual factors here again also make a huge difference to the kinds of behaviours and attitudes that are expected of or permitted to learners. Studies of national cultural groups of learners, (as opposed to the relatively few studies of teachers in this way), have attempted to characterise these. As Reid (1999:303) reports:

> For example, Japanese EFL students have been described as group-oriented, focused on consensual decision-making, reserved, formal and

cautious; these characteristics emerge from schooling – they are stressed even in Japanese pre-schools.

A number of points are worth making about the above. The first is that words like 'formal' or 'cautious' and so on are necessarily relative, chosen by the user against his or her background taken-for-granted 'norm', that will have been contextually acquired. Here the names of the writers would indicate that this is a Western interpretation. If you are Japanese or East Asian, you would probably have different ways of describing the actual observation data. You might like to think how you would describe what you imagine the contrasting appropriate behaviour of North American students to be, when Reid goes on to say:

> The characteristics preferred by North American educators and students – self-reliance, frankness, informality, spontaneity and gregariousness (Barnlund 1975) – seem in direct contrast. (Reid cited above)

So the first point to make is that in reading studies of this kind it is important to look carefully at who is doing the study as well as who is being studied. While it is very hard for someone from the same cultural group to notice what is 'normal', people from different cultural groups will inevitably both notice differences more easily, and describe them against the background of their own 'normal'. Studies which attempt to interpret behaviour in terms of its own cultural setting, that is to notice, describe factually and seek for contextual explanations are perhaps more universally useful (see, e.g. Coleman 1996; Ouyang 2000).

The second very important point is that teachers or researchers must be careful, while seeking to understand typical cultural (however defined) behaviours and preferences, not to fall into the trap of stereotyping individuals. Understanding something of typical cultural behaviours may be of more or less help in understanding something of the way groups or individual learners behave and think, but against this background, personal differences also play a very important role.

2.2 Personal differences

As in the same section under 'teachers' above, two major areas will influence personal differences between learners whatever their macro-context. These can be described as relating to experience and personality. Again there is overlap between the two (see above). The one difference here, perhaps, is that with school-age learners 'personalities' are in the process of being formed, and are therefore less fixed and more open to direct influence. This, we believe, places a great responsibility on those who will influence them! To use an analogy, you would probably agree that those in the medical profession have at a minimum the responsibility not to interfere dangerously with our bodies. More actively they should try to save lives in times of crises, and ultimately they are responsible for generally promoting and supporting health. A parallel could be made for teachers: at the very least teachers must avoid intervening dangerously in the development of young impressionable minds, more importantly teachers should be there to support minds in crisis, and to promote and support optimum conditions for minds to develop in a positive manner, however this may be culturally defined.

2.2.1 Experience

Again, we will group differences in learner experience under three main headings:

- The nature and extent of formal education already received.
- The nature and extent of informal learning: socio-economic backgrounds.
- Age, and purposes for language learning.

(i) The nature and extent of formal education already received

What messages from formal education learners have already received about what counts as learning, and therefore what has been learnt in what ways can result in great differences between learners. In addition the cultural learning from the secondary socialisation experienced during formal education will differ. The learner roles and the associated range of behaviours that learners are familiar with will affect how easy or difficult it is for them to adapt to learning with teachers who use unfamiliar methodologies. Differences can also relate to a number of other factors, including curricula, testing procedures and age (see below).

(ii) The nature and extent of informal learning: Socio-economic backgrounds

Again, learners' previous opportunities for learning in general will differentiate between them. Much relevant information can be gathered from a consideration of the socio-economic backgrounds of learners. For example, whether there are books in the home, and if there are, whether parents have had the time to read, or seen the desirability of reading to the child, as well as parents' attitude to education in general, can mean learners come to school with very different previous experiences of learning and attitudes to learning. In thinking about ELT in particular, factors such as whether, how or how much the child has been previously exposed to English, through its use in the home, in society or the media, or through contact with English-speaker visitors or travel to English speaking countries or evening classes in private language schools are all likely to be important in determining what learners already know and/or their attitudes to the language- learning process.

(iii) Age and purposes for language learning

A 6-year-old learner of English and an eighteen-year-old or adult learner, will not only behave and think differently wherever they are, but will have very different immediate needs as far as English learning is concerned as well as very different visions or purposes for learning. This is the area of difference that has perhaps been most formally recognised in programme titles, curricula or materials. As descriptions of language and theories of language learning have evolved over time (see Chapters 4 and 5), so broad specialisation has increasingly occurred to try to meet the needs of groups of learners. Roughly these can be divided into:

- specialisations according to 'purpose' (e.g. we now have ESP – English for Specific Purposes, EAP – English for Academic Purposes),
- or specialisations according to 'age' (e.g. we now have TEYL – Teaching English to Young Learners, English for 'teenagers', English Language Teaching to Adults).

2.2.2 Personality

Many 'base' personality factors can perhaps be related to macro-context (see above). Yet, however mono-cultural a classroom may be, there are bound to be differences between the learners within it, probably due to individual 'nature and nurture' differences. Although in the middle of the last century research focused on trying to identify personality traits or aptitudes favourable for learning in general or language learning in particular, a more recent trend has been to consider learner 'styles' and associated 'strategies'.

Much recent work has attempted to identify and categorise 'learner styles' so that appropriate approaches, materials and methods to suit those styles can be devised. The argument goes something like this: if teachers can identify the styles of all the students in a particular group, they can individualise the routes each student – or small group of 'same-style students' – will follow to meet the learning objectives. Within the theme of 'differentiation' (currently a requirement in the British National Curriculum for foreign languages) the term 'mixed-ability' (which suggests to some that what a child knows is a function of innate ability [only] rather than [also] of previous opportunities for learning), has been replaced by the more accurately descriptive terms: 'mixed-level' and 'mixed-style'.

We think there are several issues and problems with this idea of teaching to suit the learners' style. These include the following which are considered in more detail below:

- competing and overlapping typologies
- the question of whether styles do or should remain static
- teachers' styles
- is this still a search for 'right methods'?

(i) Competing and overlapping typologies

One problem anyone has in working with these ideas is that there are many different ways of thinking about learning styles. Which typology teachers work with will make a difference to how they think about their learners and therefore, what they do. There are however some overlaps between categories. Reid (1999) provides a useful overview of typologies of learning styles (see Table 7.2), in which many overlaps can be noticed. For example, 'field independent' and 'global' seem to be describing essentially the same thing. In addition, while there is, for example, more noticeable difference between the 'multiple intelligences' (which describe 'ability') and 'perceptual learning styles' (which describe preferred routes to learning) there do seem clear connections here too. From Table 7.2, however we see three main ideas emerge.

- People have many senses or 'intelligences' which need to be developed and used in and for learning.
- There is a need for teachers to work with new points to be learnt from the perspectives of their 'parts', as well as their 'wholes' and their place in '*the* whole'.
- Working with others and time spent working alone seem more or less important for different learners.

TABLE 7.2 Overview of some learning styles (adapted from Reid 1999:301)

	The seven multiple intelligences
Verbal/linguistic	Ability with and sensitivity to words, orally and in writing
Musical	Sensitivity to rhythm, pitch and melody
Logical/mathematical	Ability to use numbers effectively and reason well
Spatial/visual	Sensitivity to form, colour, line and shape
Bodily/kinesthetic	Ability to use the body to express ideas and feelings
Interpersonal	Ability to understand another person's moods and intentions
Intrapersonal	Ability to understand yourself, your strengths and weaknesses
	Perceptual learning styles
Visual	Learns more effectively through the eyes (seeing)
Auditory	Learns more effectively through the ears (hearing)
Tactile	Learns more effectively through touch (hands-on)
Kinesthetic	Learns more effectively through complete body experience
Group	Learns more effectively through working with others
Individual	Learns more effectively through working alone
	Field-independent/field-dependent (sensitive) learning styles
Field independent	Learns more effectively sequentially, analysing facts
Field dependent	Learns more effectively in context, holistically and is sensitive to human relationships
	Analytic/global learning styles
Analytic	Learns more effectively individually, sequentially, linearly
Global	Learns more effectively through concrete experience and through interaction with other people

Continued

TABLE 7.2 Continued

	The seven multiple intelligences
	Reflective/impulsive learning styles
Reflective	Learns more effectively when she/he has time to consider options
Impulsive	Learns more effectively when she/he is able to respond immediately

(ii) Do or should styles remain static?

Individual learning styles do not remain static since not only may they change according to task, but also with age. (Whether this change is an inevitable part of maturation, or socialised through expectations at school and elsewhere, is another issue.) It could be argued also that, even if styles did not change, teaching only to and for learners' existing styles potentially results in an unchanging educational environment, which might be deemed inappropriate in contexts where ideas of 'development' require citizens to learn new things and/or learn in new ways. Such citizens will need to be able to adapt to and cope with whatever changes the future brings. Since learning styles influence the range and type of learning strategies a learner uses, and the future is so uncertain and likely to be at least as full of rapid changes as the immediate past, it is probably safe to guess that we will all need to be able to use every learning strategy we can get. We would suggest therefore, that 'learner training' – to help extend self-awareness of styles and related strategies and add further options – is an essential aspect of the lifelong learning that has increasingly become necessary for us all. Indeed Claxton (2004) has suggested, as mentioned above, that the main purpose of all/any education system/course/programme should be to develop the 'learnacy' (ability to learn) of its students.

(iii) Teachers' styles

Teachers too have preferred learning styles, and initially at least, they tend to teach in the way which 'worked for them', which they believe helped (or would have helped) them learn. Even when they do remember that it did not work for everyone, or notice that some of their students seem to want or need a different way of working, it is not easy to change style. For example, it is difficult for teachers who are naturally global learners themselves (and therefore global teachers?) to produce analytic materials or a careful sequential lesson. Conversely it is also likely to be hard for analytic teachers who feel comfortable with the naturally more linear and sequential nature of words and language learning materials to present the language in a more global manner.

(iv) Is this still a search for 'right methods'?

In this search to categorise learners' styles and produce materials, techniques and activity-types which suit their styles, there remains a hint of the old search for 'the right method'. However, this work on learning styles is potentially useful in raising teachers' and learners' awareness of the range of styles and strategies and options open to them. In an ideal world, these ideas would additionally be incorporated into teachers' individual searches for the most appropriate approach for a particular group of learners – basing teaching on not only on what the learners already know and feel, but also on what the teacher knows about their learners' preferred styles and/or strategies.

- After reading this section, look back at the 'possible explanations' you now have for the similarities and differences between your two learners.
- Choose one similarity or one difference between your learners which interests you.
- Decide what you would need to observe, or ask your students (or their parents or other teachers), in order to decide if, or which of, your possible explanations is the correct interpretation.

3. Good language learner

Just as with teachers, researchers have tried to identify features 'of good language learners'. These studies (e.g. Naiman 1978; Rubin 1975) set out to discover the particular types of personalities, cognitive styles, attitudes, motivations, or past learning experiences that were typical of successful learners. Such studies focusing on individual learners' psychological traits were abandoned largely because they did not take context into account. More recent work (e.g. Norton and Toohey 2001) explicitly recognised the central role of context in explaining the success or otherwise of individual learners. For example Norton and Toohey (2001) explain the success of good language learners in terms of:

> their access to a variety of conversations in their communities rather than on the basis of their control of a wider variety of linguistic forms or meaning

> than their peers or on the basis of their speed of acquisition of linguistic forms and meanings. (p. 310)

This view of explaining learners' success in terms of the learning context moves away from attempting to identify the personality traits or learning styles that are better for language learning. Why then have we spent time describing various types of individual differences above? While the studies did not result in the hoped-for profile of a 'good language learner' we think they do offer a further means of understanding learners' possible starting points.

4. Teachers as learners and learners as teachers

Teachers must be principally concerned with the language learning of their learners. But we are none of us perfect and being an effective teacher – in all contexts and with every learner – is an ever-elusive goal. One of our former colleagues used to say, 'teaching is the only profession where you can go home every night and be *sure* you have failed' – failed at promoting the target learning in *all* learners. Teachers, then, are also necessarily all lifelong learners.

There is an ongoing debate about what it is essential for teachers to know (understood in a very broad sense). Writers have variously described the core knowledge for all teachers as: 'situated knowledge' (Leinhardt, 1988:146) 'craft knowledge' (Grimmet and Mackinnon 1992), 'case knowledge' (Calderhead 1991:532) and 'personal practical knowledge' (Carter 1990:300). A recent study (Ben-Peretz 2011) looked at research on teacher knowledge from the 1980s to 2009. She noted that what was included under the 'label' of 'teacher knowledge' was constantly expanding. While earlier researchers defined the term purely as knowledge of subject matter and pedagogical principles and skills, in more recent papers:

> There is the extension of the term to include societal issues. As well, one finds a growing focus on the personal aspects of knowledge. The role of context in shaping teacher knowledge plays a crucial role in the analyzed papers. (2011:8)

However teacher knowledge eventually comes to be defined, it is certain that experience of learners and interactions and classroom events are needed for teachers to learn what it is they need to know.

Therefore, it can be argued that learners are the teachers of teachers, and teachers are always learners themselves when working with learners, as in doing so they are increasing their case, craft, personal practical or situated knowledge. In this sense the main site for the learning of teaching is not the university or training college, but rather the school. Partly in recognition of this, there has been an increased emphasis on school experience in initial teacher preparation programmes. This has required trained people in schools to support the in-context/on-the-job learning, and therefore 'we have seen the birth of a new training professional: the school-based mentor' (Grenfell 1998).

As far as support for ongoing teacher development is concerned, not only some forms of mentoring (Malderez and Wedell 2007) but also 'Practitioner Research' (an umbrella term which we use to embrace the outcome of effective mentoring, as well as Action Research [Burns 2010], Exploratory Practice [Allwright and Hanks 2010], and indeed any attempt by practitioners to systematically investigate their own context, in order to inform their reasoning) seem to have potential. Indeed informal, small scale, locally focused investigations seem to us to provide a possible self-managed tool for ongoing teacher learning, supporting bottom-up or 'owned' changes in what happens in schools and classrooms.

5. Summary and task

The focus in this chapter has been on what people bring into classrooms with them. We have seen that people bring different experiences of teaching and learning with them from the wider context, and that these strongly influence what they know and are able and willing to do within the classroom. In addition of course they bring their individual personalities, styles of learning and teaching and feelings (e.g. attitudes and motivations to what is being taught /learned), all of which again influence what are likely to be considered as more or less appropriate approaches to teaching and learning. Finally we have noted that in fact in any classroom context there is the opportunity for teachers and learners to play both roles, each teaching and learning from and with the other.

Chapters 6 and 7 have touched on a very wide range of areas, for example: *Socio-cultural theories of Learning, Teacher Knowledge, Teacher Learning, Affective Factors in Language Learning, Group Dynamics, Learner Styles, Mentoring, Practitioner Research* each of which has an extensive literature. The references at the end of each chapter provide a starting point for accessing this. You will find that a lot more information is available if you decide to start digging in one or more areas.

In the first part of the next chapter we stay at the level of the classroom, but the focus will shift to the physical context.

Task:

If you are a teacher, answer the 'robust reasoning' questions above for yourself. Do your colleagues answer them in the same way? How do you explain any differences?

If you are not a teacher, predict how you think teachers in your context would answer (one or more of) the robust reasoning questions. Then talk to some teachers and check your predictions. How do you explain any differences between your prediction and what the teachers say? Why might such differences matter in your work?

References and further reading

Allwright, R. and J. Hanks. 2010. *The Developing Language Learner: An Introduction to Exploratory Practice*. Basingstoke: Palgrave-MacMillan.

Arnold, J., ed. 1999. *Affect in Language Learning*. Cambridge: Cambridge University Press.

Barnlund, D. C. 1975. *Public and private Self in Japan and the United States: Communicative Styles of Two Cultures*. Tokyo and Portland, OR: Simul Press.

Ben-Peretz, M. 2011. 'Teacher knowledge: what is it? How do we uncover it? What are its implications for schooling?' *Teaching and Teacher Education*, 27(1), pp. 3–9.

Borg, S. 2006. 'The distinctive characteristics of language teachers'. *Language Teaching Research*, 10(1), pp. 3–31.

Burns, A. 2010. *Doing Action Research in English Language Teaching: A Guide for Practitioners*. New York: Routledge.

Calderhead, J. 1991. 'The nature and growth of knowledge in student teaching'. *Teaching and Teacher Education*, 5(6), pp. 531–5.

Campbell, P. F and G. H. Wheatley. 1983. 'a model for helping student teachers'. *Mathematics Teacher*, 76(1), pp. 60–6.

Carter, K. 1990. 'Teachers' knowledge and learning to teach'. In: W. R. Houston, ed., *Handbook of Research on Teacher Education*. New York: Macmillan, pp. 291–310.

Claxton, G. 2004. 'Learning is learnable (and we ought to teach it)'. In: J. Cassell, ed., *Ten Years On*. National Commission for Education Report. London.

Claxton, G. L. 2007. 'Expanding young people's capacity to learn'. *British Journal of Educational Studies*, 55(2), pp. 1–20.

Coleman, H., ed. 1996. *Society and the Language Classroom*. Cambridge: Cambridge University Press.

Cortazzi, M. and L. Jin. 1996. 'Cultures of learning: language classrooms in China'. In: H. Coleman, ed., *Society and the Language Classroom*. Cambridge: Cambridge University Press, pp. 169–206.

Feiman-Nemser, S. 2003. 'What new teachers need to learn. Educational leadership'. *Educational Leadership,* 60(8), pp. 25–9.

Freeman, D. 1998. *Doing Teacher Research*. New York: Newbury House/Heinle & Heinle.

Freeman, D. and J. C. Richards. 1993. 'Conceptions of teaching and the education of second language teachers'. *TESOL Quarterly*, 27(2), pp. 193–216.

Grimmett, P. P. and A. M. MacKinnon. 1992. 'Craft knowledge and the education of teachers'. *Review of Research in Education*, 18, pp. 385–456.

Huberman, A. M. 1993. *The Lives of Teachers*. New York: Teachers College Press.

Jin, L. and M. Cortazzi. 2006. 'Changing practices in Chinese cultures of learning'. *Language, Culture and Curriculum*, 19(1), pp. 5–20.

Johnson, K. 1999. *Understanding Language teaching.* New York: Newbury House.

2009.*Second Language Teacher Education: A Sociocultural Perspective.* New York: Routledge.

Kagan, D. 1992. 'Professional growth among preservice and beginning teachers'. *Review of Educational Research* 2(62), pp. 129–69.

Leinhardt, G. 1988. 'Situated knowledge and expertise in teaching'. In: J. Calderhead, ed., *Teachers' Professional Learning*. London: The Falmer Press, pp. 146–69.

Malderez, A. and M. Wedell. 2007. *Teaching Teachers: Processes and Practices*. London: Continuum.

Naiman, N. M. Fröhlich, D. Stern, and A. Todesco. 1978. *The Good Language Learner* (Research in Education Series No. 7). Toronto, Canada: Ontario Institute for Studies in Education.

Norton, B. and K. Toohey. 2001. 'Changing perspectives on good language learners'. *TESOL Quarterly*, 35(2), pp. 307–22.

Oxford, R. 1990. *Language Learning Strategies: What Every Teacher Should Know*. New York: Newbury House.

Ouyang, H. 2000. 'One-way ticket: a story of an innovative teacher in mainland china'. *Anthropology and Education Quarterly*, 31(4), pp. 397–425.

Ranson, S. 1998. 'The future of educational research: learning at the centre'. In: J. Ruddock and D. McIntyre, eds, *Challenges for Educational Research: New BERA dialogues*. London: Paul Chapman, pp. 47–68.

Reid, J., ed. 1998. *Understanding Learning Styles in the Second Language Classroom*. Upper Saddle River, NJ: Prentice Hall Regents.

Reid, J. 1999. 'Affect in the classroom: problems, politics, and pragmatics'. In: J. Arnold, ed., *Affect in Language Learning.* Cambridge: Cambridge University Press, pp. 297–306.

Richards, J. C. 2008. 'Second language teacher education today'. *RELC*, 39(2), pp. 158–76.

Roberts, J. 1998. *Language Teacher Education*. London: Arnold.

Rubin, J. 1975. 'What the "good language learner" can teach us'. *TESOL Quarterly*, 9, pp. 41–51.

Schon, D. 1987. *Educating the Reflective Practitioner.* San Francisco, CA: Josey Bass.

Wallace, M. 1991. *Training Foreign Language Teachers: A Reflective Approach.* Cambridge: Cambridge University Press

— 1998. *Action Research for Language Teachers.* Cambridge: Cambridge University Press.

8

Schools and classrooms: Physical and cultural contexts

Introduction

In this chapter we return primarily to the context of place, and consider how this can and does affect what people (can) do and how they think. We start by briefly considering physical conditions and facilities in language classrooms and how these may affect what happens there. We then look more closely at one common complaint about classroom conditions often made by language teachers, that of large classes.

We move next to the level of the school or organisation. We discuss how the visible physical surroundings and the use made of them can reveal features of the less visible values and assumptions of a school or organisation (its culture). This culture will in turn strongly influence teachers' and learners' ways of working.

The extent to which people think that the physical aspects of the place in which they work are suitable for teaching and learning, will of course affect how they behave in classrooms. However, the messages that the institution sends about what is or is not 'possible' in the context is just as important an influence on what people actually do. How people behave in classrooms is therefore affected by visible and invisible features of the institutional context. Both need to be understood by teachers (and other educational professionals) when considering how feasible a proposed change might be in a particular context.

As you read this chapter, you might like to think about whether

- *the physical elements of the classrooms in which you work affect how you teach and/or the learning opportunities available to your learners, and*

- *you can see any relationships between your understanding of the values and assumptions that characterise the institution in which you work and what you do and/or how you behave in the classroom.*

1. Visible features of the classroom or institutional context

You would be an unusual teacher if you have never complained, however privately, about the conditions you work in. Perhaps you have said (to yourself or others) 'If only I had a whiteboard/ smaller classes/ better facilities/ data projection/ internet access in the classroom/ a staffroom/ my own classroom/a photocopier/ enough books for all the children . . .'

In this section, we will take just one of the 'moans' often made by teachers about their conditions of work, and use this as an example to begin to explore some relationships between immediate physical surroundings and teaching and learning in classrooms, and between these and the wider context. We have chosen to consider 'large classes' here because this is one of the most common complaints that we have heard from English teachers worldwide (Coleman 1989; Watson-Todd 2006). That said, many of the issues raised by exploring this one 'condition' can equally well apply to many other observable classroom conditions which may affect teachers' and learners' work. You might like to consider some of the other 'moans' you thought of above as you read the following discussion of 'large' class sizes and of some reasons why these exist.

We begin by trying to understand the reasons for the complaint itself, then consider whether there is any evidence to suggest that it affects teachers' thinking and practices and/or learners' achievement. Finally we look at some important aspects of the wider macro or immediate micro context that may contribute to the 'large' size of so many (English) classes worldwide.

1.1 Some reasons why teachers might think that a class is 'large'

'Large' means different things to different people. Kuchah and Smith (2011) reported on an English class of 235 in Cameroon. Wang and Zhang (2011) say that in China a 'large' class refers to one holding 50–100 students, while Smith and Warburton (1997) suggest that in the United Kingdom, 25–30 pupils represent a 'large' class.

Why are there such differences in what counts as 'large'? We can see three possible reasons, discussed below, for teacher's judgement of a class as large.

1.1.1 Because they are unable to use their preferred teaching practices

Thirty students in one group will seem 'large' to a teacher who believes in a dialogic approach to teaching-learning and who wants to be able to interact personally with every student, mark all their homework regularly and carefully (so as to understand and plan appropriate further individualised support) and so on. On the other hand, to a teacher holding a transmission approach, who is perhaps used to lecturing to classes of, say, 100, 'only' 30 might seem a small class.

This does not necessarily mean that a dialogic teacher will revert to, or adopt, only practices associated with a 'transmission' approach if they perceive a class to be 'large'. However there is research which suggests that teachers do adapt their classroom methodology (what they do in their classroom) even if not their underlying approach (their beliefs about the nature of language and learning) according to class size.

Coleman (forthcoming) discusses research by Shamim (1993) in the Pakistani context. She makes a distinction between 'core' and 'enhancing' activities, see Table 8.1.

TABLE 8.1 'Core' and 'Enhancing' activities (Shamim 1993)

'Core activities'	**'Enhancing activities'**
• T reads the text aloud • T translates text into L1 (Urdu) • T explains meaning of text and gives word meanings • Ss sit quietly apparently listening with heads bent over their notebooks. • Individual SS answer questions when nominated. • T checks SS' 'copies' (exercise books)	• SS read the text aloud • T tells a story • T uses visual aids • SS work in groups (e.g. to discuss a poem or find 'difficult' words • Vocabulary extension (T does not simply provide meanings but also elaborates on other related vocabulary) • T encourages SS to make links between background knowledge and text. • T asks SS to share information with each other. • SS read the text individually

Shamim suggests that all teachers use 'core' activities most of the time, however large or small they perceive the class size to be.

> As class size decreases (in the teacher's perception) teachers begin to feel that it may be possible for them to add some enhancing activities . . . [and] the scope for supplementing the central core of classroom practice increases as class size decreases. (Coleman, forthcoming)

Looking at what are counted as 'core' activities used by 'most teachers most of the time', we get the impression that at the time of this research the prevailing approach to (beliefs about) English teaching in Shamim's context was of the type which underpins a 'grammar-translation' method (set of practices). The 'enhancing' activities, which if seen happening daily in most classrooms might indicate that teachers were trying to implement a more interactive, communicative approach, seem in this large class context to have been an occasional and optional 'add-on'.

In contrast, O'Sullivan (2006) reports that some 'good' primary teachers in Uganda, again working in 'large classes', were able to use practices associated with a more interactive approach as the basis for their day-to-day teaching. They had, for example, developed routines for group formation and work which children were familiar with, they scanned the classroom constantly to maintain eye-contact with as many children as possible and used repetition in imaginative and meaningful ways.

The important point is that there is no automatic connection between 'large' classes and transmission-based teaching. Depending on the strength or depth of teachers' beliefs in their own approach (their own more or less conscious answers to the questions below the line in the table that concludes Chapter 5) they will try to find and/or develop methodologies (personal teaching practices) consistent with their approach that are appropriate for whatever size of class they teach. By 'strength and depth' of belief we mean for instance, how robust teachers' reasoning is, whether their approach was learnt consciously or implicitly and whether or not they have had opportunities to discover what underpins their practice and to question it (see Chapter 6).

1.1.2 Because of what they are 'used to' – their previous experience and their resulting expectations and perceptions

Teachers in different school contexts will often have had very different previous learning and teaching experiences. These will influence their expectations of what a 'normal' class size is. These expectations will in turn strongly influence their perceptions of whether the classes they are expected to teach are 'large' or not.

Even within a single school if one teacher is teaching a class of 32 but the teacher next door has a class of 29, that difference may take on great significance in the first teacher's mind. The teacher with three more students may feel that they are teaching a larger class than their colleague in the next room.

1.1.3 Overcrowding, when the number of students in a room is greater than the room was designed for

There is also another, more obviously physical, reason why almost any number of students in one class can be thought of as a 'large' class. This has to do with the degree of overcrowding in the classroom, which may limit options and/or affect the teacher's 'managerial' role. Overcrowding can lead to a number of, mostly practical, problems, further discussed below.

- *Furniture and facilities:* Most rooms, and the furniture and facilities within them, are more or less explicitly designed for a particular number of people. Where a larger-than-expected number of learners are in the room either additional furniture and facilities will need to be provided (if available and if space allows) or learners will have to share the existing (insufficient) facilities. In either case, the space in the room will be less than is needed to accommodate the learners comfortably, which is bound to affect teaching and learning. The opposite is of course also true – it can feel uncomfortable to teach or learn in a group which fills only a small part of a large hall.
- *Circulation and movement:* In an overcrowded classroom, space for movement will be restricted. In very overcrowded classrooms, it may be impossible for both students and teacher to move around the classroom at all during the lesson. How much this affects a teacher's normal methodology will of course vary. A teacher from a more transmission-based educational culture may find such overcrowding less difficult to deal with than one who has a more 'dialogic' approach. However, it will restrict teaching possibilities, particularly for the dialogic teacher.
- *Possibilities for communication*: In an overcrowded classroom with restricted movement, communication possibilities will also be

restricted. The overcrowding will affect who can talk to whom, who can hear whom and what or who can be seen, by whom. In other words, overcrowding can affect teacher and learner audibility and visibility, as well as how possible it is to group learners for interaction and/or and the range of ways in which this can be done. Audibility and visibility problems are of course not unique to overcrowded or large classes, but in such contexts they are likely to need explicit consideration.

Some other physical aspects of the place context that may affect audibility and visibility in any classroom are shown in Table 8.2.

There may also be one final impact of 'overcrowding'. This is the psychological one of people being made to feel uncomfortable by having to be physically closer to other people than they would normally choose to be. What distance is comfortable probably varies from culture to culture, or even person to person and is therefore independent or semi-independent of any of the above physical realities of the classroom or the school.

TABLE 8.2 Factors that may affect audibility and visibility in any classroom

Audibility may be affected by:	Visibility may be affected by:
The acoustic properties of the materials from which the room is constructed.	The levels and types of lighting in the classroom
The presence or absence of intrusive noise from outside the classroom or school (e.g. industry, heavy traffic, airports, etc.).	The colours of the walls and ceiling.
Whether the physical structure of the school makes it necessary to think about the effects of noise generated in one classroom on other classrooms (which may, in part, explain, e.g. the Head teacher's approval/ disapproval of noise from classrooms).	The size of the physical space in relation to the size of the objects and/or script that need to be seen.
Characteristics of different speakers' voices.	Individuals' eyesight and whether or not those who need them have appropriate glasses or contact lenses.

2. Some reasons why 'large' classes exist

If the complaint about 'large' classes is so widespread, and has prompted specific research, why are 'large' classes still so widespread? As you might expect there is no simple answer. Below, we consider a number of different reasons which may explain why such classes continue to exist. You will see that the majority of reasons relate to the wider macro-context in which all educational institutions exist.

2.1 Lack of agreement about whether 'small' classes lead to greater achievement

You may be surprised to learn that researchers do not agree on whether there is a direct relationship between 'small' class size and student achievement, when comparing achievement across or between national education systems.

Many researchers have looked for evidence of a clear relationship between class size and achievement and concluded that there is little consistent evidence that learners' achievement or academic motivation or the quality of teachers' instruction have been improved by smaller classes (e.g. Tomlinson 1989a,b). In the United Kingdom, the report '*Class Size and the Quality of Education*' looked at reports on the quality of learning and teaching from school inspectors between 1993 and 1995, covering the teaching of mathematics, science, geography and history in almost 48,000 primary classrooms and nearly 43,000 secondary classes. The report concluded that: *no simple link exists between the size of the class and the quality of the teaching and learning within it.* (OFSTED 1995:4)

Researchers have found the above to be true ever since. The most recent research on the issue by OECD, reported on the BBC news in March 2012, confirms that reducing class sizes to below 35 appears to have little effect on student achievement. Instead, it is the quality and motivation of the teachers and the type of educational culture that are more important. As an example they point to Korea, a country where student achievement is high despite school class sizes that would be considered large by Western standards. (in 1996, 56.9 students per class in mathematics and 48.8 in science; Benbow et al. 2007:5). The OECD report attributes this success to teacher salaries being high (making teaching a career of choice for high quality applicants) and to Korean cultural values which strongly support educational achievement.

Of course, this whole argument about the relationship between class size and learner achievement depends, to be consistent, on comparing learners using standardised tests (e.g. PISA, TIMMS). Inevitably, results from these tests represent only a partial picture of what might count as learner 'achievement'. They cannot, if they are to be standardised, take into account the 'other learning' that children 'achieve' through their experience of the way in which the formal curriculum is enacted in their education culture (see Chapter 2). Neither can such standardised transnational tests take into account the learning 'achieved' by learners through the 'hidden curriculum', the secondary socialisation process that is part of and fundamental to any education system.

Are teachers misguided, then, in thinking that class size matters? Do the 'moans' have more to do with teachers' own comfort than their pupils' learning? If we think about large classes not in terms of individual teachers but of education systems as a whole, there are reasons to think that attempts to reduce class sizes might be counterproductive.

Individual teachers might well be right in thinking that smaller classes would be 'better' *for them* and *their learners* – especially if they know why they want a smaller class, and what they could do differently (better) if they had fewer learners in the classroom. However, having small classes throughout an education system might not necessarily turn out to be of benefit to the system as a whole in the long term, since ensuring that smaller classrooms lead to better outcomes across a whole education system is a complicated, expensive and time-consuming undertaking. For example, smaller classes require more teachers and more classrooms. Thus more money is needed, for teachers' salaries and teacher training places, and also for building more classrooms. Any demand for smaller classes in a context then, is in fact also a demand for other contextual changes also.

The economic argument is a very powerful one. Teachers' salaries are by far the biggest component of the budget of all education systems. According to recent OECD statistics from 42 countries, including those with large populations such as India and China, teachers' salaries account for an average of 79 per cent of educational expenditure (2011:64). A reduction of class size by, say, five pupils across a whole nation therefore, potentially has enormous financial implications in terms of paying the extra teachers required (apart from the difficulty of finding, and the costs of training, those extra teachers).

2.2. *Other contextual reasons*

We will now briefly list some further contextual reasons which may result in classes that are 'large', researched over many years by our colleague Hywel

Coleman. The first three have already been suggested in the discussion above: finances, number of teachers, and number of classrooms.

2.2.1 Financial factors

As noted above financial factors are by far the biggest issue influencing class sizes and also many other visible aspects of educational contexts such as buildings and resources. Here we consider broad issues regarding possible relationships between class size and budgets and funding at school level.

- *Budget:* A higher student–teacher ratio is one of the options a school has to help it 'balance the books'. Bigger classes may be judged preferable to, say, doing without a library or a toilet block.
- *Government allocations:* The systems governments use to allocate funds to schools may be connected to the numbers of pupils in a school or in a class, as was the case in the 'old' South Africa.

> In the black primary school system in South Africa, no formal limit is placed in class size, and in fact the government allocates funding to schools according to the number of pupils accommodated. There is thus a powerful incentive for school administrators to increase the size of their classes. (Peachey 1989:1)

- *Individual salaries:* In some places, the head teacher's salary depends on the number of pupils in the school – another incentive to keep numbers high. In others, individual teachers' salaries are so linked. In 1989 our colleague wrote this about Indonesia:

> In the case of [an] Indonesian situation with which I am familiar, for example, staff shortages provided only part of the explanation for the fact that classes were so large. It seemed that however many new teachers were recruited – ostensibly with the purpose of reducing class size – the classes continued to be very big. Somehow bureaucratic decisions were being taken which continued to make large classes for language teaching inevitability. How was it that those decisions came to be taken? (Coleman 1989:19)

He discovered later that teachers were being paid salary increments as their class sizes increased. Not surprisingly, in a context where salaries were probably low, they were unwilling to give the increments up for the sake of having a smaller class.

2.2.2. Teacher availability

Whether or not an education system has sufficient teachers will depend on the adequacy of its systems for initial teacher preparation and support for ongoing teacher development as well as on the relative contextual 'attractiveness' of teaching as a profession. The attractiveness of teaching in a particular national or regional context can change quite rapidly, due to the influence of changes in the geopolitical layers of the surrounding macro context. In Eastern Europe, for example, prior to the huge political changes of 1989/90, English teachers considered themselves to be reasonably paid. However, post-1990, teachers' salaries in many countries compared so unfavourably with those of other professions or other job opportunities which opened up (especially for English speakers) that many English teachers left the profession, despite the increased demand for learning English.

2.2.3 Accommodation

If there are not enough school classrooms, and if money or community effort is not available to build them, then overcrowding is inevitable.

2.2.4 Overall school size

It is fairly obvious that if a school has only, say a 100 pupils in total, while still dividing up learners into classes according to age, class sizes will be 'small'.

2.2.5 Location of school

Urban schools in many parts of the world tend to have larger classes than their rural counterparts. This is partly because of movement into the towns and generally lower population densities in the countryside, but it may also be due to social reasons too. In rural areas, for example, there may be more absenteeism as parents need children, especially at certain times of year, to work in agriculture. In the rapidly growing towns, however, parents may prefer their children to 'stay out of trouble', and so send them to school even if, as the quote below suggests, the educational benefits may be limited.

> As African cities continued to increase in size during the 1980s and 1990s, their declining economic situation led to a precipitous decline in the supply of basic infrastructure and urban services. In many African cities . . . [s]chools are becoming so overcrowded that many students have only minimal contact with their teachers. . . . (UNHCS 1996:91)

2.2.6 Global, national or regional demographics

Fluctuations in the numbers of children needing schooling can lead to more or less temporary overcrowding. Benbow et al. (2007) point out that between 1990 and 2000 the world's primary school age population grew from 600 to 648 million and that by 2015 that number could exceed 700 million. Increases in children attending school may also be a result of national policy decisions made in response to global resolutions. For example the United Nations Millennium Development Goals include an aspiration for primary education for all by 2015. To meet these goals, school fees in some countries have been reduced or removed, leading to increases in numbers attending school and so to larger class sizes.

Within a country population movements from rural to urban areas can, as we saw above, create different challenges for class sizes in different parts of the country. The population of a whole country may also increase unpredictably for various further socio-political reasons. 'New arrivals' of various kinds – refugees fleeing conflict, or people crossing newly opened borders, can cause education systems to become overcrowded. Population explosions or 'baby booms' may cause overcrowding for particular periods of time. These are often linked to an atmosphere of political or economic optimism within a context (such as the 'baby boom' that occurred throughout much of Europe after the Second World War). However, they may also be the result of other more culturally embedded reasons in a particular context. In China for example, the most 'propitious year' for people to be born – the year of the Dragon – occurs every 12 years, and regularly produces a significant 'boom'.

2.2.7 Social reasons

The kinds of opportunities for work and for play that exist outside school in a given society can make a difference to how long children stay in school. For example, in some places the immediate social environment holds significant 'risk' that young people will be attracted into undesirable activities (for example, drugs, smuggling, prostitution, and teenage marriages). In such places, as the following quote from China suggests, parents may prefer their children to be in school than outside, regardless of their academic prospects.

> I do not think the parents have many expectations of teachers' work. We are baby sitters. They must be satisfied if their children do not bully others, fight with each other, do not abuse drugs or steal others' belongings, and still quietly sit down in the classroom every day. (Wei 2010:170)

Lack of employment opportunities in their immediate context may cause young people to consider emigration, and so see the acquisition of the qualifications that schooling and education can provide as an essential passport to life elsewhere. They may choose to repeat years at school (and contribute to overcrowded classes) in a determined effort to obtain necessary qualifications. In other places, young people may deliberately 'fail years' at school or college, (and therefore repeat years and increase numbers) so that they can continue to take advantage of school facilities (for example access to sporting or musical opportunities) that would otherwise not be available to them outside the education system.

2.2.8 Reputations – of schools or individual teachers

Finally, but importantly, in education systems where there is some flexibility about which school learners attend, the high reputations of particular teachers or schools may attract large numbers of (suitably qualified) pupils, and so cause overcrowding. In cases like this we have the anomaly that it is the schools which are considered the best that have the largest classes.

The various headings above begin to create a framework for developing questions that can help you to think about any of the 'moans' you may have in terms of your immediate and wider context. If you do use this framework to examine the context of your 'moan' more closely, you may be able to identify changes you could make to begin to improve your situation. Alternatively (in the 'worst case scenario') you might find that as a teacher there is nothing that you can do to change matters, and that therefore you will just have to accept them as they are and work out how you can live with them (e.g. here, how you can adapt and extend your methodology so that it remains consistent with your approach whatever size of class you have). Some of your 'moans' may be issues over which you do have some influence. For example, if your moan is 'learners don't do their homework', a consideration of the issue using relevant features of the framework above may lead you to for example adjust the amount or type of homework you set, or devise workshops for parents.

From thinking primarily about physical conditions in classrooms, the next section looks more closely at influences on those classrooms that result from often less visible features of the school environment.

3. School/institutional culture

Our work has often taken us out of the United Kingdom to work with teachers in their own countries and we have been lucky enough to work in or visit schools in many different parts of the world. While there is much that is recognisable as a 'school' in all of these places, the design, layout and contents of these institutions vary considerably from one part of the world to another. In part, this has to do with geographical features such as climate, or available building materials, or with the influence of the wider socio-economic context. Some differences have clear links (to us) with the surrounding macro-culture, such as, for example, the presence of a Hindu shrine in a school compound. Other features however, such as how the available space is used, how accessible the school leaders' offices are to members of staff or to learners, the choices made regarding the overall décor, the form and content of the notices that can be seen and where these are placed, may reflect more subtle differences between the particular micro-cultures of the individual schools.

To put this (very/too) simply, while the physical structure of schools will often reflect the broader cultures of the place and the education system in which the school is situated, the way the spaces and buildings are used, decorated and kept will reflect the 'unique culture' of the particular institution.

We have found it useful when thinking of school cultures to remember the words of the American cultural anthropologist, Clifford Geertz, whose work influenced early culture researchers:

> Man is an animal suspended in webs of significance he himself has spun; I take culture to be those webs, and the analysis of it therefore not to be an experimental science in search of law, but an interpretative one in search of meaning. (Geertz 1973:5)

In other words, the interpretation of visible aspects of schools and what can be seen happening within them depends to a large extent on who is looking and interpreting. For example, Prosser (1999) talks about insider and outsider 'perceived culture'. He suggests that what is 'seen' and how things are interpreted will be affected by whether the interpreter is a member of the school community or not. So if you are going to try to understand your own school culture it might be an idea to enlist the help of an 'outsider' to add to your own 'insider' interpretation. Or, if you are an 'outsider' trying to make sense of a particular school culture, it would be worth also getting an 'insider' perspective.

We will turn now to the literature on organisational culture. Although this has mostly been developed in the field of management, it provides anyone (whether insider or outsider) with a rich source of ideas for beginning to understand the 'unique cultures' of different institutions, and how these 'cultural' differences may influence the success or otherwise of particular (educational) practices.

4. Cultures of organisations

In this section, we draw heavily on the ideas from two influential writers on organisational culture, Charles Handy and Edgar Schein. Although their ideas were originally conceived some time ago they remain influential, as can be seen by the new editions of their work that have appeared since their ideas were first published. As you will tell from the language used, they, in common with most other writers in the field, have their background in business rather than educational contexts, but we feel that their ideas can be useful 'thinking tools' as we consider 'the cultures' of our own institutions. We also look again at the work of Hofstede (see Chapter 2) whose 'cultural difference model', although talking about 'cultures' in general, provides some other ways of thinking about organisational and school cultures.

4.1 Handy's organisational cultures

The ideas we discuss first are drawn mainly from the work of Handy and colleagues (1993, 2009). They describe four main types of organisational culture: the Club or Power culture, the Role culture, the Task culture and the Existential or Person culture. They argue that it is appropriate that the cultures of organisations should differ, and suggest that many of the difficulties that particular organisations experience stem from various kinds of cultural 'mismatch'. Some examples for ELT in the educational context might be:

- Expecting an organisation to behave in ways which it finds culturally inappropriate. (For example, introducing an ELT approach that requires informal teacher-student relationships in a school that prides itself on is formality and on learners displaying visible signs of respect for anyone with the title of 'teacher'.)
- Trying to impose a certain *type* of organisational culture in inappropriate circumstances. (For example, suddenly decentralising educational decision making; giving schools full responsibility for designing the syllabus and choosing the materials used to teach the English curriculum, after decades during which they have only been allowed to act on the basis of instructions from central government.)

We will summarise key features of each of Handy's four main organisational types below.

The Club or Power culture

- is frequently found in small organisations.
- is a proud and strong organisation: it thinks fast and acts quickly.
- metaphor: a web: if the organisation grows too rapidly, or tries to do too many different things, the web can break and the organisation is destroyed.
- individuals are judged by results; and are not asked too many questions about how they achieved them.
- the culture depends on:

a) a centralised leadership: power and influence spread out from this central figure to a few key individuals who exercise control.

b) trust and empathy between its members: there are few rules, little bureaucracy and few meetings.

The Role culture

- is often stereotyped as a bureaucracy.
- metaphor: a Greek temple, upper stories and roof are supported by huge stone pillars (the departments). These provide strength to the organisation, and enable it to grow very large.
- has clear procedures which control the work of the departments and the way they interact. All members understand their role and, for instance, the appropriate ways to communicate with others.
- has managers on the 'upper stories' who co-ordinate activities and plan.
- views job descriptions as more important than individuals: people are frequently chosen to match roles rather than for their personal qualities.
- is successful in a stable environment: does not respond well to rapid change: if there is such rapid change, the temple may collapse.

The Task culture

- is job or project orientated.
- seeks to bring together the human and material resources needed to complete the job and then to let individuals get on with it.
- metaphor: net. Just as too many holes in a net can make it ineffective, so a lack of the 'right people' in the organisation can lead to fail.
- emphasises team work, has a flat hierarchy influence is widely spread and power is based on expertise; individuals working on the job, rather than top managers, have day-to-day control over their work.
- is very adaptable, and is appropriate where flexibility and sensitivity to the context are needed.
- moves quickly, thrives in a fast-changing environment and encourages individual talent.

The Existential or Person culture

- is unusual, since it is based on individuals who decide to collaborate for a particular purpose.
- doesn't need a lot of structure.
- is rarely found in organisations, as their goals are usually bigger than those of individuals.
- influence is shared and the power comes from expertise.
- ends when individuals decide to leave it.

Thinking about these four different organisational cultures, which description most closely matches the organisation you work for and why do you say this? If you were able to choose, which sort of organisational culture would you feel most comfortable working in, do you think, and why?

4.2 *Hofstede's cultural difference model*

Another tool that provides a way of thinking about features of (organisational) cultures is provided by Hofstede's 'cultural difference model'. The most recent version of the model is made up of six dimensions along which he suggests any culture may be placed. We visualise the labels given to these 'dimensions' as representing the extreme ends of a continuum. The first four dimensions were in the original model. The last two have been added more recently, drawing on the work of Bond (1991) and Minkov (2010), both cited in Hofstede et al. (2010)

The dimensions are as follows:

- **High or low power distance** – The extent to which the wider culture expects there to be a widely differing degree of power between those working at different levels within it. A high power-distance culture is one in which it is considered normal for there to be an established, agreed hierarchy and considerable difference in power and status between those working 'higher up' and 'lower down' in the society (or the organisations within it). A low power distance culture reflects a belief in the desirability of all members sharing more equal rights and status.
- **High or low uncertainty avoidance** – The extent to which members of a culture are comfortable with and accept ambiguity and risk. High uncertainty avoidance suggests an aversion to risk.
- **Individualism or collectivism** – Individualist cultures emphasise the important role of the individual and expect people to take initiative and be responsible for their own lives and work. More collectivist cultures are those whose decision making prioritises the good of the group, and which are therefore likely to discourage spontaneous individual initiatives.
- **Masculinity or femininity** – A more masculine culture holds values that in the West were traditionally viewed as male – competitiveness, assertiveness, ambition and concern for material success. A feminine culture would reflect a more nurturing orientation, emphasising consideration of others and their feelings.
- **Long- or short-term orientation** – Members of cultures with a long-term orientation recognise that what is true will depend on situation, context and time. They are willing and able to adapt existing traditions to changed conditions, and realise that it can take time to achieve results. Cultures with a shorter-term orientation are generally more concerned with establishing the absolute truth (a best or right way to do things). They respect traditions, have clear norms and focus on achieving quick results.
- **Indulgence or restraint** – Indulgent cultures recognise the need to allow members to follow their natural human drives to enjoy life

and have fun. More restrained cultures tend not to encourage (and maybe even to suppress) such needs, and regulate their members' behaviour through establishing strict social norms.

While these dimensions of cultural difference were not originally conceived for the study of the cultures of particular schools or organisations, we believe that they provide a further useful framework for thinking about features of such cultures.

If you drew six lines to represent the six dimensions above, where on each continuum would you place your organisation?
Does this help to explain any features of your institutional culture that you were not (consciously) aware of?

5. School leadership

Any school culture will be strongly influenced by the leadership/management style of the head teacher (as leader of the cultural group), as well as by the wider culture.

Surprisingly, the idea of providing specific training or education for school leaders/managers is a relatively recent one. The leadership style of most existing head teachers/institutional leaders will, therefore, only rarely be based on evidence-based principles of effective school leadership. Instead it will be most strongly influenced by a combination of existing cultural assumptions and practices in the wider context and their own personality or character type. If, for example, a new leader's previous successful experience as a teacher has been as 'person-fulfilling-a role' in a role culture, then once they are promoted to the role of head teacher they are likely to perpetuate that type of culture in the institution for which they are now responsible (regardless of whether it is or remains appropriate for that context). Depending on their level of personal awareness and whether they have had access to formal leadership training, this decision will be a more or less conscious.

Again, particularly in business settings, attempts have been made to describe different leadership styles and we turn to these next. Handy (1993) draws on Maccoby's (1976) study of managers in American corporations, to identify four character types of leaders or managers. These are as follows.

The Jungle Fighter: Jungle Fighters need power and see life as a battle for survival. They are protective of 'family', ruthless to competitors, domineering and create enemies easily.

The Company Person: *Company People* are orientated to the organisation, concerned with the human side of the company and committed to organisational integrity. They are disciplined and conservative.

The Games Player: *Games Players* take calculated risks and thrive on challenges. They are team players and good communicators who look for glory rather than riches.

The Craftsperson: Craftspeople are creators who are self contained and exacting. They are good 'masters' but poor team players.

We recognise that of course labels designed to apply to the leaders of American manufacturing companies are unlikely to be an exact 'fit' for the leaders of educational institutions all over the world. We introduce them only to illustrate some continua along which individual leadership styles may differ from one person to another. Thus, using ideas from all of the above, even within schools we can recognise principals, head teachers or school inspectors who may be more or less:

- aware of, and keen to demonstrate, their authority.
- straightforward in their relationships with their staff.
- determined to make their school 'the best'.
- willing to make enemies to get their own way/climb the promotion ladder.
- willing to take risks and/or difficult decisions.
- likely to blame others for their own mistakes.
- likely to openly praise good work from their staff or students.
- caring about/interested in staff members and students as people.
- positive about new challenges.
- good communicators (orally and/or in writing).
- dependent on others for their sense of self-worth.
- willing to delegate responsibility.
- conservative and reluctant to change.
- flexible about how they interpret rules.
- hardworking and/or good administrators.
- able (and willing) to justify their decisions.

It might seem that certain leadership characteristics are particularly appropriate for certain types of organisational culture. However, although there are likely to be overlaps between leadership types and organisational cultures, (for instance conservative leaders who like to be able to justify their decisions according to the 'rules' are likely to suit a Role culture, while flexible leaders, willing to delegate and take risks will probably be better suited to a Task culture) it is rare that they overlap entirely.

At this point you might like to pause and consider your own position. Even if you have no formal 'leadership' role in your school or organisation, as a teacher you are a leader in your own classroom. What kind of a leader are you? To decide on your answer, you might like to consider the following:

- *Which of the characteristics, listed next to the bullet points above, do you think that your students would say are most true of you? Which least true?*
- *Do you have any evidence for your answers?*
- *Do you feel that these characteristics clearly place you in one of the above four categories of leadership types?*

In this section, we have looked at the idea that different organisational cultures and types of leader exist and considered ways of describing these. We have suggested that there are relationships between organisational culture, leadership style and the layout and use of the premises in which the organisation exists: for example,

a) an organisational culture may influence both the type of leader (head teacher) considered appropriate to manage a school and the design and use of the premises

b) leadership style may influence which type of organisational culture exists in a particular institution, and how the premises are used

c) the existence of particular kinds of premises and traditions of use may, if unquestioned, suggest or even impose a particular kind of culture and leadership.

However, if you tried to use the frameworks above to make sense of your own context, you no doubt discovered that schools and people do not necessarily fit neatly into predetermined categories. In addition, the section above does not suggest what kind of evidence to look for or why. The final part of this chapter, therefore introduces the work of Schein (1992), as summarised by Hatch (1997). This contains useful guidance for some of the areas which you might think about and/or observe to deepen your analysis of the culture of your school.

6. Schein's levels of organisational culture

Schein proposes three levels of organisational culture which might be investigated. These, proceeding from the most visible to the invisible, are

1. artefacts;
2. espoused beliefs and values; and,
3. underlying assumptions.

The 'artefacts level,' the most visible of the three, is the easiest to observe. A school's artefacts can be such things as,

- how school members carry out daily rituals like assemblies or roll-calls,
- what sorts of habitual behaviour the school expects, such as lining up to go into classes after breaks, ringing bells or playing music to signal different times of the day,
- the way the school is decorated,
- the types of posters or notices that can be seen on public display,
- the school smells (disinfectant? school food?).

While 'insiders' may take all of these artefacts, the things they see, hear or smell every day, for granted, outsiders are likely to be more 'struck' by visible features at this level of culture. Trying to notice your institution's artefacts with an outsider's eye, and thinking about what they tell you about what is thought to be more or less important, can provide some insight into the next level of school culture.

The 'values and beliefs level,' according to Schein defines the basic organisational character of the school. This level lies as it were on the line between the visible and the invisible. For example, statements of school values (e.g. no tolerance of bullying) are sometimes explicitly posted on notice-boards or more widely published (in brochures for prospective students or the school websites). However, the extent to which such visible public statements correspond with the school's actual cultural values can usually only be inferred by observing the actual behaviours of the people within the culture.

It is not simply what is said or written that can reveal an organisation's values and beliefs, but also how it is said – the language that is used. For example in our context nowadays, the language that is used to talk about teaching and learning seems to be becoming ever more business-like (e.g. increasing numbers of educational organisations now talk about 'delivering modules' of teaching). To us, this language suggests values that are not primarily based on current beliefs about education, for instance 'deliver' suggests a transmission view of teaching and learning.

At the deepest, least tangible and visible level of organisational culture are 'underlying assumptions' – the deep drivers of members' behaviour that are taken for granted, largely unstated, and about which most members of the institution are unlikely to be consciously aware. They can only begin to become describable when somebody (usually an outsider or a newcomer) is struck by, and so questions/comments on, the behaviour that the assumptions give rise to. For example, in almost all educational cultures (and their wider cultures) there is a taken for granted assumption that testing will inevitably support learners' learning and that it is therefore appropriate (even necessary) to spend a significant proportion of classroom time on preparing for, administering and 'going over' tests. Also, in many contexts learners' test results are assumed to be a reliable and valid measure of how 'good' a teacher is. We believe these assumptions need to be questioned, although this seems unlikely to happen soon.

Schein suggests a number of questions that can help develop an understanding of the values and assumptions that underpin an organisation's culture. You will notice that some of these below (adapted from Hatch 1997:212), are similar to ideas already mentioned above.

How does the organisation see itself in relationship to other similar organisations within its environment?

- For example, does it see itself as 'dominant' (regarding itself and acknowledged as important and successful) 'submissive' (willing to take second place), or 'harmonising' (trying to fit in)?

How does it see the 'correct' way for people to behave?

- For example, does it expect them to be pro-active and take initiative, or does it expect them to await instructions and then carry them out?

How does it see the nature of time?

- Does the organisation always plan ahead, is it very much focused on the present or does it look back to the 'good old days' of the past?
- What 'units of time' are most important to the daily running of the organisation? For example, does it seem to manage its affairs day by day, or does it organise itself by the week, the month, the term, the year?

What kinds of human relationships does the organisation encourage?

- Does it see life and human relationships as cooperative or competitive?
- Does it encourage individualism or group decision making?
- Does it believe that the best way of managing the organisation is through expecting staff to follow decisions made by senior leaders or through collegial and participative shared decision making?

Does the organisation value diversity or homogeneity among its members?

- Does the organisation consciously try to employ a range of different types of people or does it recruit from a narrow group of people of a more or less similar kind?
- Are individuals within the organisation expected to conform to the particular organisational norms or are they encouraged to be different or innovative?

7. Summary and task

This chapter has tried to start from what is most 'visible' in schools and classrooms. We have suggested that at the level of classroom, how teachers teach may both influence and be influenced by what teachers think of the facilities and physical conditions in which they work. Although we could argue that the cognitive and affective contexts of teaching and learning are the most important (see Chapters 6 and 7), these will inevitably be affected by, and so cannot be entirely separated from, physical contexts. We also began to see that because of the interdependent nature of the relationships between the various layers of any context, even seemingly small changes to classroom conditions might have knock-on effects into, or require bigger changes in, the wider context. The need to understand the importance of establishing coherence between contexts at all levels becomes clearer in the chapter that follows.

The outward, visible, physical design and structure of a school, influences and is influenced by cultures at many levels. The design, layout, décor and use of school space can send messages. It can reveal values deriving from the wider and/or immediate cultures about who or what is regarded as important. An understanding of such values can contribute towards developing a more or less accurate picture of the institutional culture that a particular school may have.

We then considered some organisational culture and leadership types. We noticed that different organisational cultures and leaders with particular characteristics are likely to vary considerably in how they view their organisations, their relationships with those they 'lead' and in their attitudes to and so their approaches to the planning and implementation of significant changes.

The next chapter will look more closely at some aspects of the process of planning for and managing educational changes.

Task:

Look at Schein's questions above. Try to answer some or all of them for your own organizsation.

References and further reading

BBC. 2012. Does Class Size matter? [accessed 14 March 2012]. Available from: http://news.bbc.co.uk/today/hi/today/newsid_9703000/9703679.stm.

Benbow, J., A. Mizrachi, D. Oliver, and L. Said-Moshir, 2007. *Large Classes in the Developing World: What Do We Know and What Can Be Done.* USAID(US Agency for International Development) .

Coleman, H. 1989. *The Study of Large Classes* (Project Report 2). Leeds: Lancaster-Leeds Language Learning in Large Classes Research Project.

Coleman, H., ed. 1996. *Society and the Language Classroom.* Cambridge: Cambridge University Press.

Coleman, H. (in process). *Class Size and the Context of English Language Teaching.*

Geertz, C. 1973. *Interpretation of Cultures.* New York: Basic Books.

Glass, G. V. and M. L. Smith. 1978. *Meta-Analysis of Research on the Relationship of Class Size and Achievement*. San Francisco, CA: Farwest Laboratory for Educational Research and Development.

— 1979. 'Meta-analysis of research on class size and achievement'. *Educational Evaluation and Policy Analysis*, 1(1), pp. 2–16.

Handy, C. B. and R. Aitken. 1990. *Understanding Schools as Organisations*. Harmondsworth: Penguin.

Handy, C. B. 1993. *Understanding Organisations* (4th edn). London: Penguin.

— 2009. *Gods of Management: The Changing Work of Organisation*. London: Arrow Books/Random House.

Hashim, N. H. 1994. *Investigating the Problems of Materials and Resources in Large Classes*. Unpublished PhD thesis, School of Education, University of Leeds.

Hatch, M. J. 1997. *Organisation Theory*. Oxford: Oxford University Press.

Hofstede,G., G. J Hofstede and M. Minkov.2010. Cultures and Organizations: *Software of the Mind: Intercultural Cooperation and Its Importance for Survival* (3rd edn). New York: McGraw-Hill Professional.

Kuchah, K. and R. C. Smith. 2011. 'Pedagogy of autonomy for difficult circumstances: from practice to principles'. *International Journal of Innovations in Language Learning and Teaching*, 5(2), pp. 119–40.

Maccoby, M. 1976. *The Gamesman: The New Corporate Leaders*. New York: Simon & Schuster.

O'Sullivan, M. 2006. 'Teaching large classes: the international evidence and a discussion of some good practice in Ugandan primary schools'. *International Journal of Educational Development*, 26(1), pp. 24–37.

OECD. 2011. *Education at a Glance 2011: Highlights*. OECD Publishing.

OFSTED. 1995. *Class Size and the Quality of Education*. OFSTED report for academic years 1993/94 and 1994/95. London: Office for Standards in Education.

Peachey, L. 1989. *Language Learning in Large Classes: A Pilot Study of South African Data* (Project Report 8). Leeds: Lancaster-Leeds Language Learning in Large Classes Research Project.

Prosser, J. 1999. *School Culture*. London: Paul Chapman.

Schein, E. H. 1992. *Organisational Culture and Leadership* (2nd edn). San Francisco, CA: Jossey-Bass.

— 2010. *Organizational Culture and Leadership* (4th edn). San Francisco, CA: Jossey Bass Publishers.

Shamim, F. 1993. *Teacher-Learner Behaviour and Classroom Processes in Large ESL Classes in Pakistan*. Unpublished PhD thesis, School of Education, University of Leeds.

Shamim, F., N. Negash, C. Chuku, and N. Demewoz, 2007. *Maximising Learning in Large Classes: Issues and Options*. Addis Ababa: British Council.

Sheath, R. H. 1970. 'Administrative and educational decisions affecting the cost of school buildings'. *Buildings for Education: Technical Notes*, 2, 1970, pp. 3–18. Colombo: Asian Regional Institute for School Building Research.

Sitkei, G. E. 1968. *The Effects of Class Size: a Review of the Research*. Research Report 4, Research Study Series 1967–8. Los Angeles County Superintendent of Schools, Division of Research and Pupil Personnel Services. ERIC Document Reproduction Service No. 043124.

Slavin, R. 1990. 'Class size and student achievement: is smaller better?' *Contemporary Education*, 62(1), pp. 6–12.

Smith, M. L. and G. V. Glass. 1980. 'Meta-analysis of research on class size and its relationship to attitudes and instruction'. *American Educational Research Journal*, 17, pp. 419–33.

Smith, P. and M. Warburton. 1997. 'Strategies for managing large classes: a case study'. *British Journal of In-service Education*, 23, pp. 253–66.

Tomlinson, T. M. 1989a. 'Class size and public policy: Politics and panaceas'. *Educational Policy*, 3(3), pp. 261–73.

— 1989b. 'Class size and public policy: the plot thickens'. *Contemporary Education*, 62(1), pp. 17–23.

Trompenaars, F. and C. Hampden-Turner. 1997. *Riding the Waves of Culture: Understanding Cultural Diversity in Business* (2nd edn). London: Nicholas Brealey.

United Nations Centre for Human Settlements (HABITAT). 1996. *An Urbanizing World: Global Report on Human Settlements.* Oxford: Oxford University Press.

Wang, Q. and N. Zhang. April 2011. *Teaching Large Classes in China – English as a Foreign Language* (Notes). China: Beijing Normal University.

Watson-Todd, R. 2006. 'Why investigate large classes?' *Reflection*, 9, pp. 1–13.

Wei W. 2010. *The washback and impact of a high-stakes test on classroom teaching: A case study from China.* Unpublished PhD thesis. University of Leeds

A useful resource for recent thinking about 'large' classes in ELT is the University of Warwick's Teaching English in Large Classes (TELC) website [accessed 1 July 2012], from: http://telcnet.weebly.com/.

9

Planning and implementing classroom change

Introduction

In Chapter 1, we established three central dimensions for thinking about the term 'context'. In this chapter the perspective of *time* is again particularly relevant. This is because as time passes, it inevitably brings changes of all sorts with it – not only in the visible environment, but also in people and in ideas about what is important or how things should be done (see Chapters 3–7). Often these changes in people and ideas then lead to a desire to introduce other changes in classrooms or education systems and, as Hopkins (below) points out, the process of introducing these will *take time*.

> Rarely does policy take cognizance of implementation: there is an implicit assumption that implementation is an event that change occurs next Tuesday or in September, rather than it being a process that extends over a period of years. That recognition needs to be built into policy. (Hopkins 1987:195)

This need to recognise change as a process, taking time, often remains insufficiently acknowledged, even 25 years later, by those initiating change whether in a single classroom or an entire education system.

The main purpose of this whole book has been to enable and encourage you (teachers) to understand your contexts better for two reasons. First, so that you can make informed decisions about which types of small-scale changes might be appropriate, feasible and successful in your own classrooms. Second, because understanding more about your context can help you to manage your own expectations, feelings and responses to externally initiated changes. These changes, as many of you will know from experience, often require teachers to *do* things (sometimes very) differently, often without planners apparently realising that in order to do so successfully teachers will need to *think* differently too.

In this chapter, we begin by briefly considering teacher-initiated changes to what happens in classrooms. In the rest of the chapter, we discuss changes initiated by those outside the classroom and often also outside the school (externally initiated – often imposed – change). Within this, we discuss reasons for change, educational change in ELT as cultural change, attitudes to change and some implications of all this for models of change planning and change leadership. We end the chapter by proposing an outline for a parallel learning model for planning and managing a change process.

1. Teacher-initiated classroom changes

There is a sense in which all (English) teachers are making small, reactive and intuitive changes in response to what is happening in their classrooms all the time. In addition, when thinking about how best to support their learner's learning (see, e.g. Chapters 3 and 6), teachers may decide that they need to change, for example, the way they give instructions, the materials or types of activities they use with students or how they assess student progress. Like larger scale externally initiated changes, consciously planned teacher changes of this kind will almost always take time to 'get right', that is they take time to work in the ways, or have the effects, that the teacher hoped they would.

Millions of teachers make such small-scale, planned changes every day. However, books or articles explicitly describing and/or discussing teachers' reasons for, or processes for, introducing these types of changes are not numerous. The vast majority of all English teachers don't write about these small scale changes: to do so is not traditionally seen as part of a teacher's role and, anyway, most teachers have more than enough to do without having to write about it too!

Nonetheless, there have been several published stories, or case studies by (usually exceptionally dedicated and /or imaginative) teachers that have related their experiences of initiating and managing small-scale changes in their classrooms (e.g. Appel 1995; Badhekha 1999; Kuchah and Smith 2011). However, since such data are so scarce, we do not know of any attempt to consider such teacher data as a body of evidence from which it is possible to draw transferable conclusions. In addition, since each teacher's context is to some (maybe crucial) degree unique, the data that is available does not match a research approach which until quite recently (see Chapter 4) aimed to discover generalisable 'truths', rather than generate potentially transferable insights.

There are also publications by academics or teachers of teachers reporting on specific teachers' experiences of using a guiding framework of some kind (e.g. action research or exploratory practice) to structure the process of planning and implementing classroom changes (Burns 2009; Dadds 1995; Farrell 2007). However, such reports rarely relate to 'normal' classroom teachers, with most teachers either being personally exceptional in some way or participants in an 'out-of-the-ordinary' experience (e.g. participating in teacher learning programmes, or funded research projects). Overall therefore, there is little documentation of factors that affect the huge numbers of 'ordinary' teachers as they 'tinker' and make small-scale planned changes in their classrooms to try out ways of better supporting their learners' learning.

In addition, there is a wide and relevant literature in related areas such as teacher learning, teacher cognition, conceptual change, reflective practice, the discipline of noticing, exploratory practice and others (Alwright and Hanks 2008; Borg 2008; Malderez and Wedell 2007; Mason 2002). Such sources help illuminate the kinds of thinking and noticing processes individual teachers (might) more or less consciously undergo and/or might usefully undertake, first when deciding to initiate change in their own classrooms and then when going through the process of doing so. Some of this literature was referred to in Chapters 6 and 7.

While the literature directly related to factors influencing small-scale, teacher-initiated change may be sparse, there is an extensive literature that discusses various aspects of the process of planning and implementing larger scale externally initiated changes. This is understandable since such changes often require massive human and financial investment and so there is pressure to consider the extent to which they have been successful. We now turn to this literature, and especially the parts which highlight aspects of change implementation which we think are relevant to both large and small-scale classroom changes.

2. Externally initiated classroom changes

Here we first explore some main reasons why externally initiated changes might occur as, in our experience, the rationale or motivation for being asked to make such changes is rarely communicated to teachers. This only makes trying to carry out the changes even more difficult, because if teachers are to 'get something right' in their own classrooms, they need to have developed *their own* initial purposes for trying to do it. Consequently, if externally initiated changes are not to be perceived as an imposition, teachers need to be helped to understand the 'spirit of the reform' and to develop personal purposes for implementing the changes in their own classroom contexts.

We then look at the idea that educational change can often require culture change (see Chapter 2) and at how this contributes to making implementation very complex and time-consuming. If you as a teacher are finding it difficult to teach as you think you are supposed to, and feel that changing what you do is taking a very long time, this could be normal. In the following section, we consider ways of thinking about the planning of large-scale changes and why it is important for planners to find out about and be responsive to your needs as teachers, in much the same way as you are to your learners' needs. Here it is useful to remember that planners in any one education system are having to try to support many more teachers (and other people) than you do in your classroom (and that's difficult enough!). Next we look at people's feelings about externally initiated changes. If you have ever felt insecure or stressed when asked (or told) to make what are for you big changes in your classroom, you will know that you are not alone. We also consider the important role of leadership in a change process. Finally, we return to the idea that large- scale, externally initiated changes involve and affect many other groups of people in the (educational) culture, and discuss how, for successful implementation, everyone needs to learn in parallel.

2.1 Some reasons behind externally initiated changes

As you might imagine, there are potentially many reasons for initiatives that try to promote change in classrooms 'from the outside'. Here we discuss three of the most common.

2.1.1 To meet the challenges posed by globalisation

Globalisation, and the consequent perceived need for the citizens of any country to be able to use English to access and make use of all available knowledge resources worldwide (see Chapter 3), is frequently cited by policy-makers when justifying initiatives aimed at producing changes in English language classrooms. The example below is from Argentina.

> The reformed curriculum, which encouraged multilingualism and multiculturalism, viewed English as the language for international communication that would give its speakers access to many cultures and would thereby empower future Argentine generations with the necessary symbolic resources needed to fully function in the global market. English was thus seen as necessary to every Argentine citizen. (Zappa-Hollman 2011:618–19)

Furthermore this same globalisation makes it ever easier for policy makers to access (each others') ideas, increasing, as Hallinger suggests below, the extent to which similar educational changes are being introduced, using similar rationales in different parts of the world, often with little regard as to whether they are contextually appropriate.

> Advances in communication technologies have enhanced the formation of a global network of policy-makers with ready access to the same platform of educational innovations and reforms . . . there seems to be an inherent pressure to 'keep up with one's neighbours' which leads to the adoption of very similar reforms around the region and throughout the world. (Hallinger 2010:409)

2.1.2 To support equity and social cohesion within a country

English education within state school systems has over time developed in ways that do not provide equal opportunities for all learners. For example in many countries rural schools and learners tend to be less well served (in terms of resources, funding and teaching staff) than those in the cities. These inequities have the potential to create or exacerbate the kinds of divisions within societies that can lead to a lack of social cohesion and possibly even contribute to unrest. Some educational change initiatives are therefore specifically aimed to try to rebalance provision. Indeed Fullan (2003) suggests that introducing large-scale educational change of any kind is ultimately only justified if it contributes to helping to narrow the gaps that already exist between and within educational institutions in most countries.

2.1.3 'Looking Good'

A third reason for deciding to announce educational change initiatives is more obviously political. Since education is so important to parents and so to the whole society (the voters), it is tempting for politicians or leaders to use popular and seemingly beneficial initiatives (whether informed or not) to try to gain favour with and/or positive publicity among the people-as-voters. For example, at this point in the context of *time* in ELT, an announcement that a country aims to be bilingual within ten years, or that all learners will have access to English from their first year at primary school may provide good 'headlines' for those doing the announcing. Goodson (2001) calls such change initiatives, when they are announced with little thought as to their appropriacy for the context or to the practicalities of actual implementation, 'symbolic, triumphalist action'. He points out that any ensuing 'triumph' is likely to be superficial and short lived.

Whatever the stated reasons for the proposed changes (which may include some of the above as well as further contextually specific reasons), policy makers need to be able to explain them. They will therefore ideally develop robust reasoning (see Chapter 7) about the rationale for the change, to be able to confidently and clearly explain the 'why' of change to the many different groups of people who may be directly or indirectly affected.

The need to be able to provide such explanation becomes clear as we turn to a consideration of what educational (and particularly most current ELT) change entails, and of the challenges it poses.

2.2 *Educational change as culture change*

In previous chapters (1, 2 and 8) we have discussed the idea that cultures exist at different levels of context, and that that people's beliefs and behaviours are strongly influenced by the cultures to which they belong. Any member of a national culture is also, more or less directly, a member of the educational culture that prevails in that national context. Teachers and learners, for example, are likely to be strongly and directly influenced on a day-to-day basis by the national and regional educational culture, as interpreted by the organisation within which they work. Other adults in society, such as parents, are more peripheral members.

TABLE 9.1 Some features of an educational culture continuum (adapted from Wedell 2010)

Individuals within an institution feel they cannot (and do not) influence decisions made about their work	Individuals feel they can (and can and do) influence decisions made about their work.
Strict subject delineation	Subject boundaries are fuzzy and learners are encouraged to see links between areas
Subject matter is seen as a finite body of factual content knowledge to be 'delivered'.	Subject matter is seen as consisting of content knowledge and of the skills and understandings needed to be able to learn and use it.
Competition assumed between learners (and teachers)	Collaboration assumed between learners (and teachers)

TABLE 9.1 Continued

Individuals within an institution feel they cannot (and do not) influence decisions made about their work	Individuals feel they can (and can and do) influence decisions made about their work.
Hierarchical organisational culture. Changes almost always occur in response to 'top–down' initiatives from 'leaders'.	A fairly flat hierarchy within the organisation. Changes may be (and often are) initiated by teachers, from the 'bottom–up'.
Teacher as expert knower/transmitter of knowledge	Teacher as creator of learning opportunities and supporter of learning.
Learners as more or less identical empty vessels	Learners as individuals with personal prior experiences, existing knowledge learning styles and purposes.
Organisations and individuals with little experience of professional change, since teaching-learning approach and body of knowledge remains stable over time.	Organisations and individuals familiar with change since alterations to practices, knowledge and its uses are a permanent feature of professional life.

As first mentioned in Chapter 1, one way of thinking about how educational cultures may differ is to imagine them existing along a continuum whose extremes represent very different views of 'education' and its practices. Table 9.1 represents some aspects of behaviour, belief and experience that might be found at the extremes of such an 'educational culture continuum'.

No educational culture we have encountered has ever been consistently in only one column for all of the above categories. Most cultures do though tend towards one end of the continuum or the other. Therefore, if administrators, teachers and learners whose existing professional experience is towards the left-hand column in Table 9.1 are suddenly expected to implement changes that imply beliefs and behaviours more typical of the right-hand column, then this can amount to a culture change for all of them. Some examples of what this transition might mean for teachers and learners in an English language classroom are given in Table 9.2.

Over recent decades the stated aim of virtually all large-scale ELT (and other educational) change initiatives has been to 'move' classroom (language) teaching closer to the right-hand column in Table 9.2. Achievement of such an aim has, for most implementers in most educational contexts, represented

TABLE 9.2 Transmission-based and dialogic ELT classrooms (adapted from Wedell 2010)

	Transmission-based classroom	Dialogic classroom
Main content of the 'lesson'	The written text in the coursebook and the grammar structures and vocabulary items that are exemplified.	The experience of engaging in and talking about a variety of tasks and activities (some of which may be in a textbook), aimed at developing skills, communicative competences, or the use of specific language items.
How learning is assumed to take place	Through the teacher presenting the lesson, with explanations of new grammatical structures and vocabulary items, which learners then 'learn' outside the classroom. Formally correct performance is expected and once achieved (often through a single assessment by the teacher), learning is assumed to have occurred.	Through the learners engaging with experiential, task or problem solving based activities, to be carried out as far as possible in English. Formally incorrect language used during oral or written classroom activities is regarded as evidence of learning taking place. Unless it impedes communication, it is usually not commented on during activities. Commonly occurring language problems will be noted by the teacher and used to inform future lesson planning.
Types of classroom interaction	Teacher presents information abut the language and/or asks learners grammar, vocabulary or comprehension questions, they answer.	Teachers and learners interact (including asking each other questions). Learners may work alone or interact with one another in pairs or groups in order to complete learning tasks.

TABLE 9.2 Continued

	Transmission-based classroom	Dialogic classroom
Assumption about learner needs and behaviour	All learners have the same language learning needs and will learn in the same way.	Learners have different language (learning) needs and learning styles. It is expected that individuals or different groups will respond to tasks and activities in different ways.
Where learning takes place	Learning, understood mainly as memorisation, is expected to take place outside the classroom. In the classroom the teacher tests the extent of learning.	Learning takes place through working with and using language both in the classroom and outside it.
Classroom focus	On the teacher as the provider of knowledge about the subject.	On the learners and their development as competent communicators. (The teacher's main role is to be a skilled and responsive provider of appropriately sequenced and focused opportunities for all learners to learn.)

a culture change. Despite decades of educational research, and numerous attempts to introduce more 'communicative', 'learner centred' approaches to education systems worldwide, many features of (language) teaching and learning in most systems remain at, or gravitate back towards, features of the left- hand column in Table 9.2.

This is not entirely surprising for two main reasons. First, since rapid change in many visible material and technological aspects of life seems increasingly to be the norm worldwide, educational planners have often expected the visible outcomes of their change initiatives to be achieved within a similarly short time-span. However, if, as we believe and explain below, seeing visible evidence of different classroom ELT behaviours depends on implementers working through a process of invisible culture change, this is bound to take considerable time. Second, cultural changes in education systems do not occur in isolation. They have implications for the present and future actions and behaviours of large numbers of people both within education and outside it. These implications are rarely taken sufficiently into account (or understood?) by planners, resulting in slow progress or disappointing (or unanticipated) change outcomes, which may lead policy-makers to radically adjust or halt the original initiative.

For example, imagine that a national change initiative does develop a means of successfully supporting most teachers to learn to teach in responsive, dialogic ways, and so enables most young adults to develop as creative, independent and critical thinkers. What impact might this have over time on ideas about the existing structures of the education system and the wider society? What are the implications for the existing national social and/or political status quo? Then there is the question of 'standardisation' (of e.g. materials and the rate of 'covering' them). A common justification for 'standardisation' within education relates to equity of provision. This is an argument that often presupposes the need for transmission-view of teaching and learning. Current understandings of the learning process with their focus on responding to the needs of every learner however imply a move away from the simple ways of trying to ensure 'standardisation' as above. In that case, when individual teachers are using different materials and doing different things in their classrooms, will parents still believe each child has access to the same opportunities? What about the testing system and will it be possible to maintain reliable, measureable standards to show who has 'passed' and who has not? What effects might a lack of such standards have on future social and/or political developments within society at large? If possible answers to these questions (and others like them) have not been sufficiently taken into account from the beginning of a change planning process, it is easy to imagine that political decisions might be taken to halt a change if unanticipated (and 'undesirable') results become evident. Such a halt would leave any teachers who have invested time and energy in their own 'reculturing', frustrated and disillusioned.

At this point, you might wonder whether large-scale, externally initiated changes can ever be successful, and indeed many have not been – but read on!

2.3 Planning effective educational change

Let's start with an idea we have discussed before: any education system and the institutions through which it carries out its roles (ministries, bureaux, commissions, education offices, schools and colleges) is part of and represents a variety of cultures.

Before we go on, you might like to think back to Chapter 2 and consider

- *the cultures that your education system is part of, and*
- *the cultures that exist within your system.*

At all layers of these cultures, there will be beliefs and ways of behaving that are both shared across layers and specific to a particular layer. Educational planners need to consider these multiple and overlapping existing cultures when planning changes that will affect them. Fullan (1992) calls any change that requires teachers (and other education professionals) to change their professional (and possibly also personal) invisible beliefs and visible behaviours to be successful, 'complex educational change'. We believe that in many contexts ELT change falls into this category.

If you have been teaching English for any length of time, you will probably have experienced some curriculum reforms. Did these challenge your existing ways of teaching, require you to learn different or new skills, and /or behave differently in the classroom or school? If so, they were asking you to make a complex change.

So what are core issues that change planners need to consider when planning 'complex' educational change? We suggest three below.

2.3.1 The need to allow time and support for implementers to think and rethink their ideas about teaching and learning

Plans are often made to introduce for example, a new curriculum, testing system or textbook based on a new approach into an education system. If the new approach is very different to that which already exists, success will depend on the extent to which teachers (and also administrators, leaders, learners and their parents) are able to *rethink* at least some of their ideas about and expectations of teaching and learning (pedagogical beliefs), and *adapt* their (classroom) behaviour and expectations accordingly.

Such rethinking takes time, usually more time than planners acknowledge. In part this is because to be able to rethink, the people involved need to have 'thought' – discovered and articulated what they already 'think' – in the first place. Many may never have consciously thought about some of the fundamental ideas about teaching and learning that are challenged by complex educational changes.

For example, when we discussed (language) learning in Chapters 4 and 5, did you already have answers to the questions about what language and/ or (language) learning is, in a form which consciously guided your classroom decision making? If you did not, you would still have been planning your teaching according to some 'taken-for-granted' understandings of 'language' and '(language) learning', acquired from your previous experiences as a learner and teacher in your context. So, if you were expected to implement an ELT change that introduced new ideas about language and learning, before you could begin any 're-thinking' you would first need to 'think' (become conscious of your existing taken-for granted views).

Such thinking and rethinking is not easy or quick, and often needs or is helped by someone who can scaffold the process. Similarly, learning new teaching skills and practices takes time, and needs support, even when the rethinking that has been done means that a teacher does see the new skills as desirable. These processes of rethinking and learning the use of new skills probably develop together over time, with teachers perhaps encouraged to 'complete' their processes of rethinking if they notice positive effects of their use of new skills and practices on learners' learning.

Planning according to the timescales necessary to support such a process is in itself often very difficult, because educational changes can rarely be separated entirely from national political contexts, which will themselves often change several times within the sorts of time-scales needed for educational change. Research suggests (e.g. Fullan 2007; Polyoi et al. 2003) that depending on the degree of culture change that a complex educational change represents for the education system as a whole, it can take from 5 to 25 years to implement. The need to shrink educational change planning timescales to fit political time-scales is we believe one frequent reason for the generally unsatisfactory outcomes of large-scale change initiatives. A way of freeing change processes from such constraints would be for national politicians to agree to make education a national rather than a political issue and so enable longer term planning to occur. While this has previously been suggested (Cox and Le Maitre 1999), there is as yet little sign of the idea being accepted in any context.

2.3.2 The need to try to ensure that as many implementers as possible have positive attitudes to change

Positive attitudes to the idea and reality of any proposed change, on the part of the individuals and institutions affected by it, are bound to be one of the most important factors (perhaps even more important than existing knowledge or skills) in determining whether or not changes have the hoped-for effects or, in extreme cases, whether they actually take place at all.

Attitudes to change are likely to be affected by a large number of contextual factors at the personal and institutional level. First of all, attitudes to making the effort needed for the rethinking and skill development that a change requires will be affected by whether or not, and the extent to which, individuals and institutions have previous experiences of educational changes, and whether these have been positive or negative. Next, there is the extent to which people feel dissatisfied with the present situation (Kennedy 1988; Whitaker 1993) and so feel that the proposed change is needed and will actually improve matters. For example, many people in the countries of Eastern and Central Europe were initially very open to the idea of educational change in 1989–90 when they underwent major political changes, because of dissatisfaction with their previous education systems.

Attitudes to change are, of course, not fixed, and may themselves change, for better or worse in response to how the change process is planned and implemented. They may change for the better if the purpose and benefits of the proposed changes are clearly stated in comprehensible terms, or if the change process is given wider legitimacy by being openly supported by the institutional leadership or by respected leaders in the wider educational or socio-economic environment. One factor that seems to be particularly influential in developing positive attitudes to change among institutions and individuals is clear evidence that people who most teachers respect as 'key leaders' (Henry and Walker 1991) within the profession are 'early adopters' of the proposed changes (Markee 1997; Waters 2006). The support of such 'key leaders' within an institutional context may similarly provide an important impetus for teachers who wish to introduce personally initiated change in their own classrooms.

You might like to think about which members of the national English teaching profession in your context you would regard as a 'key leaders'. Would their clear support for a change influence you and your fellow professionals in a positive way? Would you know how to find out their opinion of a proposed ELT change?

Positive attitudes to change may also be encouraged by evidence that the change planners are being realistic and that their planning is taking the successful implementation of the changes seriously. Such evidence may be provided by, for example:

- canvassing teachers' and other professionals' opinions about the appropriacy/desirability of the proposed changes, and listening to their views in a genuine consultation process;
- a clear commitment to, for example, adequate funding throughout the lifetime of the change process;
- signs that they have spent time and (informed) thought on designing appropriate systems and programmes of professional support for the rethinking and new learning that implementers will need to undergo;

- signs that the time-scales for the various stages of the process are realistic (sufficient, informed).

Evidence that the national planners are taking the change seriously is likely to encourage implementers to have a more positive attitude towards the change and take it seriously too. The opposite is also true. Desired attitudes need to be modelled and are 'infectious'.

We suggest that most of the above also holds true for changes that you might wish to introduce in your classroom and/ or institution. If the changes expect your learners to behave in significantly different ways from those they are used to from their teaching-learning experiences in other classrooms, you too will need to start with the changes *they* would like to see, discuss and agree what *their* purposes are, and how changes will benefit *them*. Even having done so, you cannot expect all learners to adopt and fully understand the changes from one day to the next. You may find that you need to introduce the changes more slowly than you would like to, and so allow learners to feel comfortable and secure about the implications of one stage of the change process before being expected to cope with the next.

Finally, and perhaps most obviously, attitudes to change are more likely to be positive when those affected by change can see that it brings personal and/or professional and/or material gains with it. As we said above, complex educational change requires a lot of work. This usually means that, for several years implementers have to work harder, in terms of both the time and the mental effort that they devote to their job. Most teachers, however dedicated they may be, will only be willing to consistently spend this extra time and use up this extra energy over number of years if they feel that what is being gained in some way outweighs what they are losing in terms of personal comfort.

Gains may be concrete, in the form of better working conditions due to investment in new facilities and resources, or higher status resulting from salary increments or promotion. Gains may also be less tangible in the sense of feeling that the changes really do help provide a better education for the learners, or make the classroom atmosphere friendlier, and so result in increased job satisfaction. Whatever forms gains may take however, change planners at any level need to recognise that *those affected* by change must perceive gains of some kind if they are to remain committed to positively supporting the change project. This is especially true, since as discussed in the next section, there are many ways in which people can feel threatened by complex change.

The above is, of course, again also true in for changes you may wish to introduce in your classroom. Learners are more likely to engage with whatever new behaviours or ways of thinking the change demands of them, if they can see clear advantages, to them personally, from doing so. A promise that the changes will eventually help them learn X or Y, for example, is not enough. As the process unfolds learners have to experience their involvement as worthwhile to them: for example, they have more fun, 'don't notice time passing', find lessons more interesting. In addition, the new practices do actually have to result in more/better learning for more learners, and learners have to realise that this is so. You may often need to think about how to help learners to recognise the progress they have made as a result of the change, and so come to this realisation.

2.3.3 The need to understand how implementers may experience change

However appropriate the planning, change involves people and their feelings. Fullan (2007) repeats what he said in 1981,1991 and 2003 when he suggests that underlying the relative failure of so many hoped-for educational changes is insufficient consideration of how the proposed changes will be experienced by the actual implementers.

> Neglect of the phenomenology of change – that is how people actually experience change as distinct from how it might have been intended- is at the heart of the spectacular lack of success of most social reforms. (p. 4)

For those professionally affected by a complex change, the process of thinking and rethinking is not purely rational. It is likely to affect their beliefs, which are connected to their attitudes, values and feelings. Untangling one from the other is difficult (see, e.g. Woods 1996).

Others (e.g. Fullan 2001; Hutchinson 1991; Markee 1997) have also pointed out that the introduction of complex educational change can generate feelings of insecurity, vulnerability and potential stress among implementers. They suggest that this is because, unsurprisingly (especially early on in the change process) many implementers feel that they are not yet as competent at (and so confident about) the 'new' ways of, for example, teaching or administering, as they are at their 'old' existing ways of working.

Blackler and Shinmin (1984) propose the idea that change is often viewed negatively because it threatens people's 'key meanings' (which we see as including a range of other labelled concepts such as identity, sense of self-efficacy, values and beliefs). They suggest that it is key meanings that provide human beings with their day to day stability and security, and affect how they perceive themselves and their relationships with others. Since complex educational changes often require substantial rethinking of professional beliefs as well as learning of new behaviours throughout the layers of an education system, they are potentially threatening to, for example, implementers' feelings of competence and so to (some aspects of) their existing professional (and personal) identities and relationships (key meanings). These threats can lead to an understandable resistance to change on the part of those so affected.

> To protect key meanings we will defend the contexts within which they developed. Reason, persuasion, argument by others are not enough to help people adjust to significant losses, for no-one can solve for someone else the crisis of re-integration that disruptive changes impose. (Blackler and Shinmin 1984:84)

Although different individuals will of course react differently to the pressures of change, the greater the extent to which the proposed change requires implementers' to alter their existing ways of thinking and working, the greater its potential to destabilise existing key meanings. If participation in the change process makes most implementers *feel* vulnerable and insecure they are unlikely to participate with much enthusiasm.

Once again, it is important for you to be aware of how your learners may feel about any changes you introduce to your classroom. If you try to alter aspects of your practice in ways that make it necessary for them to 'rethink' their behaviour and beliefs about their role, for example being expected to take more responsibility for their own English learning, or to participate more in classroom tasks and activities, learners will probably respond differently. Some learners may find the 'new role' more unsettling than others (especially if teachers in other classes are not making similar changes), and so will react in different ways when you begin to make the change, and accommodate to it to different extents and at different speeds.

Although it is impossible to anticipate in advance exactly how a given group of teachers, administrators or learners will respond to the demands of a complex change, it is important to recognise that most people find challenges to their accustomed ways of doing things unsettling. This again emphasises the importance of giving educational change time, and also suggests the need to provide implementers with ongoing support of the psychosocial kind (such as that provided by effectively trained mentors). If too much change is introduced too quickly, too many existing key meanings may be challenged simultaneously, and the result is likely to be a negative rather a positive attitude to the change process.

Planning change bearing all of the above issues in mind suggests the need for exceptional leadership. In the next section, we discuss some desirable characteristics and behaviours of change leaders.

2.4 *Leading educational change*

Here we discuss the ideas of leadership mainly in the context of large-scale, externally initiated changes. However, as before, many ideas are relevant to teachers as change leaders in their own classrooms`.

> Of all of the MDGs [Millennium Development Goals], universal access to basic education is surely the easiest to achieve. The technology is the best understood and most straightforward. (Sachs 2008:301–2 in McGrath, 2010:246)

The above quote represents a still common, rational or technical view of educational change planning and implementation. It gives an impression of change leaders who control and direct the 'technology' to implement their preplanned changes to achieve predetermined aims against which successful outcomes can be clearly measured. Such change leaders therefore, in theory at least, know where they are going, how they are going to get there and when they have arrived.

As will be apparent from all we have said so far, educational change processes are rarely so straightforward. More recent, evolutionary, views of such processes (e.g. Levin 2008) recognise the need to take account of the issues raised in the previous section (e.g. the actual experiences and attitudes of the many people involved) as the process evolves. Such views therefore recognise that the speed, the manner of proceeding, and the extent to which the aims of the change are ultimately achieved, will depend on the, itself everchanging (often in very unpredictable ways), implementation context. Leaders of such a process cannot know, in advance, exactly how change implementation will develop or indeed what the final outcomes will be. At any given stage of the implementation process, they depend on obtaining information about the current stage to plan and manage subsequent stages. Important change leadership characteristics therefore include:

- A high tolerance for uncertainty about the exact manner in which the change will be implemented.
- The mental ability to cope with the very complex inter-relationships between all the variables that need to be considered at every stage of the change implementation process (Bennett 1996).
- Deep coping skills (Beare et al. 1992) to face up to and deal with unexpected challenges by, for example, changing strategy or timing, rather than just ignoring them, hoping that they will go away, or abandoning the original purpose for the change.

Leaders cannot plan the implementation of complex educational change in isolation. First, they need to be clear about the change aims and the reasons behind them. Then they need a thorough understanding of their own educational context, to be able to communicate aims and reasons appropriately to implementers of all kinds (e.g. administrators, institutional leaders and teachers). If educational change is viewed as an evolutionary process, implementers' understanding of the change aims, and their willingness to report honestly on implementation progress at any given stage, are crucial for change leaders to plan future stages appropriately. Leaders therefore also need to create an implementation 'climate' in which honesty is valued, whether what is reported is positive or not.

What we have said about leadership so far is also relevant to you as leaders of smaller scale changes in your own English classrooms. Before introducing change, you need to be clear about:

- what, given your understanding of your context, it is feasible for you, probably alone or with one or two colleagues in the first instance, to change;
- who, if anyone, needs to be/could usefully be informed about your proposed change;
- why you feel the changes that you wish to introduce will be worthwhile; and
- how you will introduce and explain the need for the changes to learners, colleagues, parents and anyone else who may question you/need to be informed, about them

Once you begin to introduce change, you need to be confident enough in what you are doing to:

- consciously seek out information about others' reactions to the changes you have introduced, and
- be able to cope flexibly with those reactions, particularly with different learners' reactions to your change(s).

Being a change leader, whatever the scale of the change, is an extremely demanding role. The literature suggests three responsibilities likely to be common to complex change leaders in all contexts. These are discussed below.

2.4.1 Ensuring good communication

We have said that implementers are likely to enter the change process with different attitudes to change, and are likely to experience change in different ways. It is essential therefore for leaders to establish effective systems of communication, using regular meetings and/or information bulletins to share their current understanding of the changes, their plans for the next stage of the change process and the ultimate aims of the changes with the implementers. In an evolutionary change process, feedback from those taking part in the actual implementation process itself will provide an important source of information for current understandings and future plans. Leaders therefore also need to ensure that mechanisms exist to ensure that implementation of the change is monitored systematically enough to provide insights and information from implementers and learners in a form that can be used to help inform the next stage of the process.

If you are introducing changes in your classroom, you will need to think of ways of finding out about how your learners are experiencing the change. It might be useful to hold regular brief discussion sessions or to provide time for learners to give written reactions, so that they can talk, or write, about their experiences of the changes that you have introduced. Their responses will help inform both your planning for subsequent stages and the pace at which you make the changes.

2.4.2 Involving as many people as possible

Ideally the largest possible (and practical) number of potentially concerned and affected people ought to be involved in initial decisions about the aims of any educational change, and how they might begin to be achieved. Such involvement makes it more likely that there will be a mass of committed people (a 'critical mass'; Markee 1997) who understand the aims of the change, available to actually implement it (Wedell 2009). Broad agreement that change is desirable and about how, in outline, it might be achieved does not mean that everybody involved has to agree completely about every aspect of the change or the implementation process. In fact, Henry and Walker (1991) and Hutchinson (1991) both suggest that the more different, but committed, points of view there are, about how to work towards the aims, the wider the available range of potential strategic options. If different points of view and strategies are discussed, it is more likely that any problems that arise will be dealt with positively and effectively (see group dynamics, Chapter 6).

Leaders genuinely wanting to encourage implementers' involvement during the change process must also be willing to share some of their responsibility with those who are willing and able to take it. Shared responsibility will help implementers to feel that they have some control over the change process, and personal responsibility for the decisions that are made. Psychologists use the term 'internal locus of control', while sociocultural theorists (e.g. Wertsch 1993) use the term 'agency' to refer to the feeling of having some control over and responsibility for what happens in the (work) environment. The more 'agency' implementers feel they have, the more likely they are to feel satisfied with the ongoing effects of the change process.

In practice, large-scale involvement from the very beginning of the change planning process rarely happens. One reason may be the great physical (and particularly social) distance that exists between national level planners and the other layers of implementers in the many educational cultures that are 'high power-distance' (see Chapter 8). Another is the strong belief in rational top-down models of educational change planning and implementation that continues to be held by change planners in many contexts.

At the classroom level, distance between planners (the teacher) and implementers (teachers and learners together) need not exist to the same degree. Some negotiation and discussion between teacher and learners about what changes to introduce, the aims of doing so and how to achieve them ought, in principle, to be much more possible when the prevailing approach is, or is becoming more learner or learning-centred. How easy it is to carry out in practice will be influenced by how the culture in a given context views the appropriate roles of teachers and learners (Wright 1987).

2.4.3 The need for 'training' and support for professional development

We have often mentioned that implementers need to be supported by change leaders as they work their way through the change process. Leaders will need to consider firstly what support systems will be necessary to enable implementers to be able to *learn* to do what is required by the change, and then what conditions will need to exist in their working environment to support them in doing it. For example, for teachers, the conditions provided to support the learning element need to be more than just a one-off workshop or a series of lectures about the principles underlying the change and a demonstration of the practices associated with it (Hayes 2000; Malderez and Wedell 2007; Van Veen and Sleegers 2006; Waters 2005). Conditions must be established that will enable the learning process to be supported over time, while teachers go through the thinking/rethinking work mentioned above, and have access to repeated scaffolded cycles of skill development work. Other types of 'learning conditions' (apart from time) will also need to be considered for all involved, such as, for example, where the learning takes place, who will do the supporting and how prepared these supporters are for their roles.

Since complex change takes time, leaders need to try to design ongoing 'learning' programmes that give implementers opportunities to come together at various points in time during the implementation process. At such meetings they will be able to support, reinforce or challenge each others' developing understanding of what the changes mean, as they reassess their existing beliefs in the light of their implementation experience. These opportunities for frequent meetings to reassess with others what implementation actually entails can contribute greatly to developing confidence and feelings of ownership among implementers, and so to the ultimate success of the change process.

Teachers making changes in their classrooms will also need to take time to support learners in the development of whatever new skills and understandings are needed to be able to participate fully in the proposed changes. For example, if a teacher wants or is being expected to introduce practices associated with a communicative approach in the classroom, this will involve some use of pair and group-work. Learners will need support over time to adapt their behaviour to these scenarios, and to learn how to work effectively in pairs and groups.

So what might a model for planning and implementing change which supports a view of change as an evolutionary process look like? We propose such a model below.

3. A parallel learning model

There are two important features of large-scale complex educational change. The first is that although a particular change initiative is thought of as a single project, a number of different types of people play different roles in the process: it is a whole with many parts. The second is that learning is central.

We see three main types of learning that need to occur in any change process. First, everyone involved will, throughout the process, need to be learning the new ways of thinking and new practices that the initiative aims to bring about. Second, because the context is a whole with different parts, so the change process must affect all the parts in a congruent way. As noted above, throughout the change process those working in each role will need to get information from others in different roles so that they can both manage their part of the process responsively and maintain 'the whole'. This obtaining of information is a second kind of learning – an ongoing updating of the understanding of context as the change process unfurls.

Third, again because all participants are working together on a single change process, the outcomes of the learning that takes place in each separate role as a result of attempting to implement the next stage of the process also need to be shared, in appropriate ways, across roles, so that what has been learned in one role can be taken into account (in whatever ways are relevant) by those working in other roles. For example, 'teachers of teachers' may discover (learn) that the existing planned support for teachers has not enabled them to reach the stage in the learning process that was envisaged. They not only pass this information (with evidence) on to those responsible for the planning and allocation of resources for this strand of the project (as in the second type of 'learning' above), but also pass on their interpretations of what the problem was and what solutions might be possible (the third type of learning). The planners, in turn, might (also using other available information) then decide, for example, to provide different facilities or materials, change the timing, duration or format of teacher support, change the site, group size and/or provide further support for the teachers of teachers.

Finally, to enable people to do the second and third types of learning, they may need to be supported in learning to develop appropriate ways of discovering information from others, understanding what it means (and what it does not mean) and using the meanings to support the decision-making that their role in the process demands.

Ideally any model for planning and managing a change process will take into account the need for these various types of learning to occur, which will enable congruence to be maintained across the whole system. This 'whole', change system, putting, as is appropriate in education, the learner at the centre, could be viewed as another 'onion' (Figure 9.1).

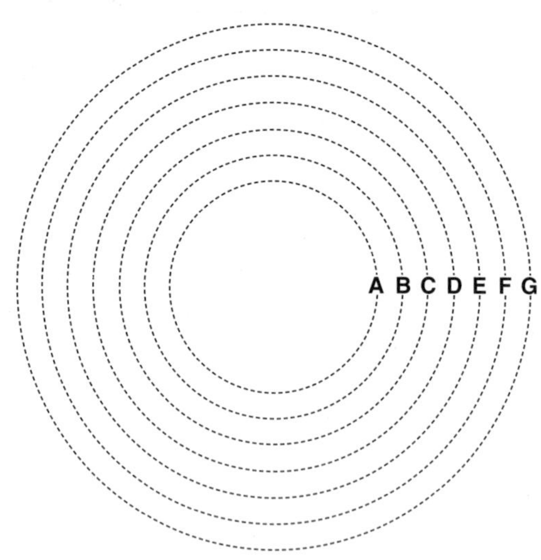

A. Learners
B. Teachers
C. School Leaders
D. Local Education Officers
E. Teacher Trainers, Inspectors
F. Regional Education Officers
G. Policy–makers, National Planners

FIGURE 9.1 *The change context 'onion'.*

At the outer layer – the one furthest away from the learners, and the one that contains and constrains all others – are the national policy-makers and planners, usually found in ministries. At the next layer in, regional or provincial education officers can usually be found together with those responsible for support for teacher development of one kind or another (e.g. inspectorate, 'researchers' or 'teacher trainers'). Further still, there are usually more local versions of these at city, or district level. Next come the leaders in institutions, then teachers, and finally, the central target of any change, the learners. This education 'onion' is of course situated within the wider society whose members (especially parents) will also need to learn.

Assuming the aim of the reform is contextually appropriate, then recognising that the process needs to be considered and planned for as a coherent whole is the only way of enabling the broad aim of the reform, the spirit of it, to be reflected in locally appropriate ways in all classrooms and so benefit most learners' learning. Judgement of whether a change process is effective should not be based on whether implementation is identical in every classroom. Instead, an effective process is one where, over time, all those involved develop a shared understanding of the purposes and potential benefits of the change, shared principles for working out how these can best be adjusted for local classroom contexts, and agreement about what evidence could be looked for, when and from whom, to make judgements about the success or otherwise of the (stage in the) change process.

We call a model which allows all the above types of learning to take place across and between all the layers a parallel learning model. We call it this because all people involved in all layers of the onion need to be learning in all the above ways (appropriate to their role) more or less simultaneously (in parallel) throughout the process.

If planning on the basis of this model is to stand any chance of being appropriate, national planners will first need a full understanding of their context and of the principles of evolutionary approaches to change. They will need a thorough understanding of the whole 'onion', of the types (and amount) of information that each layer will need to engage with, and of the likely learning needs of those working at each layer. They will also need to block in meetings of various kinds for members of each layer, and consider communication systems between layers. The flows of information between layers serve (at least) three important purposes. First, they allow members of each layer to gain insights into the lived experiences of colleagues in other layers ('learn'). Next they are the basis for ongoing responsive planning of implementation processes. Finally, they can provide data for evaluating the overall initiative through documenting evidence of learning at all layers over time.

How can such a process be organised? Whatever the scale of the proposed complex changes (which require people to change how they think and what they do) over the first years of the change process, national planning in a parallel learning model will need to:

i) *Provide multiple opportunities for people involved at every layer to come together and be supported in:*

- exchanging experiences and information/data about their experiences so far of trying to support those in their inner layer(s) in implementing the changes;
- considering what other helpful information they might be able to obtain in future and ways of obtaining it;
- considering relevant information from other layers or the wider context;
- making decisions about how to proceed and/or adjust tentative plans in the light of all this information;
- making requests for any further information or learning opportunities they need in order to either make such decisions or carry out their plans;
- receiving such learning opportunities/training as are requested/ needed when they need them; and
- formulating appropriate ways of passing on what they have learnt and the actions taken or planned as a result to adjacent layers.

Many of the above will require explicitly working to establish a systemic atmosphere or ethos in which people feel able to be honest about, for example, contextual realities, what they don't know/can't do, what has not been successful and so on. This in itself will represent, in most contexts, a substantial culture change, and ways of supporting this may need to be planned.

ii) *Plan the frequency and timing of such meetings for an initial period so that the flow – both ways – of the outcomes of the learning is smooth.*

When it comes to making initial decisions about the number, frequency and timing of meetings of members of each layer, some contexts may reasonably decide, for example, that meetings of people working in the inner layers need to be more frequent, because their closeness to the direct implementation of the change will mean that they have more immediate practical and affective needs than those working in outer layers. In addition, because those working in the outer layers will be dealing with more and more complex information, this will take time to amass and process and so meetings can be less frequent. Also, whatever plans they make will affect a larger number of people and so it is important that they have enough time to digest information and to plan appropriately. Here too though in some contexts people in these outer layers may feel that, in the first instance at least, that they too need to meet more frequently, to get help to develop the skills (e.g. data analysis) they (will) need to be able to carry out their roles appropriately. Even when the concept of the model is fully understood, just making these kinds of early planning for implementation decisions appropriately is challenging since they will need to be responsive to contextual realities. How the change process planning evolves over time will of course need to be responsive to actual events and emerging needs.

This is a very different approach to and model of leading and managing educational change to ones that most people in most educational systems are familiar with. Most current models (e.g. the still very popular cascade model) remain based on a view of educational change as a largely rational linear process. They focus on getting the teachers to *do* things differently, and don't sufficiently recognise that all involved in the process will need to change, change how they *think* not just how they behave. Also it is rare for those working within the different layers to seek to understand how the change will affect or is affecting the experiences of others (the phenomenology of change mentioned above). The parallel learning model, by making learning central, does highlight the need to pay attention to the learning processes of people at every layer and across the whole. It focuses on providing those conditions for supporting learning of the type that we have discussed in earlier chapters (scaffolding; noticing and being responsive and assessing what is valued, not just what is measurable) in other words, creating a version of the trusting dialogic classroom culture at the macro-level of context.

Any model of managing change represents a way of *thinking* about making change happen. Like an approach in ELT (see Chapter 5), it is based on more or less explicit answers to a series of questions (What is educational change? How does educational change happen? What can be done by whom to support people in making the necessary changes?). Different models will result in different practices and methodologies. In addition, just as in classrooms achieving perfect match between what is said and what is done is challenging (see Chapter 6) so, and to a greater degree because of the scale, is achieving a match between using a parallel learning model (or any model) for planning change and the practices of its implementation or evaluation.

Examples of practices that would not be a match for a parallel learning model would include evaluating the progress/success of the change initiative purely by apparently measurable 'outputs' such as for example, the numbers of 'teachers trained' or the banks of 'materials' that have been developed by 'experts' for implementers to use. Evidence of such outputs expressed in terms of numbers and tangible products are often demanded by the politicians who instigate and fund most large-scale educational change, even though they do not necessarily tell anyone anything about any learning that has occurred. Some, such as materials externally developed for implementers to use may even prevent learning (see Chapters 3 and 6, 'scaffolding' and the need **not** to 'do things FOR learners'). A parallel learning model will (also) need other evaluation practices which document and provide evidence of learning and change (e.g. 'most significant change' MSC technique; Davies and Dart 2005).

This discussion of a model for managing externally initiated change may seem a long way from your concerns as teachers. However, this model puts teachers and their learners at the centre of the change process, and makes information about how the change is actually impacting on classrooms central to the success. Teachers are used to being evaluated on whether or not they are 'doing it right', and typically, will want to try to show, or say that they are. In a parallel learning model of change management, evaluation of teachers' performance in this way is not needed and would, in fact, be unhelpful. What people in outer layers need from teachers is honest information about what is happening in classrooms where attempts are being made to implement the change, and about how the teachers and learners involved are feeling and thinking, and why teachers think this is so. Without such information, they cannot plan appropriate support for teachers and learners. We recognise, of course, that providing honest information is much easier said than done and that expecting the model to work as smoothly and ideally as described above, is unreasonable given the numbers of people in every layer all involved in their personal culture changes at the same time. Therefore, for such information to be obtainable, some teachers, at least, will need to be courageous enough to be honest, and they will need allies and support to be so.

We think it is important that you, as a teacher, try to find out as much as possible about the model being used to manage any change process you are involved in, for two main reasons. First, so that, should you be asked about how it is going in your classroom, you know how to tailor your response. Your automatic reaction might be to assume that the inquirer wants to hear that everything is going well (and that they will judge you negatively if you say anything else) but in a parallel learning model they will genuinely want and need your honest descriptions and thoughts. Second, so that you realise that whatever others may say, whether the reform goes well or not is not just teachers' or your responsibility. As long as you feel you are doing the best *you* can to help your learners learn in contextually appropriate ways that match *your* understanding of what is expected of you, and are taking full advantage of any support opportunities that are provided, there is no more anyone can ask of you.

In addition, when you are the initiator of changes in your own classroom, effectively you are the outer layer of a two-layer onion, and many of the points we make above, for example about seeking and exchanging information and about creating a trusting change environment will be relevant to you too.

4. Summary and task

In this chapter, we have considered the role of context (particularly the aspect of time, and then people) in planning educational changes, whether initiated by a single teacher for his/her own classroom, or by national planners for an entire system. Important points to remember include:

- All change takes time and is a process not an event.
- The greater the gap between people's current attitudes, thinking and behaviour and the attitudes, thinking and behaviour needed if the change is to be successful, the more time is needed.
- A large-scale change directly involves a lot of people at different layers of the educational system, as well as indirectly affecting others in the broader society.
- Since so many people playing so many different roles in the change process are involved, it is important to maintain coherence through effective communication between the parts and the whole.
- All people involved will need to learn (in all its complexity – not just imitate or use the new language) so that they can bridge the gap (and be supported in doing so) if they are to make the change successfully.
- Leaders having the original ideas for change initiatives need to understand their context to know where change is needed (and new learning needs to happen). If they are o understand the focus and type of change being aimed for, they need to do more than quote the contemporary global educational rhetoric.
- Planning a complex educational change process needs to be based on a model such as the parallel learning model proposed, that bears all the above in mind.
- The implementation of such a model needs to employ practices that are consistent, coherent and responsive to emerging needs over time.

In the final chapter we return to our title and, drawing on ideas from all chapters, summarise how an understanding of the language classroom context is a starting point for planning change and an ongoing key concern.

Task:

Think about any large-scale educational change initiative you have experienced. How did you feel at the time? Was it clear to you what was wanted and why? Did the experience change you? Why might this be? Can you trace any of your current reasoning or classroom practices back to that time? Overall, do you consider it was successful or not, from the government point of view? What makes you think so?

If you are a teacher, think about a small scale classroom change that you initiated. Why did you decide to make the change? Did you take account of context when you made the decision to change things? How involved were your learners in the decision-making and the process of change? Did you engage in any learning specifically in order to make the change? How much time did you allow before you decided if the change had worked or not? Was the change successful, do you think? Why/why not?

References and further reading

Allwright, R. and J. Hanks. 2008. *The Developing Language Learner: An Introduction to Exploratory Practice*. Basingstoke: Palgrave Macmillan.

Appel, J. 1995. *The Diary of a Language Teacher*. Basingstoke: Macmillan.

Badheka, G. 1999. *Diwaswapna*. New Delhi: National Book Trust.

Beare, H., B. J Caldwell, and R. Millican. 1992. 'Dimensions of leadership'. In: M. Crawford, L. Kydd and C. Riches, eds, *Leadership and Teams in Educational Management*. Buckingham: Open University Press, pp. 24–39.

Bennett, N. 1996. 'Analysing management for personal development: theory and practice'. In: L. Kydd, M. Crawford, and C. Riches, eds, *Professional Development for Educational Management*. Buckingham: Open University Press, pp. 60–73.

Bennett, N. and C. Carre. 1995. 'Teachers' early experiences of the implementation of the British National Curriculum'. In: D. Carter and M. O'Neill, eds, *Case Studies in Educational Change: An International Perspective*. London: Falmer Press.

Borg, S. 2008. *Teacher Cognition and Language Education: Research and Practice*. London: Continuum.

Burns, A. 2009. *Doing Action Research in English Language Teaching: A Guide for Practitioners*. London: Routledge.

Cox, C. and M. J. Lemaitre. 1999. 'Market and state principles of reform in Chilean education: policies and results'. In: G. Perry and D. Leipziger, eds,

Chile: Recent Policy Lessons and Emerging Challenges. Washington, DC: World Bank Institute of Development Studies, pp. 149–88.

Dadds, M. 1995. *Passionate Enquiry and School Development: a Story about Teacher Action Research*. Basingstoke: Burgess Science Press.

Davies, R. and J. Dart. 2005. *The 'Most Significant Change' (MSC) Technique: A Guide to Its Use* [accessed 22 June 2012]. Available from: http://scholar.google.co.uk/scholar?q=Davis+and+Dart+MSC+technique&btnG=&hl=en&as_sdt=0%2C5&as_vis=1.

Farrell, T. 2007. *Reflective Language Teaching: From Research to Practice*. London: Continuum.

Fullan, M. and A. Hargreaves, eds. 1992. *Teacher Development and Educational Change*. London: Falmer Press.

Fullan, M. G. 1991. *The New Meaning of Educational Change* (2nd edn). London: Cassell.

— 1992. 'Causes and processes of implementation and continuation'. In: N. Bennett et al., eds, *Managing Change in Education. Individual and Organizational Perspectives*. London: Paul Chapman, pp. 109–31.

— 1993. *Change Forces. Probing the Depths of Educational Reform*. London: Falmer Press.

— 1999. *Change Forces: The Sequel*. London: Falmer Press.

— 2001. *The New Meaning of Educational Change* (3rd edn). London: Routledge Falmer.

— 2007. *The New Meaning of Educational Change* (4th edn). New York: Teachers College Press.

Gaziel, H. H. and I. Weiss. 1990. 'School bureaucratic structure, locus of control and alienation among primary school teachers'. *Research in Education*, 44, pp. 55–66.

Goodson, I., 2001. 'Social Histories of Educational Change'. *Journal of Educational Change*, 2, pp. 45–63.

Hallinger, P. 2010. 'Making education reform happen: is there an "Asian" way?' *School Leadership and Management*, 30(5), pp. 401–18.

Hatch, M. J. 1997. *Organisational Theory*. Oxford: Oxford University Press.

Hayes, D. 2000. 'Cascade training and teachers' professional development'. *English Language Teaching Journal*, 54(2), pp. 135–45.

Henry, J. and D. Walker, eds. 1991. *Managing Innovation*. London: Sage.

Hopkins, D. 1987. *Improving the Quality of Schooling*. Lewes: The Falmer Press.

Hutchinson, T., 1991. 'The management of change'. *Teacher Trainer*, 5(3), pp. 19–21.

Kennedy, C. 1988. 'Evaluation of the management of change in ELT projects'. *Applied Linguistics*, 9(4), pp. 329–42.

Kuchah, K. and R. Smith. 2011. 'Pedagogy of autonomy for difficult circumstances: from practice to principles'. *International Journal of Innovations in Language Learning and Teaching*, 5(2), pp. 119–40.

Lamb, M. 1995. 'The consequences of INSET'. *English Language Teaching Journal*, 49(1), pp. 72–9.

Levin, B. 2008. *How to Change 5000 Schools: a Practical and Positive Approach to Leading Change at Every Level*. Cambridge, MA: Harvard Education Press.

Louis, K. and M. Miles. 1992. *Improving the Urban High School*. London: Cassell.

Malderez, A. and M. Wedell. 2007. *Teaching Teachers: Processes and Practices*. London: Continuum.

Markee, N. 1997. *Managing Curricular Innovation*. Cambridge: Cambridge University Press.

Mason, J. 2002. *Researching Your Own Practice: The Discipline of Noticing*. London: Routledge.

McGrath, S. 2010. 'The role of education in development: an educationalist's response to some recent work in development economics'. *Comparative Education*, 46(2), pp. 237–53.

Polyoi, E., M. G. Fullan, and J. P. Anchan, 2003. *Change Forces in Post-Communist Eastern Europe*. London: Routledge Falmer.

Schon, D. 1983. *The Reflective Practitioner: How Professionals Think in Action*. New York: Basic Books.

Van Veen, K. and Sleegers, P. 2006. 'How does it feel? Teachers' emotions in a context of change'. *Journal of Curriculum Studies*, 38(1), pp. 85–111.

Waters, A. 2009. 'Managing innovation in Language Teaching'. *Language Teaching*, 42(4), pp. 421–58.

Waters, A. 2006. 'Facilitating follow up in ELT INSET'. *Language Teaching Research*, 10(1), pp. 32–52.

Waters, A. 2005. 'Expertise in teacher education: helping teachers to learn'. In: K. Johnson, ed., *Expertise in Second Language Learning and Teaching*. Basingstoke: Macmillan, pp. 210–29.

Wedell, M. 2009. *Planning for Educational Change: Putting People and Their Contexts First*. London: Continuum

2010.*Managing Educational Change in a Turbulent Environment: Hungary 1991–1998*. Saarbrucken: Lambert Academic Publishing.

Wertsch, J. V., P. Tulviste and F. Hagstrom. 1993. 'A sociocultural approach to agency'. In: E. A. Forman, N. Minick and C. A Stone, eds, *Contexts for Learning: Sociocultural dynamics in children's development*. Oxford: Oxford University Press, pp. 336–68.

Whitaker, P. 1993. *Managing Change in Schools*. Milton Keynes: Open University Press.

White, R. 1987. 'Managing innovation'. *English Language Teaching Journal*, 41(3), pp. 211–18.

Wright, T. 1987. *Roles of Teachers and Learners*. Cambridge: Cambridge University Press.

Zappa-Hollman, S. 2011. 'EFL in Argentina's schools: teachers' perspectives on policy changes and instruction'. *TESOL Quarterly*, 41(3), pp. 618–24.

10

Conclusions: On understanding language classroom contexts and the process of change

Introduction

This book is about education and education is about planning for systems and processes that will support learning. Any classroom or externally initiated change involves another planning process whose main aim must be to *improve* support for learning processes.

Until very recently, achieving improved support for learning has often been seen as telling people to do things differently. This is typical of a top–down and rational view of change, managed by a vertical hierarchy, in which each level instructs the level below it in what needs to be done in a cascade model. This view of the change process is consistent with a broadly transmission view of learning. How important is/was an understanding of language classroom contexts in this view? The short answer is, not very. In extreme circumstances, change initiators' 'understanding of context' may be limited to a (more or less conscious) desire to be seen to keep up with changing global ideas about language teaching.

However, many of the hoped-for outcomes of educational change today (e.g. development of communicative abilities, or reflective teachers) are inconsistent with a transmission view of learning. If the change planning and implementation model continues to be underpinned by a transmission view, but the change outcomes require a different view, this results in very mixed messages and a lack of congruence. For example, if as a teacher you are told to make your classrooms learning and learner-centred but the conditions in which you are supposed to (learn to) do so are *not* themselves learning and learner-centred, how are you supposed to interpret what is expected of you? Although some individual implementers at various levels of a top down model of change may in such circumstance do their best to adjust their practices to take account of these conflicting views of learning, this is not enough to make the change process successful.

The parallel learning model proposed in Chapter 9 is, we believe, more appropriate for those (many) situations where the views of learning implied by change outcomes are different from those prevalent within the existing system. It views the traditional vertical change planning hierarchy horizontally, because of the need in such a situation for all layers to be learning (in senses mentioned in Chapter 9, which include learning the new view of learning) in parallel. For such parallel learning to be possible, an initial and ongoing effort by all involved to understand all aspects and layers of 'the language classroom context' is needed.

1. Summarising the book

The subtitle for this book is 'the starting point for change', and as is clear from the above, whatever model or scale of change is envisaged, an understanding of the language classroom context is helpful before the initiation of any change to determine appropriate desired outcomes. In an evolutionary parallel learning model of change which recognises that the context itself will be changing over time (both 'naturally' and because of the effects of the initiative) it will also be necessary to continually update the understanding of the context.

Chapter 1 attempted to outline the main visible and invisible aspects of context that it will be necessary to understand. Chapter 2 went into more detail about the crucial but difficult to notice (and so often underestimated) aspect of culture. Understanding as much as possible about the culture(s) of a context is so important since, as we discussed in the previous chapter, successful complex educational change affects and requires change in the existing cultures of the context. Chapter 3 highlighted the importance of language in a view of learning which requires dialogic interaction and which leads to culture learning, and also explored some relationships between attitudes to the learning of particular languages and their roles and use in a context. Chapters 4 and 5 explored how changes over time in ideas about language, language learning and how it is supported have resulted in changes in practices which can be observed in classrooms. Here we highlighted the connections between approach (beliefs), whether articulated or not, and classroom practices. Chapters 6 and 7 explored many of the various ways that people in one language classroom may be different from people in another and so create more or less unique classroom cultures. They also discussed the possible contextually influenced origins of such differences. Chapter 8 looked at how both visible and invisible (cultural) features of the institutional context can influence what happens in classrooms. Finally, in Chapter 9 we focused specifically on change in educational contexts and on how, given the need for large numbers of people to be learning over time, educational change might be managed.

If you have read these chapters and carried out the various suggested tasks, you will by now have quite a full understanding of important features of your context (including details about, e.g. the people, existing views of learning, existing classroom practices, likely learning needs, the place, the resources, the leaders, the physical environment, societal expectations and many more). This will not be complete, or remain true over time, but it should provide a useful starting point for you to:

a) Identify what it is that you might usefully change (from 'what existing state/practice' to 'what desired state/practice').

b) Consider the gap between the two, the time and resources available to effect the change and whether it is in fact feasible.

c) Further develop your arguments for wishing to make changes, and perhaps reconsider your target in the light of (b).

d) Make use of your understanding of the context to make decisions about how implementation might take place.

Then, in order to monitor progress and adjust the initial plans made at (d) above in the light of what actually happens and, importantly, how the people involved actually experience the changes, continuous updating of your understanding of the now (rapidly you hope) changing context will be necessary. At some point in the future (at some time 'after' the active change process is deemed complete) you will probably want to assess whether in fact the change has become a new 'normal' for most of those involved. To do so, you will need to have had a picture of the context before you began the change process so that you can compare it with how things are at that future point. Such a comparison will give you a sense of what has actually changed, and may trigger thinking about the 'what' (see (a) above) of a new change process.

All of our experiences in education have convinced us of the importance of context. This is particularly true of those experiences which have involved participation of one kind or another in planned educational change initiatives in a range of different countries. When context *has* been explicitly taken into account in such change contexts, it has generally focused on only some of the aspects of context as labelled in Chapters 1 and 2 (and further described in the rest of this book). The aspects that tended (and tend still) to be referred to have been some features of the 'visible' (e.g. descriptions of what teachers do in classrooms, availability of resources or physical features of institutions). On occasion there has been reference to surface level and stereotypical macro cultural traits (e.g. 'Confucian heritage culture learners are passive'). It has been (and remains) very rare for an explicit understanding of the all-important existing cultures at the various levels of context (e.g. view of learning, prevailing ELT approach, prevailing school cultures, etc.) to be taken into account.

2. And finally . . .

There are other current theoretical frameworks which try to unpack and explain the relationships between many of the ideas discussed in this book, such as Activity Theory (Engeström 1987) or Actor Network theory (see, e.g. Fenwick and Edwards, 2010). Any readers engaged in academic study might find these useful to explore. However, since these academic frameworks are still evolving and our aim has been to make these ideas accessible to as wide a readership as possible, we chose not to use them in this book. Our overall framework is one that has been developed from our own experience, rather than being based on that of others. In this sense, the way we have presented and ordered the material is itself a product of our own particular context. You might like to consider how your own contexts may have influenced the sense you have made of these chapters. Lastly, perhaps as you read you had ideas for changes in your own practices, and your investigation of your context led you to believe that they would be feasible. If so, what might be the first steps towards making the changes happen?

We said above that our experience has convinced us of the importance of context. If you were already convinced, we hope this book has added to your understanding of the types of things that can be understood about a context, as well as provided some ideas about why they matter and how you can begin to investigate them. If you were not convinced before, we hope this book has begun to make you more so!

References and further reading

Engeström, Y. 1987. *Learning by Expanding: An Activity-Theoretical Approach to Developmental Research*. Helsinki: Orienta-Konsultit Oy.

Fenwick, T. and R. Edwards. 2010. *Actor-Network Theory in Education*. Abingdon: Routledge.

Index